Building Telephony with OpenSIPS
Second Edition

Build high-speed and highly scalable telephony systems using OpenSIPS

Flavio E. Goncalves

Bogdan-Andrei Iancu

BIRMINGHAM - MUMBAI

Building Telephony Systems with OpenSIPS
Second Edition

First published: January 2010

Second edition: January 2016

Production reference: 1250116

Published by Packt Publishing Ltd.
Livery Place
35 Livery Street
Birmingham B3 2PB, UK.

ISBN 978-1-78528-061-0

www.packtpub.com

Credits

Authors
Flavio E. Goncalves
Bogdan-Andrei Iancu

Reviewers
Saúl Ibarra Corretgé
Vyacheslav Kobzar
Mfawa Alfred Onen
Ali Pey

Commissioning Editor
Neil Alexander

Acquisition Editor
Kevin Colaco

Content Development Editor
Amey Varangaonkar

Technical Editor
Pranil Pathare

Copy Editor
Tasneem Fatehi

Project Coordinator
Suzanne Coutinho

Proofreader
Safis Editing

Indexer
Monica Ajmera Mehta

Graphics
Disha Haria

Production Coordinator
Conidon Miranda

Cover Work
Conidon Miranda

About the Authors

Flavio E. Goncalves was born in 1966 in Brazil. Having a strong interest in computers, he got his first personal computer in 1983, and since then, it has been almost an addiction. He received his degree in engineering in 1989 with a focus on computer-aided designing and manufacturing.

He is also the CTO of SipPulse Routing and Billing Solutions in Brazil—a company dedicated to the implementing of small-to-medium telephone companies, VoIP providers, and large-scale new generation telephony systems. Since 1993, he has participated in a series of certification programs and been certified as Novell MCNE/MCNI, Microsoft MCSE/MCT, Cisco CCSP/CCNP/CCDP, Asterisk dCAP, and some others.

He started writing about open source software because he thinks that the way certification programs have worked is very good for learners. Some books are written by strictly technical people who sometimes do not have a clear idea on how people learn. He tried to use his 15 years of experience as an instructor to help people learn about the open source telephony software. Together with Bogdan, he created the OpenSIPS boot camp followed by the e-learning program, OpenSIPS eBootcamp.

His experience with networks, protocol analyzers, and IP telephony combined with his teaching experience gave him an edge to write this book. This is the fourth book written by him. The first one was *Configuration Guide for Asterisk PBX*, by *BookSurge Publishing*, the second was *Building Telephony Systems with OpenSER*, by *Packt Publishing*, and the third was *Building Telepopny Systems With OpenSIPS 1.6*, by *Packt Publishing*.

As the CTO of SipPulse, Flavio balances his time between family, work, and fun. He is the father of two children and lives in Florianopolis, Brazil—one of the most beautiful places in the world. He dedicates his free time to water sports such as surfing and sailing.

Bogdan-Andrei Iancu entered the SIP world in 2001, right after graduating in computer science from the Politehnica University of Bucharest, Romania. He started as a researcher at the FOKUS Fraunhofer Institute, Berlin, Germany. For almost four years, Bogdan accumulated a quick understanding and experience of VoIP/SIP, being involved in research and industry projects and following the evolution of the VoIP world closely.

In 2005, he started his own company, Voice System. The company entered the open source software market by launching the OpenSER/OpenSIPS project—a free GPL-SIP proxy implementation. As the CEO of Voice System, Bogdan pushes the company in two directions: developing and supporting.

The OpenSIPS public project (Voice System being the major contributor and sponsor of the project) creates professional solutions and platforms (OpenSIPS-based) for the industry. In other words, Bogdan's interest was to create knowledge (through the work with the project) and to provide the knowledge where needed (embedded in commercial products or raw format as consultancy services). In the effort of sharing the knowledge of the SIP/OpenSIPS project, he started to run the OpenSIPS Bootcamp in 2008 together with Flavio E. Goncalves, which is intensive training dedicated to people who want to learn and get hands-on experience on OpenSIPS from experienced people. Bogdan's main concern is to research and develop new technologies or software for SIP-based VoIP (this is the reason for his strong involvement with the OpenSIPS project) and pack all these cutting-edge technologies as professional solutions for the industry.

About the Reviewers

Saúl Ibarra Corretgé started working in the VoIP industry over a decade ago. He has worked in many different areas and projects, from development and configuration to deployment.

In 2006, when OpenSER 1.0.0 (the project where OpenSIPS was forked from) was released, Saúl began to experiment with it. Several years later, he started using it heavily and contributing with code until he became an OpenSIPS core team member in 2010. His contributions to the project have been diverse but mainly focused on improving the presence part.

He also maintains several projects on GitHub (`https://github.com/saghul`) and you can contact him through his website (`http://bettercallsaghul.com`) or on Twitter (`@saghul`).

When not in front of the computer, he likes to travel around the world.

Vyacheslav Kobzar is the chief of software development at Modulis.ca Inc. He graduated from Donetsk State Technical University in 2006, where he was studying software development. Right after graduation, he started to work as a freelance developer on different projects, mostly web development. Since 2008, he started to work remotely in the Canadian company, Modulis.ca Inc. He moved to Canada in 2009 where he continued working at Modulis.ca Inc as a developer on multiple web projects.

He started to work on VoIP in 2011, mostly with Asterisk. He has been working on AGI and AMI modules for different VoIP projects. He was certificated with Asterisk dCAP in 2012. In 2014, Vyacheslav participated in the OpenSIPS eBootcamp session. He has been an OpenSIPS's Foundation member since 2014.

In 2013, he participated in the designing and developing of the Modulis VoIP start-up project, which was later successfully deployed in multiple companies and organizations in Quebec. OpenSIPS is the core part of the project along with other VoIP technologies and protocols (UNIStim, Skinny, and others).

Being a Linux user for almost 10 years, Vyacheslav contributes to different open source projects on GitHub and also works on his own.

I'd like to thank OpenSIPS developers and contributors for this amazing project. I would also like to thank the Modulis team for sharing their knowledge and ideas and always being open for new challenges. Finally, I would like to thank my wife, Anna, for her support and patience.

Mfawa Alfred Onen is a system administrator with more than 6 years' experience in the field of UNIX/Linux system administration. He studied electrical and electronics engineering in his bachelor of engineering undergraduate program and has continued to venture into the area of telecommunications with a postgraduate certificate from Birmingham City University, UK. He currently resides in Nigeria and has worked with both private and education sectors, including numerous consulting jobs for clients at home and abroad.

Being a software developer and having an operations background, he is heavily involved with cloud computing (DevOps) using open source software such as OpenStack, OpenShift, Docker, Asterisk, OpenSIPS, and FreeSWITCH, to name a few. He also helps to manage a Google Developer Group (GDG Bingham University), where software developers and technology enthusiasts come to learn Google developer tools and services in the form of Developer Festivals (DevFest), Hackathons, and Code labs.

When Mfawa is not busy with technology, he is an avid gamer (Call of Duty, NFS, and Forza) and a blogger at `http://www.maomuffy.com/` with much content on OpenShift, OpenStack, RADIUSDesk, Linux/UNIX system administration, and so on.

My special thanks goes to my family (Professor Alfred Ikpi Onen, Mrs. Jummai Alfred Onen, Dr. Eno Alfred Onen, Williams Alfred Onen, and Ikpi Alfred Onen Jnr.), friends (Aderogba Otunla, Alhamdu Bello, Suzanne Coutinho, and others) and well-wishers.

Ali Pey is a senior software engineer architect with more than 23 years experience in telephony, networking, and VoIP. He has an electronics engineering degree with a focus on telecommunication and software design. He has worked for companies such as Nortel, TalkSwitch, and j2 Global, and has been developing VoIP solutions since the start of the technology. He has developed software for proxy servers, registrar servers/clients, user agents, and other VoIP components in both SIP and H.323 protocols. Currently, Ali is an independent consultant and has successfully used OpenSIPS and other open source applications such as Asterisk and FreeSWITCH to provide global telephony cloud solutions.

www.PacktPub.com

Support files, eBooks, discount offers, and more

For support files and downloads related to your book, please visit www.PacktPub.com.

Did you know that Packt offers eBook versions of every book published, with PDF and ePub files available? You can upgrade to the eBook version at www.PacktPub.com and as a print book customer, you are entitled to a discount on the eBook copy. Get in touch with us at service@packtpub.com for more details.

At www.PacktPub.com, you can also read a collection of free technical articles, sign up for a range of free newsletters and receive exclusive discounts and offers on Packt books and eBooks.

https://www2.packtpub.com/books/subscription/packtlib

Do you need instant solutions to your IT questions? PacktLib is Packt's online digital book library. Here, you can search, access, and read Packt's entire library of books.

Why subscribe?

- Fully searchable across every book published by Packt
- Copy and paste, print, and bookmark content
- On demand and accessible via a web browser

Free access for Packt account holders

If you have an account with Packt at www.PacktPub.com, you can use this to access PacktLib today and view 9 entirely free books. Simply use your login credentials for immediate access.

Table of Contents

Preface

This book will be your companion when working with OpenSIPS using a case study for an Internet Telephony Service Provider (ITSP). With the help of this book, you should be able to build a system that is able to authenticate, route, bill, and monitor VoIP calls. Topics and advanced scenarios such as TCP/TLS support, load balancing, asynchronous processing, and more are discussed in depth in this book. You will create dynamic dialplans, route calls using advanced routing, integrate OpenSIPS with a media server, account calls and generate CDRs, provision the system using a Web GUI, and use tools to monitor and check the health of your server. You will also learn some advanced topics such as support for TLS/TCP and the newest technology called asynchronous callbacks.

By the end of this book, you should be able to build a system that is able to authenticate, route, bill, and monitor VoIP calls. Whenever you are thinking big on telephony, OpenSIPS is your savior and this book is your friend!

What this book covers

Chapter 1, *Introduction to SIP*, introduces you to the SIP server. You will see how to recognize a SIP request and reply according to RFC 3261, identify the mandatory SIP headers, and describe the SIP routing process for initial and sequential requests.

Chapter 2, *Introducing OpenSIPS*, shows you how OpenSIPS is used in the market, the basic architecture of the system, use cases, and the main target market.

Chapter 3, *Installing OpenSIPS*, shows you how to download the OpenSIPS source and its dependencies, compile and install OpenSIPS with MySQL and Radius support, and configure the Linux system to start OpenSIPS at boot time.

Chapter 4, OpenSIPS Language and Routing Concepts, introduces you to the OpenSIPS scripting language and OpenSIPS routing concepts. After reading this chapter, you should be able to recognize the OpenSIPS script language, describe its mains commands, process initial requests, and drop or route requests.

Chapter 5, Subscriber Management, shows you how to manage subscribers in the system using the subscriber, location, group, and address databases. You will learn how to implement a multidomain system that is able to support multitenant implementations.

Chapter 6, OpenSIPS Control Panel, demonstrates how to install a web GUI to help with the provisioning of users, dialplan, routes, and other information that is required to run OpenSIPS. You will see how to install, use, configure, and customize the OpenSIPS control panel.

Chapter 7, Dialplan and Routing, enables you to integrate OpenSIPS with PSTN through gateways, selecting the best gateway, and failing over automatically if a response code is negative.

Chapter 8, Managing Dialogs, shows you how to activate the dialog module, limit the number of simultaneous calls, disconnect hanged calls, impose a maximum duration time for a call, and implement SIP session timers integrated with the dialog module.

Chapter 9, Accounting, demonstrates how account calls generate a CDR (Call Detail Record), account correctly forwarded calls, prevent calls without BYE, and add extra fields to the CDR.

Chapter 10, SIP NAT Traversal, helps you implement an OpenSIPS solution for clients behind NAT. You will see how to implement OpenSIPS in a data center such as Amazon AWS where all the servers are behind NAT.

Chapter 11, Implementing SIP Services, implements services such as call forward, forward on busy, and forward on no answer in cooperation with a media server and SIP phone.

Chapter 12, Monitoring Tools, enables you to detect performance issues using the built-in statistics. These include protocol issues using SIP trace, database issues using the benchmark module, script issues using the script trace, and software and hardware issues using GDB.

Chapter 13, OpenSIPS Security, shows you how to increase the security of your OpenSIPS installation.

Chapter 14, Advanced Topics with OpenSIPS 2.1, covers some advanced topics that can be important for specific installations. Topics such as asynchronous processing, TCP and TLS support, binary replication, and NoSQL integration for clusters are discussed.

What you need for this book

All you need for this book is a working installation of OpenSIPS on either Linux or Debian. We will go through the installation of OpenSIPS in detail in this book.

Who this book is for

System integrators who need to scale their VoIP projects, universities, and other entities who need to provide large-scale communication systems based on the SIP protocol can make the best use of this book.

Conventions

In this book, you will find a number of text styles that distinguish between different kinds of information. Here are some examples of these styles and an explanation of their meaning.

Code words in text, database table names, folder names, filenames, file extensions, pathnames, dummy URLs, user input, and Twitter handles are shown as follows: "It also contains a parameter called branch that identifies this transaction."

A block of code is set as follows:

```
P-Asserted-Identity: "John" sip:+554833328560@sip.com
P-Asserted-Identity: tel:+554833328560
```

When we wish to draw your attention to a particular part of a code block, the relevant lines or items are set in bold:

```
if (is_method("INVITE")) {
  setflag(ACC_DO); # Do accounting
  setflag(ACC_FAILED); # Account failed transactions
}
```

Any command-line input or output is written as follows:

```
opensipsctl fifo ps
opensipsctl fifo debug 4
```

New terms and **important words** are shown in bold. Words that you see on the screen, for example, in menus or dialog boxes, appear in the text like this: "In the following **Select your location** screen, choose your location to be used in the installation process."

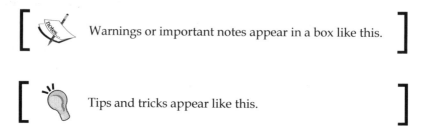

Warnings or important notes appear in a box like this.

Tips and tricks appear like this.

Reader feedback

Feedback from our readers is always welcome. Let us know what you think about this book—what you liked or disliked. Reader feedback is important for us as it helps us develop titles that you will really get the most out of.

To send us general feedback, simply e-mail feedback@packtpub.com, and mention the book's title in the subject of your message.

If there is a topic that you have expertise in and you are interested in either writing or contributing to a book, see our author guide at www.packtpub.com/authors.

Customer support

Now that you are the proud owner of a Packt book, we have a number of things to help you to get the most from your purchase.

Errata

Although we have taken every care to ensure the accuracy of our content, mistakes do happen. If you find a mistake in one of our books—maybe a mistake in the text or the code—we would be grateful if you could report this to us. By doing so, you can save other readers from frustration and help us improve subsequent versions of this book. If you find any errata, please report them by visiting http://www.packtpub. com/submit-errata, selecting your book, clicking on the **Errata Submission Form** link, and entering the details of your errata. Once your errata are verified, your submission will be accepted and the errata will be uploaded to our website or added to any list of existing errata under the Errata section of that title.

To view the previously submitted errata, go to https://www.packtpub.com/books/ content/support and enter the name of the book in the search field. The required information will appear under the **Errata** section.

Piracy

Piracy of copyrighted material on the Internet is an ongoing problem across all media. At Packt, we take the protection of our copyright and licenses very seriously. If you come across any illegal copies of our works in any form on the Internet, please provide us with the location address or website name immediately so that we can pursue a remedy.

Please contact us at copyright@packtpub.com with a link to the suspected pirated material.

We appreciate your help in protecting our authors and our ability to bring you valuable content.

Questions

If you have a problem with any aspect of this book, you can contact us at questions@packtpub.com, and we will do our best to address the problem.

1
Introduction to SIP

Before we dive into OpenSIPS, it is very important to understand some important concepts related to **Session Initiation Protocol (SIP)**. In this chapter, we will cover a brief tutorial regarding the concepts used later in this book. By the end of this chapter, we will have covered the following topics:

- Understanding the basics of SIP and its usage
- Describing the SIP architecture
- Explaining the meaning of its components
- Understanding and comparing main SIP messages
- Interpreting the header fields' processing for the **INVITE** and **REGISTER** messages
- Learning how SIP handles identity and privacy
- Covering the Session Description Protocol and Real-Time Protocol briefly

SIP was standardized by **Internet Engineering Task Force (IETF)** and is described in several documents known as **Request for Comments (RFC)**. The RFC 3261 describes SIP version 2. SIP is an application layer protocol used to establish, modify, and terminate sessions or multimedia calls. These sessions can be audio and video sessions, e-learning, chatting, or screen sharing sessions. It is similar to **Hypertext Transfer Protocol (HTTP)** and designed to start, keep, and close interactive communication sessions between users. Nowadays, SIP is the most popular protocol used in **Internet Telephony Service Providers (ITSPs)**, IP PBXs, and voice applications.

The SIP protocol supports five features to establish and close multimedia sessions:

- **User location**: Determines the endpoint address used for communication
- **User parameters negotiation**: Determines the media and parameters to be used
- **User availability**: Determines if the user is available or not to establish a session
- **Call establishment**: Establishes parameters for caller and callee and informs about the call progress (such as ringing, busy, or not found) to both the parties
- **Call management**: Facilitates session transfer and closing

The SIP protocol was designed as a part of a multimedia architecture containing other protocols such as **Resource Reservation Protocol (RSVP)**, **Real-Time Protocol (RTP)**, **Real-Time Session Protocol (RTSP)**, **Session Description Protocol (SDP)**, and **Session Announcement Protocol (SAP)**. However, it does not depend on them to work.

Understanding the SIP architecture

SIP has borrowed many concepts from the HTTP protocol. It is a text-based protocol and uses the same Digest mechanism for authentication. You will also notice similar error messages such as 404 (Not found) and 301 (Redirect). As a protocol developed by the IETF, it uses an addressing scheme similar to **Simple Mail Transfer Protocol (SMTP)**. The SIP address is just like an e-mail address. Another interesting feature used in SIP proxies are aliases; you can have multiple SIP addresses for a single subscriber such as the following:

- johndoe@sipA.com
- +554845678901@sipA.com
- 45678901@sipA.com

In the SIP architecture, there are user agents and servers. SIP uses a peer-to-peer distributed model with a signaling server. The signaling server only handles the SIP signaling, while the user agent clients and servers handle signaling and media. This is depicted in the following figure:

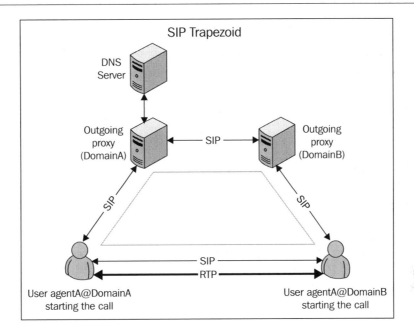

In the traditional SIP model, a user agent, usually a SIP phone, will start communicating with its SIP proxy, seen here as the outgoing proxy (or its home proxy) to send the call using a message known as INVITE.

The outgoing proxy will see that the call is directed to an outside domain. According to RFC 3263, it will seek the DNS server for the address of the target domain and resolve the IP address. Then, the outgoing proxy will forward the call to the SIP proxy responsible for DomainB.

The incoming proxy will query its location table for the IP address of agentB if its address was inserted in the location table by a previous registration process. It will forward the call to agentB.

After receiving the SIP message, agentB will have all the information required to establish an RTP session (usually audio) with agentA sending a 200 OK response. Once agentA receives the response from agentB, a two-way media can be established. A BYE request message can terminate the session.

Here, you can see the main components of the SIP architecture. The entire SIP signaling flows through the SIP proxy server. On the other hand, the media is transported by the RTP protocol and flows directly from one endpoint to another. Some of the components will be briefly explained in the sequence.

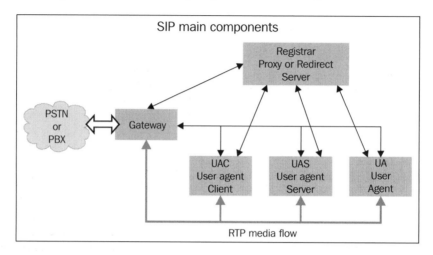

In the preceding image, you can see the following components:

- **UAC (User Agent Client)**: A client or terminal that starts the SIP signaling
- **UAS (User Agent Server)**: A server that responds to the SIP signaling coming from a UAC
- **UA (User Agent)**: A logical entity that can act as both UAC or UAS, such as a SIP endpoint (IP phones, ATAs, softphones, and so on)
- **Proxy Server**: Receives requests from a UA and transfers to another SIP proxy if this specific terminal is not under its domain
- **Redirect Server**: Receives requests and responds to the caller with a message containing data about the destination (302, Moved Temporarily)
- **Registrar Server**: Provides the callee's contact addresses to the proxy and redirect servers

The proxy, redirect, and registrar servers are usually available physically in the same computer and software.

The SIP registration process

The SIP registration process is shown as follows:

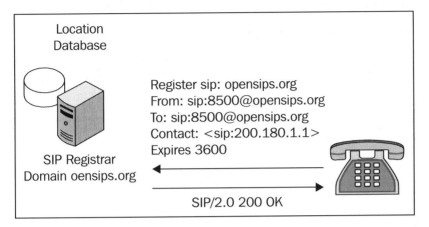

The SIP protocol employs a component called **Registrar**. It is a server that accepts REGISTER requests and saves the information received in these packets on the location server for their managed domains. The SIP protocol has a discovery capacity; in other words, if a user starts a session with another user, the SIP protocol has to discover an existent host where the user can be reached. The discovery process is done (among others) by a Registrar server that receives the request and finds the location to send it. This is based in a location database maintained by the Registrar server per domain. The Registrar server can accept other types of information, not only the client's IP addresses. It can receive other information such as **Call Processing Language (CPL)** scripts on the server.

Before a telephone can receive calls, it needs to be registered with the location database. In this database, we will have all the phones associated with their respective IP addresses. In our example, you will see the sip user, **8500@opensips. org**, registered with the IP address, **200.180.1.1**.

RFC 3665 defines best practices to implement a minimum set of functionalities for a SIP IP communications network. In the following table, the flows are defined according to RFC 3665 for registration transactions. According to RFC 3665, there are five basic flows associated with the process of registering a user agent.

Message flow	Description
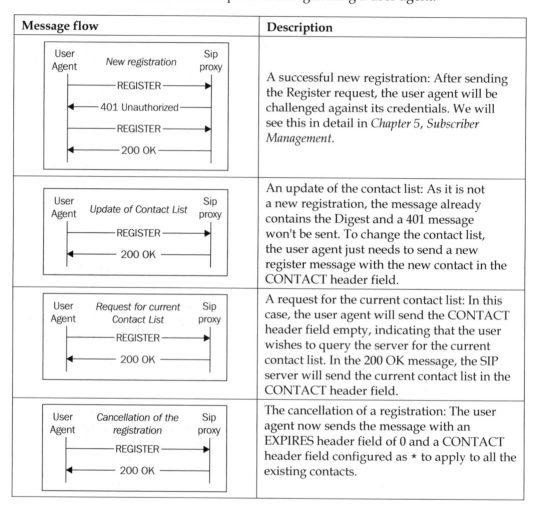	A successful new registration: After sending the Register request, the user agent will be challenged against its credentials. We will see this in detail in *Chapter 5, Subscriber Management*.
	An update of the contact list: As it is not a new registration, the message already contains the Digest and a 401 message won't be sent. To change the contact list, the user agent just needs to send a new register message with the new contact in the CONTACT header field.
	A request for the current contact list: In this case, the user agent will send the CONTACT header field empty, indicating that the user wishes to query the server for the current contact list. In the 200 OK message, the SIP server will send the current contact list in the CONTACT header field.
	The cancellation of a registration: The user agent now sends the message with an EXPIRES header field of 0 and a CONTACT header field configured as * to apply to all the existing contacts.

Message flow	Description
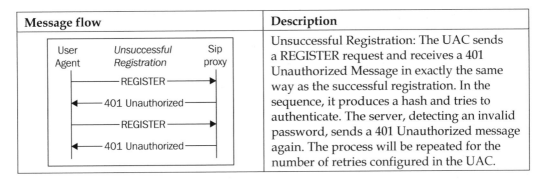	Unsuccessful Registration: The UAC sends a REGISTER request and receives a 401 Unauthorized Message in exactly the same way as the successful registration. In the sequence, it produces a hash and tries to authenticate. The server, detecting an invalid password, sends a 401 Unauthorized message again. The process will be repeated for the number of retries configured in the UAC.

Types of SIP servers

There are a few different types of SIP servers. Depending on the application, you can use one or all of them in your solution. OpenSIPS can behave as a proxy, redirect, B2BUA, or Registrar server.

The proxy server

In the SIP proxy mode, all SIP signaling goes through the SIP proxy. This behavior will help in processes such as billing and is, by far, the most common choice. The drawback is the overhead caused by the server in the middle of all the SIP communications during the session establishment. Regardless of the SIP server role, the RTP packets will go directly from one endpoint to another even if the server is working as a SIP proxy.

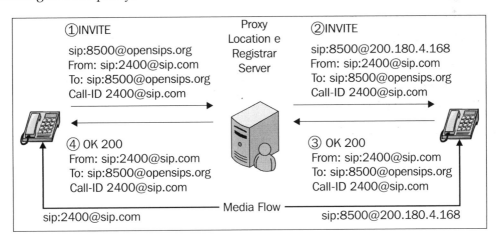

The redirect server

The SIP proxy can operate in the SIP redirect mode. In this mode, the SIP server is very scalable because it doesn't keep the state of the transactions. Just after the initial INVITE, it replies to the UAC with a 302 Moved Temporarily and is removed from the SIP dialog. In this mode, a SIP proxy, even with very few resources, can forward millions of calls per hour. It is normally used when you need high scalability but don't need to bill the calls.

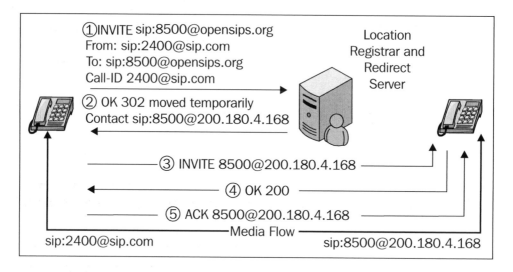

The B2BUA server

The server can also work as a **Back-to-Back User Agent (B2BUA)**. B2BUAs are normally applied to hide the topology of the network. They are also useful to support buggy clients unable to route SIP requests correctly based on record routing. Many PBX systems such as Asterisk, FreeSwitch, Yate, and others work as B2BUAs.

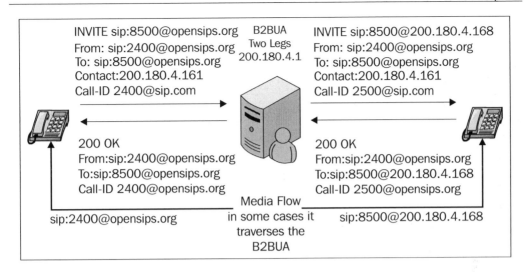

SIP request messages

There are several types of message requests. SIP is transactional, communicating through requests and replies. The most important types of requests are described in the following table:

Message	Description	RFC
ACK	Acknowledges an INVITE	RFC 3261
BYE	Terminates an existing session	RFC 3261
CANCEL	Cancels a pending registration	RFC 3261
INFO	Provides mid-call signaling information	RFC 2976
INVITE	Session establishment	RFC 3261
MESSAGE	Instant message transport	RFC 3428
NOTIFY	Sends information after subscribing	RFC 3265
PRACK	Acknowledges a provisional response	RFC 3262
PUBLISH	Uploads the status information to the server	RFC 3903
REFER	Asks another UA to act on **Uniform Resource Identifier (URI)**	RFC 3515
REGISTER	Registers the user and updates the location table	RFC 3261
SUBSCRIBE	Establishes a session to receive future updates	RFC 3265
UPDATE	Updates a session state information	RFC 3311

Most of the time, you will use REGISTER, INVITE, ACK, BYE, and CANCEL. Some messages are used for other features. For example, INFO is used for **Dual-tone Multi-frequency (DTMF)** relay and mid-call signaling information. PUBLISH, NOTIFY, and SUBSCRIBE give support to the presence systems. REFER is used for call transfer and MESSAGE for chat applications. Newer requests can appear depending on the protocol standardization process. Responses to these requests are in the text format as in the HTTP protocol. Some of the most important replies are shown as follows:

Description	Code	Examples	
Informational or provisional response	1XX	100 Trying 180 Ringing 181 Call Is Being Forwarded	182 Queued 183 Early Media
Success	2XX	200 OK 202 Accepted	
Redirect	3XX	300 Multiple Choices 301 Moved Permanently 302 Moved Temporarily	303 See Other 305 Use Proxy 380 Alternative Service
Client Errors	4XX	400 Bad Request 401 Unauthorized 402 Payment Required 403 Forbidden 404 Not Found 405 Method Not Allowed 406 Not Acceptable 407 Proxy Authentication Required 408 Request Timeout 409 Conflict 410 Gone	411 Length Required 413 Request Entity Too Large 414 RequestURI Too Large 415 Unsupported Media Type 420 Bad Extension 480 Temporarily not available 482 Loop Detected 483 Too Many Hops 484 Address Incomplete 485 Ambiguous 486 Busy Here
Server Errors	5XX	500 Internal Server Error 501 Not Implemented 502 Bad Gateway	503 Service Unavailable 504 Gateway Timeout 505 SIP Version not supported
Global Errors	6XX	600 Busy Everywhere 603 Decline	604 Does not exist anywhere 606 Not Acceptable

The SIP dialog flow

Let's examine this message sequence between two user agents as shown in the following figure. You can see several other flows associated with the session establishment in RFC 3665:

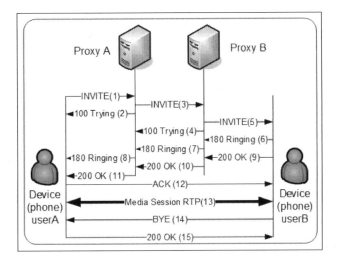

The messages are labeled in sequence. In this example, **userA** uses an IP phone to call another IP phone over the network. To complete the call, two SIP proxies are used.

The **userA** calls **userB** using its SIP identity called the SIP URI. The URI is similar to an e-mail address, such as `sip:userA@sip.com`. A secure SIP URI can be used too, such as `sips:userA@sip.com`. A call made using `sips:` (Secure SIP) will use a secure transport, **Transport Layer Security (TLS)**, between the caller and callee.

The transaction starts with **userA** sending an **INVITE** request addressed to **userB**. The INVITE request contains a certain number of header fields. Header fields are named attributes that provide additional information about the message and include a unique identifier, the destination, and information about the session.

INVITE from A->B

```
INVITE sip:userB@sipB.com SIP/2.0
Via: SIP/2.0/UDP moon.sipA.com;branch=z9hG4bK776asdhds
Max-Forwards: 70
To: userB <sip:userB@sipB.com>
From: userA <sip:userA@sipA.com>;tag=1234567890
Call-ID: a84b4c76e66710@moon.sipA.com
CSeq: 314159 INVITE
Contact: <sip:userB@sun.sipB.com>
Content-Type: application/sdp
Content-Length: 142
(SDP not shown)
```

The first line of the message contains the method name and request URI. The following lines contain a list of header fields. This example contains the minimum set required. The header fields have been described as follows:

- **Method and Request-URI**: In the first line, you have the request URI also referred to as RURI. It contains the current destination of the message and is often manipulated by the proxies to route a request. It is the most important field in a SIP request.

- **Via**: This contains the address to which userA will be waiting to receive responses to this request. It also contains a parameter called `branch` that identifies this transaction. The Via header defines the last SIP hop as IP, transport, and transaction-specific parameters. Via is used exclusively to route back the replies. Each proxy adds an additional Via header. It is a lot easier for replies to find their route back using the Via header than to go again in the location server or DNS.

- **To**: This contains the name (display name) and SIP URI (that is, `sip:userB@sip.com`) in the destination originally selected. The To header field is not used to route the packets.

- **From**: This contains the name and SIP URI (that is, `sip:userA@sip.com`) that indicates the caller ID. This header field has a tag parameter containing a random string that was added to the URI by the IP phone. It is used for the purposes of identification. The tag parameter is used in the To and From fields. It serves as a general mechanism to identify the dialog, which is the combination of the Call-ID along with the two tags, one from each participant in the dialog. Tags can be useful in parallel forking.

- **Call-ID**: This contains a globally unique identifier for this call generated by the combination of a random string and it may contain the hostname or IP address of the UAC. A combination of the To, From, and Call-ID tags fully defines an end-to-end SIP relation known as a SIP dialog.

- **CSeq**: The CSeq or command sequence contains an integer and a method name. The CSeq number is incremented to each new request in a SIP dialog and is a traditional sequence number.

- **Contact**: This contains a SIP URI, which represents a direct route to contact userA, usually composed of a user name and **fully qualified domain name (FQDN)**. It is usual to use the IP address instead of the FQDN in this field. While the Via header field tells the other elements where to send a response, the Contact tells the other elements where to send future requests.

- **Max-Forwards**: This is used to limit the number of allowed hops that a request can make in the path to their final destination. It consists of an integer decremented by each hop.

- **Content-Type**: This contains a body message description.
- **Content-Length**: This contains a byte count of the body message.

Session details such as the media type and codec are not described in SIP. Instead, it uses the **Session Description Protocol (SDP)** (RFC 2327). This SDP message is carried by the SIP message, similar to an e-mail attachment.

The phone does not know the location of userB or the server responsible for domainB. Thus, it sends the INVITE request to the server responsible for the domain, sipA. This address is configured in the phone of userA or can be discovered by DNS. The server sipA.com is also known as the SIP proxy for the domain sipA.com.

The sequence is as follows:

1. In this example, the proxy receives the INVITE request and sends a 100 Trying reply back to userA, indicating that the proxy received INVITE and is working to forward the request. The SIP reply uses a three-digit code followed by a descriptive phrase. This response contains the same To, From, Call-ID, and CSeq header fields and a `branch` parameter in the header field, Via. This allows for the userA's phone to correlate the INVITE request that is sent.

2. ProxyA locates ProxyB consulting a DNS server (NAPTR and SRV records) to find which server is responsible for the SIP domain sipB and forwards the INVITE request. Before sending the request to proxyA, it adds a Via header field that contains its own address. The INVITE request already has the address of userA in the first Via header field.

3. ProxyB receives the INVITE request and responds with a 100 Trying reply to ProxyA indicating that it is processing the request.

4. ProxyB consults its own location database for userB's address and then it adds another Via header field with its own address to the INVITE request and forwards this to userB's IP address.

5. The userB's phone receives the INVITE request and starts ringing. The phone responds to this condition by sending a 180 Ringing reply.

6. This message is routed back through both the proxies in the reverse direction. Each proxy uses the Via header fields to determine where to send the response and removes its own Via header from the top. As a result, the message 180 Ringing can return to the user without any lookups to DNS or Location Service and without the need for stateful processing. Thus, each proxy sees all the messages resulting from the INVITE request.

7. When userA's phone receives the 180 Ringing message, it starts to ring back in order to signal the user that the call is ringing on the other side. Some phones show this in the display.

8. In this example, userB decides to attend the call. When they pick up the handset, the phone sends a response of 200 OK to indicate that the call was taken. The 200 OK message contains in its body a session description specifying the codecs, ports, and everything pertaining to the session. It uses the SDP protocol for this duty. As a result, an exchange occurs in two phases of messages from A to B (INVITE) and B to A (200 OK) negotiating the resources and capabilities used on the call in a simple offer/response model. If userB does not want to receive the call or is busy, the 200 OK won't be sent and a message signaling the condition (that is, 486 Busy Here) will be sent instead.

Response 200 Ok

```
SIP/2.0 200 OK
Via: SIP/2.0/UDP sipB.com
;branch=z9hG4bKnashds8;received=192.0.2.3
Via: SIP/2.0/UDP moon.sipA.com
;branch=z9hG4bK77ef4c2312983.1;received=192.0.2.2
Via: SIP/2.0/UDP phoneA.sipA.com
;branch=z9hG4bK776asdhds ;received=192.0.2.1
To: userB <sip:userB@sipB.com>;tag=a6c85cf
From: userA <sip:userA@sipA.com>;tag=1928301774
Call-ID: a84b4c76e66710@phoneA.sipA.com
CSeq: 314159 INVITE
Contact: <sip:userB@192.0.2.4>
Content-Type: application/sdp
Content-Length: 131
```

The first line contains the response code and a description (OK). The following lines contain the header fields. The Via, To, From, Call-ID, and CSeq fields are copied from the INVITE request and the To tag is attached. There are three Via fields: one added by userA, another by ProxyA, and finally, ProxyB. The SIP phone of userB adds a `tag` parameter for the To and From headers and will include this tag on all the future requests and responses for this call.

The Contact header field contains the URI by which userB can be contacted directly in its own IP phone.

The Content-Type and Content-Length header fields give some information about the SDP header. The SDP header contains media-related parameters used to establish the RTP session.

After answering the call, the following occurs:

1. The 200 OK message is sent back through both the proxies and received by userA and then the phone stops ringing, indicating that the call was accepted.

2. Finally, userA sends an ACK message to userB's phone confirming the reception of the 200 OK message. When record routing is not involved, the ACK is sent directly from phoneA to phoneB avoiding both the proxies. ACK is the only SIP method that has no reply. The endpoints learn each other's addresses from the CONTACT header fields during the INVITE process. This ends the cycle, INVITE/200 OK/ACK, also known as the SIP three-way handshake.

3. At this moment, the session between both the users starts and they send media packets to each other using a mutually agreed format established by the SDP protocol. Usually, these packets are end to end. During the session, the parties can change the session characteristics issuing a new INVITE request. This is called a reinvite. If the reinvite is not acceptable, a 488 Not Acceptable Here message will be sent, but the session will not fail.

4. At the end of the session, userB disconnects the phone and generates a BYE message. This message is routed directly to userA's SIP phone, bypassing both the proxies.

5. The userA confirms the reception of the BYE message with a 200 OK message ending the session. No ACK is sent. An ACK is sent only for INVITE requests.

In some cases, it can be important for the proxies to stay in the middle of the signaling to see all the messages between the endpoints during the whole session. If the proxy wants to stay in the path after the initial INVITE request, it has to add the Record-Route header field to the request. This information will be received by userB's phone and will send back the message through the proxies with the Record-Route header field included too. Record-routing is used in most scenarios. Without record-routing, it is not possible to account the calls and there is no control of the SIP dialog in the proxy.

The REGISTER request is the way that ProxyB learns the location of userB. When the phone initializes or in regular time intervals, the SIP phoneB sends a REGISTER request to a server on domain sipB known as SIP Registrar. The REGISTER messages associate a URI (userB@sipB.com) to an IP address. This binding is stored in a database in the Location server. Usually the Registrar, Location, and Proxy servers are in the same computer and use the same software such as OpenSIPS. A URI can only be registered by a single device at a certain time.

SIP transactions and dialogs

It is important to understand the difference between a transaction and dialog because we will use this ahead in OpenSIPS scripting. For example, there are attribute value pairs attached to transactions and dialog variables attached to dialogs. If you can't recognize a dialog and variable, it will be hard to configure the SIP server.

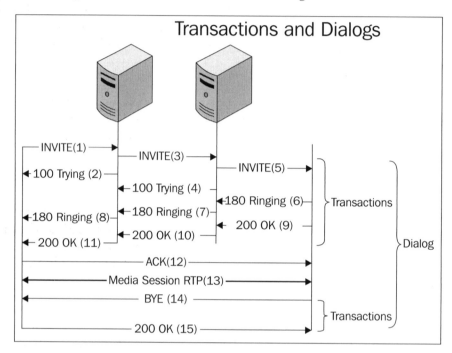

A transaction occurs between a user agent client and server and comprises of all the messages from the request to the final response (including all the interim responses). The responses can be provisional, starting with one followed by two digits (for example, 180 Ringing) or final, starting with two followed by two digits (for example, 200 OK). The scope of a transaction is defined by the stack of Via headers of the SIP messages. So, the user agents, after the initial invite, don't need to rely on DNS or location tables to route the messages.

The ACK request is a special case. For positive replies (2XX), the UAC creates a new transaction and generates a new CONTACT header and it can be sent straight to the UAS bypassing the proxy. However, for negative replies, it belongs to the INVITE transaction because it is not possible to create a new transaction without the Contact of the other part. In this case, the request is sent to the same proxy as INVITE.

According to RFC 3261, a dialog represents a peer-to-peer SIP relationship between two user agents that persists for some time. A dialog is identified at each UA with a dialog ID, which consists of a Call-ID value, local tag, and remote tag present in the From and To headers, respectively.

A dialog is a succession of transactions that control the creation, existence, and termination of the dialog. All dialogs do have a transaction to create them and may (or may not) have a transaction to change the dialog (mid-transaction). Additionally, the end-dialog transaction may be missing. (Some dialogs do end based on timeouts rather than on explicit termination.)

According to RFC 3665, there are 11 basic session establishment flows. The list is not meant to be complete but covers the best practices. The first two were already covered in this chapter, *Successful Session Establishment* and *Session Establishment through two Proxies*. Some of them will be seen in *Chapter 11, Implementing SIP Services*.

Locating the SIP servers

Similar to e-mail servers, you will need to specify which server would serve a specific domain. The location of the SIP servers is described in RFC 3263. The first objective of location is to determine the IP, port, and transport protocol for the server based on the domain name. The second objective is to determine the address of a backup for the first proxy.

To perform these objectives, we will use a Domain Name System, more specifically, **Name Authority Pointer (NAPTR)** and **Service (SRV)** records. NAPTR records are employed to determine the transport protocol. To specify a transport protocol, you should insert the DNS records in the zone file of your DNS server. (Check the documentation of your DNS server on how to do it.) In the following code, we are enabling three protocols for this domain, TLS, TCP, and UDP. If the client supports TLS and UDP, TLS will be chosen because of the defined order in the records:

```
Order   pref    flags service regexp replacement
IN NAPTR   10    50      "s"    "SIPS+D2T" ""  _sips._tcp.opensips.org.
IN NAPTR   20    50      "s"    "SIP+D2T"  ""  _sip._tcp.opensips.org.
IN NAPTR   30    50      "s"    "SIP+D2U"  ""  _sip._udp.opensips.org.
```

After selecting the transport protocol, it is time to select the preferred server, which is done as follows:

```
Service             TTL     Class P/W   Port Server
_sips._tcp.opensips.org. 86400 IN SRV 0 5 5060 sipA.opensips.org.
_sips._tcp.opensips.org. 86400 IN SRV 0 5 5060 sipB.opensips.org.
_sip._udp.opensips.org.  86400 IN SRV 0 5 5060 sipA.opensips.org.
_sip._udp.opensips.org.  86400 IN SRV 0 5 5060 sipB.opensips.org.
```

The terms in the preceding code are described as follows:

- **Service**: The symbolic name of the desired service
- **TTL**: The standard DNS time to live field
- **Class**: The standard DNS class field (this is always IN)
- **Priority**: The priority of the target host; a lower value means more preferred
- **Weight**: A relative weight for the records with the same priority
- **Port**: The TCP or UDP port on which the service is to be found
- **Target**: The canonical hostname of the machine providing the service

The configuration of the SRV records is often used to provide failovers and load sharing between the SIP servers. It is one of the easiest ways to get geographical redundancy in a SIP project.

SIP services

Beyond making and receiving calls, you can implement a series of SIP services. These services include, but are not limited to, Call Transfers, Call Pickup, Call Hold, Call Forward, and many others. Fortunately, RFC 5359 (SIP services) defines a standard way to accomplish these tasks. Most SIP phones comply with the way SIP services are implemented; however, to make them work, you need to make sure that all the components in the network support some specific RFCs. As an example, the call transfer requires the support of the REFER method defined in RFC 3515 and the Referred-By and Replaces headers defined in RFCs 3891 and 3892, respectively. If you intend to provide PBX-like services using a SIP proxy, you have to make sure that all the components, including phones and gateways, support it. SIP services are implemented in phones, gateways, media servers, and proxies. All the components must collaborate in order to implement each specific service. The following are some of the services defined in RFC 5359:

- Call Hold
- Consultation Hold
- Music on Hold
- Transfer – Unattended
- Transfer – Attended
- Transfer – Instant Messaging
- Call Forwarding – Unconditional
- Call Forwarding – Busy

- Call Forwarding — No Answer
- 3-Way Conference — Third Party Is Added
- 3-Way Conference — Third Party Joins
- Find-Me
- Incoming Call Screening
- Outgoing Call Screening
- Call Park
- Call Pickup
- Automatic Redial
- Click to Dial

It would be counterproductive to describe in detail each service here. Refer to the specified RFC for details.

The SIP identity

SIP servers are often employed to provide telephony services. However, there is a problem where **Public Switched Telephone Network (PSTN)** does not support SIP addresses containing domains and alphanumeric characters. To identify a caller identity for the PSTN, a few methods were created and applied.

The `draft-ietf-sip-privacy-04` document describes the **Remote-Party-ID** header. While it has never became a standard, it is still quite popular among gateway manufacturers and service providers. See the following example:

```
Remote-Party-ID: "John" <sip:+554833328560@sip.com>; party=calling;
id-type=subscriber; privacy=full; screen=yes
```

The preceding header sets the caller ID number as `+554833328560` and caller name as `"John"`; it is a subscriber in the proxy, the identity was verified (`screen=yes`), and the number should not be present in the destination's terminal (`privacy=full`). The draft specifies additional features and how to handle privacy requests. For the purposes of this book, Remote-Party-IDs will be used just for caller ID presentation.

The standard way to handle caller IDs and privacy came later in RFC 3325. It defines the P-Asserted-Identity, P-Preferred-Identity, and Privacy headers. See the following example:

```
P-Asserted-Identity: "John" sip:+554833328560@sip.com
P-Asserted-Identity: tel:+554833328560
```

To specify the caller ID to be present in the PSTN, you can use these headers. The gateway should match the type of caller ID and privacy used in your proxy. In an OpenSIPS server, you can add headers using the `append_hf` command. It is an extensive RFC and you can check the details in the document itself.

The RTP protocol

The **Real-Time Protocol (RTP)** is responsible for the real-time transport of data such as audio and video. It was standardized in RFC 3550. It uses UDP as the transport protocol. To be transported, the audio or video has to be packetized by a *codec*. Basically, the protocol allows the specification of the timing and content requirements of the media transmission for the incoming and outgoing packets using the following:

- The sequence number
- Timestamps
- Packet forward without retransmission
- Source identification
- Content identification
- Synchronism

Codecs

A **codec** is an algorithm capable of encoding or decoding a digital stream. The content described in the RTP protocol is usually encoded by a codec. Each codec has a specific use. Some have compression while others do not. G.711 is still the most popular codec and does not use compression. With 64 Kbps of bandwidth for a single channel, it needs a high-speed network, commonly found in **Local Area Networks (LANs)**. However, in **Wide Area Networks (WANs)**, 64 Kbps can be too expensive to buy for a single channel. Codecs such as G.729 and GSM can compress the voice packets to as low as 8 Kbps, saving a lot of bandwidth. To simplify the way you choose a voice codec, the following table shows the most relevant ones. Bandwidths do not consider the lower protocol layer headers. There are also video codecs where the most relevant ones are the H.264 series and VP8 from Google.

Codec	Bandwidth	MOS	Env.	When to use
G.711	64 Kbps	4.45	LAN/WAN	Use it for toll quality and broad support from gateways.
G.729	8 Kbps	4.04	WAN	Use it to save bandwidth and keep toll quality.
G.722	64 Kbps	4.5	LAN	Use it for high-definition voice.
OPUS	6-510 Kbps	–	INTERNET	OPUS is the most sophisticated codec ever created. It spans from a narrowband audio to high-definition music.

There are other codecs such as G.723, GSM, iLBC, and SILK that are slowly losing ground to OPUS. OPUS is the codec adopted for the WebRTC standard. Obviously, you can dig a little more into codec details; there are dozens available, but I truly believe that the four described previously are the relevant choices at the time of this book being written. **MOS** is the **Mean Opinion Score** and defines the audio quality.

MOS	Quality	Impairment
5	Excellent	Imperceptible
4	Good	Perceptible but not annoying
3	Fair	Slightly annoying
2	Poor	Annoying
1	Bad	Very annoying

Source: ITU-T P.800 recommendation

DTMF-relay

There are three ways to carry DTMF in VoIP networks: inband as audio tones, named events on RTP as defined in RFC 2833, and signaling using the SIP INFO messages. RFC 2833 describes a method to transmit DTMF as named events in the RTP protocol. It is very important that you use the same method between user agent servers and clients.

Session Description Protocol

The Session Description Protocol (SDP) is described in RFC 4566. It is used to negotiate session parameters between the user agents. Media details, transport addresses, and other media-related information is exchanged between the user agents using the SDP protocol. Normally, the INVITE message contains the SDP offer message, while the 200 OK contains the answer message. These messages are shown in the following figures. You can observe that the GSM codec is offered, but the other phone does not support it. Then it answers with the supported codecs, in this case, G.711 u-law (PCMU) and G.729. The **rtpmap:101** session is the DTMF relay described in RFC 2833.

```
⊟ Session Initiation Protocol
  ⊞ Request-Line: INVITE sip:8520@8.8.30.36:42989 SIP/2.0
  ⊞ Message Header
  ⊟ Message body
     ⊟ Session Description Protocol
        Session Description Protocol Version (v): 0
        ⊟ Owner/Creator, Session Id (o): root 10968 10968 IN IP4 8.8.1.4
           Owner Username: root
           Session ID: 10968
           Session Version: 10968
           Owner Network Type: IN
           Owner Address Type: IP4
           Owner Address: 8.8.1.4
        Session Name (s): session
     ⊞ Connection Information (c): IN IP4 8.8.1.4
     ⊞ Time Description, active time (t): 0 0
     ⊞ Media Description, name and address (m): audio 17412 RTP/AVP 0 3 18 101
     ⊞ Media Attribute (a): rtpmap:0 PCMU/8000
     ⊞ Media Attribute (a): rtpmap:3 GSM/8000
     ⊞ Media Attribute (a): rtpmap:18 G729/8000
     ⊞ Media Attribute (a): fmtp:18 annexb=no
     ⊞ Media Attribute (a): rtpmap:101 telephone-event/8000
     ⊞ Media Attribute (a): fmtp:101 0-16
     ⊞ Media Attribute (a): silenceSupp:off - - - -
```

INVITE (SDP Offer)

```
⊟ Session Initiation Protocol
  ⊞ Status-Line: SIP/2.0 200 OK
  ⊞ Message Header
  ⊟ Message body
    ⊟ Session Description Protocol
        Session Description Protocol Version (v): 0
      ⊟ Owner/Creator, Session Id (o): root 11218 11218 IN IP4 8.8.1.4
          Owner Username: root
          Session ID: 11218
          Session Version: 11218
          Owner Network Type: IN
          Owner Address Type: IP4
          Owner Address: 8.8.1.4
        Session Name (s): session
      ⊞ Connection Information (c): IN IP4 8.8.1.4
      ⊞ Time Description, active time (t): 0 0
      ⊞ Media Description, name and address (m): audio 17428 RTP/AVP 0 18 101
      ⊞ Media Attribute (a): rtpmap:0 PCMU/8000
      ⊞ Media Attribute (a): rtpmap:18 G729/8000
      ⊞ Media Attribute (a): fmtp:18 annexb=no
      ⊞ Media Attribute (a): rtpmap:101 telephone-event/8000
      ⊞ Media Attribute (a): fmtp:101 0-16
      ⊞ Media Attribute (a): silenceSupp:off - - - -
```

200 OK (SDP Answer)

The SIP protocol and OSI model

It is always important to understand the voice protocols against the OSI model to situate where each protocol fits. The following diagram demonstrates this clearly:

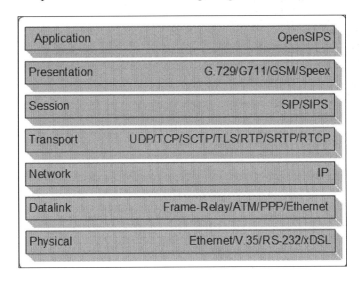

The VoIP provider's big picture

This book was created using the VoIP provider as it is the most common use case. Before we start digging in the SIP proxy, it is important to understand all the components for a VoIP provider solution. A VoIP provider usually consists of several services. The services described here could be installed in a single server or multiple servers depending on the capacity requirements.

In this book, we will cover each one of these components, from left to right, in the chapters ahead. We will use the following picture in all the chapters in order to help you identify where you are:

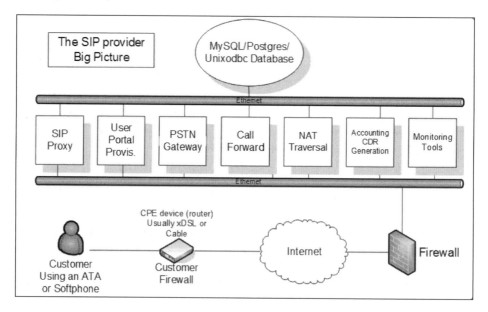

The SIP proxy

The SIP proxy is the central component of our solution. It is responsible for registering the users and keeping the location database (maps IP to SIP addresses). The entire SIP routing and signaling is handled by the SIP proxy and it is also responsible for end-user services such as call forwarding, white/blacklist, speed dialing, and others. This component never handles the media (RTP packets); most media-related packets are routed directly from the user agent clients, servers, and PSTN gateways.

The user administration and provisioning portal

One important component is the user administration and provisioning portal. In the portal, the user can subscribe to the service and be capable of buying credits, changing passwords, and verifying his account. On the other hand, administrators should be able to remove users, change user credits, and grant and remove privileges. Provisioning is the process used to make it easier for administrators to provide automatic installation of user agents such as IP phones, analog telephony adapters, and SIP phones.

The PSTN gateway

To communicate to the PSTN, a PSTN gateway is usually required, except when you have a SIP trunk. The gateway will interface the PSTN using E1 or T1 trunks. To evaluate a good gateway, check the support of SIP extensions, such as RFC 3325 (Identity), RFC 3515 (REFER), RFC 3891 (Replaces), and RFC 3892 (Referred-by). These protocols will allow unattended transfers behind the SIP proxy; without them in the gateway, it might be impossible to transfer calls.

The media server

The SIP proxy never handles the media. Services such as **Interactive Voice Response (IVR)**, voicemail, conference, or anything related to media should be implemented in a media server. There are many SIP servers fitting this purpose, such as Asterisk (http://www.asterisk.org/), FreeSWITCH (https://freeswitch.org/), Yate (http://yate.ro/), SEMS from IPTEL, and SilkServer for AG projects. The examples in this book will use Asterisk as it is, by far, the most popular.

The media proxy or RTP proxy for NAT traversal

Any SIP provider will have to handle NAT traversal for their customers. The media proxy is an RTP bridge that helps the users behind symmetric firewalls to access the SIP provider. Without them, it won't be possible to service a large share of the user base. You can implement a universal NAT traversal technique using these components. The media proxy can help you in the accounting correction for unfinished SIP dialogs that, for some reason, didn't receive the BYE message.

Accounting and CDR generation

An **Authentication**, **Authorization**, and **Accounting (AAA)** server can be used along with OpenSIPS. FreeRADIUS is a common choice. In several implementations, you can skip RADIUS and use SQL accounting. Some VoIP providers will leverage an existing AAA server while some others will prefer the low overhead MySQL accounting. Beyond accounting, there is CDR generation where the duration of the calls is calculated.

Monitoring tools

Finally, we will need monitoring, troubleshooting, and testing tools to help debug any problems occurring in the SIP server. The first tool is the protocol analyzer and we will see how to use ngrep, Wireshark, and TShark. OpenSIPS has a module called SIP trace, which we will use as well.

Additional references

The best reference for the SIP protocol is RFC 3261. To read the RFCs is a little bit boring and sleepy. (It is very good when you have insomnia.) You can find RFC at `http://www.ietf.org/rfc/rfc3261.txt`.

The OpenSIPS mailing lists can be found at `http://www.opensips.org/Support/MailingLists`.

There is a mailing list where you can post questions about SIP called SIP implementors at `https://lists.cs.columbia.edu/mailman/listinfo/sip-implementors`.

Summary

In this chapter, you learned what the SIP protocol is and its functionality. We saw different SIP components, such as the SIP proxy, SIP Registrar, user agent client, user agent server, and PSTN gateway. We also got acquainted with the SIP architecture and its main messages and processes.

In the next chapter, we will be introduced to OpenSIPS and its basic architecture and components.

2
Introducing OpenSIPS

This chapter will help you understand **OpenSIPS**. The most important thing is to clarify what OpenSIPS is in relation to the SIP ecosystem: what OpenSIPS is good for, what OpenSIPS can do, what it cannot do, and where OpenSIPS can be the answer for you. This overview is to be followed by a description of the OpenSIPS design. It is essential to fully understand OpenSIPS—from the outside and inside perspectives—before using it.

In this chapter, we will cover the following topics:

- What OpenSIPS is
- How to get the knowledge about OpenSIPS
- When to use OpenSIPS and the different usage scenarios
- What the OpenSIPS internal design and structure is

Understanding OpenSIPS

OpenSIPS is an open source, GPLed, multipurpose SIP server that is able to perform a large set of SIP-related functions, such as SIP Registrar, SIP proxy/router, Instant Messaging server, Presence server, SIP Redirect server, SIP load balancer or SIP Dispatcher, SIP Back-to-Back user agent, Call Queuing System, SIP IP gateway, SIP media controller, SIP application server, and many others.

OpenSIPS defines itself via the following three major capabilities:

- **Performance**: It is translated into a huge throughput actively measured up to 60,000 calls per second, 1.5 million simultaneous calls, 5 million registered users, and 1 million TCP connections, all in a single OpenSIPS instance running on a mid-level server

- **Feature-rich**: It is translated into more than 160 modules providing functionalities or features related to the SIP protocol, SQL or NoSQL DB operations, AAA integrations, routing algorithms (quality, prefix, load-based routing, and dial plans), management and control (events and external commands), and many others

- **Flexibility**: It is provided by the routing language; a simple but powerful scripting language (shell-like) that allows you to program OpenSIPS to handle the SIP traffic in the way you want

OpenSIPS as a SIP server is mainly about processing and handling the SIP traffic. OpenSIPS does not have media capabilities (handling RTP) at all. Nevertheless, there are external extensions that can be used to enable OpenSIPS not to handle but to control the RTP traffic, such as controlling external media relays (RTPproxy, MediaProxy, and RTPEngine) or external transcoders (Sangoma D1 transcoding cards).

There are two words that describe OpenSIPS perfectly – SIP and Engine:

- OpenSIPS is designed for SIP: From this perspective, OpenSIPS covers the providing of various transport protocol for SIP (UDP, TCP, TLS, SCTP, WebSockets, and so on) and also implementing an RFC-compliant SIP stack to handle the SIP packet (parsing, building, and changing).

- OpenSIPS means handling and processing: OpenSIPS has a powerful but flexible engine able to handle the SIP traffic in the most efficient, fast, and customized way. Any kind of routing logic can be implemented with the OpenSIPS processing engine.

The capabilities and throughput of OpenSIPS simply makes it the core entity of any SIP platform; whatever the service type is, whatever the size is, and whatever the requirements are.

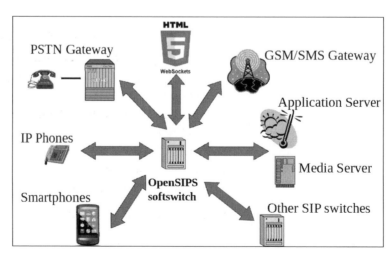

OpenSIPS capabilities

OpenSIPS was originally intended to be a Class 4 SIP switch, but during its evolution along the years, OpenSIPS exceeded the original goal and started to provide Class 5 features. It is not able to offer a complete set of Class 5 features because of being limited to the SIP signaling-related features (that is, call forwarding, call transfer, call pickup, and so on). This limitation comes from the fact that OpenSIPS does not handle media, so it cannot offer media-related features. You can find the list of capabilities offered by OpenSIPS as follows:

Capabilities	Classes
Transport-level capabilities	<ul><li>UDP / TCP / TLS / SCTP / WebSockets support</li><li>IPv4 and IPv6</li><li>Multihomed with interface exchange</li><li>IP blacklists</li></ul>
Endpoint-oriented capabilities	<ul><li>SIP registration</li><li>NAT traversal (STUN, TURN, SIP pinging)</li><li>Digest authentication (against SQL, noSQL, AAA, LDAP)</li><li>Trunking or IP authentication</li><li>Complex call accounting/CDRs</li><li>Multidomain support</li><li>User profiles (groups, attributes, flags)</li></ul>
Class 4 routing	<ul><li>SIP aliases, DID aliasing</li><li>Speed dialling</li><li>Call Processing Language (CPL) interpreter</li><li>Dialplan (text and regular expression-based)</li><li>Traffic dispatching (with multiple dispatching algorithms)</li><li>Prefix-based routing to multiple carriers (with failovers)</li><li>Load balancing</li><li>ENUM-based routing</li><li>Redirect server, redirect UAC</li><li>Geolocation-based routing</li><li>OSP integration</li></ul>

Capabilities	Classes
Class 5 routing	• Generic SIP B2B capabilities • Inbound call center with call queuing • UAC registration • UAC authentication • UAC mangling (From, To, Call-ID, CSeq) • Call managing (call forward, call hunting, call pickup, redirect) • White/Black list for inbound and outbound calls
SIP SIMPLE	• SIP Presence • BLF, SCA, BLA, MWI • XCAP support • RLS • SIP messaging and SIP chatting • SIP to XMPP gatewaying • Offline messages storing • SMS gateway (AT and SMPP)
Media/RTP-related capabilities	• Media relaying (RTPProxy, MediaProxy, RTPEngine) • Media transcoding (Sangoma D1 cards) • Codec manipulation
SIP security	• Fraud detection and prevention • Flood detection (at IP level) • SIP traffic validation • QoS control • Parallel calls and calling rate limitation
SIP-related capabilities	• Dialog support (monitor, probing, termination) • SIP DNS lookup (A, SRV, NAPTR) • DNS-based failover • SIP compression • SIP Identity • **SIP Session Timer (SST)**

Capabilities	Classes
OpenSIPS scripting capabilities	• Processing benchmarking • Script tracing • Custom data caching (from script) • Execution of external scripts/applications • LUA, Perl, and Python scripting support • Mathematical operation support • SIP traffic capturing (tracing and Homer integration)
OpenSIPS management and integration	• Event interface—subscribing and delivering events to external entities • Built-in HTTP server • Management interface (FIFO, XMLRPC, JSON, Datagram, HTTP) • SNMP support • Internal statistics
Backend support	• SQL—Berkeley, Flat File, HTTP, MySQL, Postgres, Oracle, Perl VDB, Text, and Unix ODBC • AAA—Radius and Diameter • NoSQL—Cassandra, MongoDB, Redis, CouchBase, and Memcached • LDAP • REST client

As you can see, these capabilities are grouped by classes, depending on their nature.

 Remember that OpenSIPS has no built-in media capabilities, but it can control external media engines.

An overview of the OpenSIPS project

The OpenSIPS project is an open source project with a dynamic international community, releasing its code under the GNU **General Public License version 2 (GPLv2)**.

OpenSIPS is a daemon-like application that runs on all Unix-like platforms—the BSD family, Linux, Solaris, OS X, and others. Nevertheless, the development is primarily done under Linux environments.

OpenSIPS is written in the C language with several additional helper tools written in Shell, Perl, or Python (tools to install and create DB schemas, CLI tools, and others). OpenSIPS development is completely active and there is a major release every 6 to 12 months and a minor release every 1 to 3 months. Some basic things to note here are as follows:

- The OpenSIPS project is primarily hosted on GitHub: `https://github.com/OpenSIPS`

- The code is versioned under Git: `https://github.com/OpenSIPS/opensips`

- A tracker is available for bug reports, feature requests, patch submission, or any other generic issues: `https://github.com/OpenSIPS/opensips/issues`

- The OpenSIPS project is governed by the **OpenSIPS Software Foundation (OSF)** but relies on a vast and international community in order to function.

The goal of OSF is to provide an open framework to encourage contributions that help the OpenSIPS project to flourish. The OSF activities are mainly focused on building a proper image for the project, organizing OpenSIPS-related events, and other activities related to managing and marketing the project. The OSF is not involved at all in any decisions or activities related to the code development part.

The community is the one leading and powering the project development and progress—in terms of research, code development, testing and reporting, fixing, and knowledge transfer to newcomers.

The monthly public meetings hosted on the OpenSIPS IRC channel involve the entire community in the current status of the project (transparency in terms of development) and in the decision-making for future plans:

```
#opensips on FreeNode IRC server
```

Such meetings allow the community to stay connected to the OpenSIPS project and synchronize their own plans with the development path of OpenSIPS. This makes OpenSIPS a reliable tool (in terms of code and delivery) to be used in all areas, including the most demanding grounds such as the telecom industry.

One step further, the OpenSIPS Summits are events meant to coagulate the OpenSIPS community by providing its participants with a concentrated cocktail of knowledge and understanding of the project—updates on the project, real case studies, examples of usage scenarios, tutorials, and open discussions. The OpenSIPS Summits take place two or three times per year in various locations across the world and are announced in advance via the project news channels:

`http://www.opensips.org/Community/Summits`

For coagulating purposes, the OpenSIPS project has a strong presence on various socializing portals such as LinkedIn or Facebook—this in an easy way to be up to date with the latest news or activities of the project:

- `https://www.linkedin.com/groups/164063`
- `https://www.facebook.com/opensips`

OpenSIPS knowledge transfer and support

For the OpenSIPS users, the project offers multiple ways of knowledge transfer—the Open Access to Knowledge is a mandatory complement of the open source code in an open source project. The project offers various and complete online documentations; each OpenSIPS version has its own version of documents. The documents are updated with each release. For easy browsing, the documents are structured based on the OpenSIPS versions.

The documentation section is located at `http://opensips.org/Documentation/Manuals`.

The most important subsections are as follows:

- The generic OpenSIPS manual: Information about functions, modules, and interfaces in OpenSIPS at `http://www.opensips.org/Documentation/Manual-2-1`

- Advanced tutorials: Complete and comprehensive examples of using certain OpenSIPS functionalities at `http://www.opensips.org/Documentation/Tutorials`

- Troubleshooting: How to deal with the most common problems at `http://www.opensips.org/Documentation/Troubleshooting`

- Migration: How to migrate your OpenSIPS installations at `http://www.opensips.org/Documentation/Migration`

Besides manuals, tutorials, and other written documentation, the OpenSIPS project provides you with audio/video webinars. Each webinar covers a certain topic with detailed explanations and working script examples at http://www.opensips.org/Documentation/Webinars.

Complementary to the documentation, the OpenSIPS project provides help and support to its community. There are various available channels that the users can use in order to get support from the OpenSIPS team and the rest of the community:

http://www.opensips.org/Support/Contact

The most popular channel is the mailing list, where anyone can ask and answer OpenSIPS-related questions. For similar purposes, the project has its own IRC channel that can be used for real-time discussions.

For more demanding users, the project offers training and certification programs. Starting with a fast-track self-training, the project also offers intensive boot camp training with instructors and ends with a certification exam to prove your OpenSIPS knowledge and skills at http://www.opensips.org/Support/EBootcamp and http://www.opensips.org/Support/Certification.

> *The philosophy of the OpenSIPS project is "a project for users, by users".*

Usage scenarios for OpenSIPS

The huge set of features provided by the modules combined with the powerful routing script makes OpenSIPS the best candidate for almost any SIP-related scenario.

From simple traffic switching to complex residential or trunking scenarios, from the ingress to egress of your network, OpenSIPS is able to cope with the requirements in an efficient and scalable way.

This chapter does not aim to list all the possible usage scenarios for OpenSIPS but just to scratch the surface, show the most popular usage scenarios, and give some reference points when it comes to what you can do with OpenSIPS. Let's take the classical SIP network as a case study, which typically consists of an ingress, a core, and an egress. We will inspect each of these sides in order to see what OpenSIPS can do for them.

The ingress side

In a SIP network, the ingress component sits between the SIP endpoints (registering SIP phones, SIP PBX, and SIP trunks) and the SIP core platform.

Due to its location, the ingress component must address two important issues:

- **Scalability**: The ingress SIP servers concentrate a huge volume of traffic from the endpoints
- **Security**: The SIP servers are in direct contact with the endpoints and so the ingress component is more exposed to attacks, floods, or other security issues

Usually, an ingress component is also called **Session Border Controller (SBC)**. Despite the common understanding that an SBC is responsible only for security and NAT traversal, the term of SBC is something very generic—it is a component sitting on the edge of the network and controlling the traffic crossing in and out of your network. The following figure shows OpenSIPS working as a SIP router:

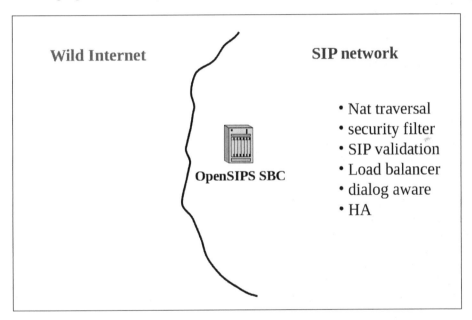

Acting as an SBC (or ingress component), OpenSIPS can address multiple requirements at the same time.

Starting from the lowest level, the *network level*, OpenSIPS is able to provide the most complex operations:

- **Network bridging**: As it is able to listen on multiple interfaces in different networks, OpenSIPS can route the traffic between different isolated networks (to perform bridging). The interface used to send out the traffic can be controlled manually from a script or automatically detected by OpenSIPS. The bridging is also available between the IPv4 and IPv6 networks.

- **NAT traversal**: With NAT autodetection functions, OpenSIPS is able to discover the traffic coming from behind NAT and translate all the SIP traffic into public IP addresses. The built-in STUN server is also available in OpenSIPS; even better, the STUN server is able to listen on the same listeners as the SIP traffic (mixing SIP and STUN on the same UDP listeners). The NAT traversal logic may be combined with media relaying by using OpenSIPS to control such external media relays.

- **Protocol conversion**: As OpenSIPS implements various transport protocols for SIP, it can take incoming traffic over TLS (towards the endpoints) and convert it to UDP (towards the core components).The OpenSIPS script gives a maximum of flexibility to detect the need of protocol conversion and also to implement it.

- **Flood detection**: By monitoring all the source IPs for the incoming traffic, OpenSIPS can detect potential sources of flood (attacks or unintended) in an efficient way. All the received packets, SIP-valid or not, over different protocols are counted in the flood detection process.

- **IP Filtering**: IPs or ranges of IPs can be configured to be discarded as sources of traffic.

Moving up on the stack, on the *SIP level*, OpenSIPS addresses multiple important issues for an SBC:

- **SIP validation**: The incoming SIP packets are subject to validation from a SIP perspective. It checks both the syntax and message contents to make sure that all the mandatory headers are present. If body is present, it checks the Content-Length and Content-Type headers. Depending on the nature of the packets (and its methods), specific consistency checks are performed.

- **Call aware**: OpenSIPS can be (optionally) call stateful, which means that it will be call aware. If configured, OpenSIPS monitors all the ongoing calls and checks the validity and health of all the SIP messages in the call. Such checks are mainly looking for broken in-call routing (for sequential requests), requests injection (attacks based on sequential requests), or hanged calls (so-called zombie calls, which were terminated only by one end).

- **Topology hiding**: On a call basis, OpenSIPS can perform IP and/or SIP topology hiding.
- **Traffic filtering**: Using regular expression patterns, OpenSIPS can filter out the SIP traffic by inspecting various fields in the SIP requests—Request URI, User-Agent, or From/To headers.
- **Media handling**: Codec filtering and reordering can be performed in combination with media pinning, transcoding, or call recording (using external media servers).
- **SIP tracing**: OpenSIPS can be instructed to selectively trace (and store) certain SIP traffic on a SIP user, source IP, or destination criteria.
- **Data replication**: OpenSIPS implements an internal data replication mechanism, which is a must in building **High Availability (HA)** solutions with hot backups (active backup) or even Active-Active solutions. Transparency and 0% losses are mandatory requirements for the SBC HA solutions.

On the top level, at the *routing level*, endpoints and traffic can be handled in almost any custom combination by OpenSIPS SBC, which acts as a **frontend** for the core components:

- **Endpoint authentication**: IP-based and Digest-based authentication can be performed against the traffic received from the endpoints.
- **Traffic shaping**: The traffic received from the endpoints may be subject to limitations based on the number of concurrent calls or the calling rate.
- **Dialplan**: For the incoming traffic, OpenSIPS can offer a simple dialplan. This provides you with the ability to perform inspection and changes over the dialled or dialling numbers (or SIP URIs).
- **Dispatching/Load-balancing**: As a frontend for the core components, OpenSIPS can provide the function of distributing the incoming traffic across multiple back servers (such as application or media servers); the distribution is also combined with a failover mechanism. OpenSIPS monitors and detects when one of the core servers is down and reroutes the traffic to the remaining back servers.
- **Custom routing**: The selection of the core servers may be done via different custom logics, such as inspecting the SIP domain, source IP, dial number, or any other part of the incoming SIP traffic.

A frontend (or SBC) OpenSIPS may be part of a SIP network design from day zero or it may be added later in order to solve problems such as scaling and distribution of the existing SIP platform.

There is a large set of deployments based on PBX-oriented SIP servers, such as FreeSwitch, Asterisk, or Yate. Such deployments are focused on delivering rich services to the end users (usually enterprises), but later face the problem of scalability. Such PBX-based services are quite limited in terms of users or active calls. The natural solution to scale them is to add more similar servers, but in order to manage the resulting pool/cluster of core servers, it is a must to add a frontend server to take care of distributing the traffic.

The ability of OpenSIPS to perform the frontending task makes it one of the best solutions when it comes to scaling or geographically distributing the existing SIP platforms.

The core side

The core component of a SIP platform is usually called an application, telephony, media, or feature server. It is basically responsible for implementing the actual service in the way that it is seen by the end users.

There are several classes of services such as residential (end user-oriented), hosted PBX, or enterprise (company-oriented), trunking (traffic exchange), or origination/termination (inbound or outbound gateways).

OpenSIPS is the perfect platform to build core services such as **Residential** and **Hosted PBX** services also known as end user-oriented services. Such services are more demanding as they combine the need for a rich set of advanced features (addressing the needs of the end users) with the carrier-level scaling in terms of traffic and location presence.

OpenSIPS offers a rich feature set and an ability to mix everything together via a flexible routing script. It also offers the following end user-oriented features:

- Endpoints management
- DID management
- Advanced call routing (forward, filter, DND, and star codes)
- Presence and messaging
- Class 5 calling (virtual PBX)
- Call center (call queuing)
- CDRs and pre/postpaid billing

Such features are the building blocks of the end user-oriented services. However, OpenSIPS offers basic (or simple) features that you can use, reuse, and combine via the routing script. Mastering the routing script gives you the ability to create new and custom rich features.

 Not all the features are built-in modules; most of them result from pure scripting (combining several basic abilities of OpenSIPS).

Even more, the end user-oriented services offer both SIP-oriented features and non-SIP features. This leads to integration issues; for such purposes, OpenSIPS offers several mechanisms or interfaces to integrate with the external entities:

- A management interface to execute commands in OpenSIPS
- An event interface for OpenSIPS to deliver events to external parties
- An HTTP/REST interface
- An external script/apps execution

The **Trunking** services demand a high throughput, reliability, failure detection, handling of large amounts of data, precise CDRs, and billing. All these requirements are met by OpenSIPS, thanks to its scalability and flexibility.

Modules such as `permissions`, `ratelimit`, and `dialog` allow OpenSIPS to route, partition, and limit the SIP traffic to more than 10,000 SIP trunks on a single instance.

Even if OpenSIPS does not offer built-in billing engines, it generates accurate and real-time CDRs that can be pushed to external rating engines. Based on its ability to control the calls (to be dialog stateful), OpenSIPS can implement prepaid scenarios and precisely terminate ongoing calls on demand.

When dealing with multiple trunks, each having its particularities, there is a need of a complex dialplan to check and unify (as a format) all the dialled calls. OpenSIPS offers both built-in and scripting capabilities of achieving such operations.

In all the cases, whatever the service is, the access to the database(s) is a strong requirement. OpenSIPS offers a variety of backend to different kinds of databases listed as follows:

- SQL
- NoSQL
- Radius and Diameter AAA
- LDAP

OpenSIPS allows you to combine the usage of all these DB types in your routing logic and connect to different types of servers at the same time (using MySQL and Postgre at the same time or MongoDB and Redis).

The DB access can be transparent (hidden by modules offering encapsulated functionalities) or explicit from the routing script level.

The egress side

The egress side of a SIP platform is typically responsible for interfacing the platform with third-party SIP services such as termination providers (PSTN and IP gateway). Nevertheless, the egress side may also interface with the end users when it comes to delivering PSTN calls to the users. In relation with the termination providers (or carriers), OpenSIPS egress is responsible for doing the so-called **PSTN prefix-based routing**, which means selecting the proper carrier/gateway to terminate the call based on the dialled number.

In OpenSIPS, the PSTN routing logic has two logical parts:

- Based on the longest matched prefix (from the dialled number), OpenSIPS selects a set of gateways offering termination to this destination number.

- One gateway is chosen from the selected set — which one? It depends on the order in which the gateways are provisioned in OpenSIPS. If the order reflects cost, it means that you have to do **Least Cost Routing (LCR)**. If the order reflects quality, you get quality-based routing.

The mechanism to select the destination gateway is combined with a failover mechanism (so-called **gateway failover** or **gateway redundancy**). If the chosen gateway is found as failed (not answering or generating server errors), OpenSIPS can retake the call to the next gateway from the set selected for the destination prefix.

In terms of gateway failover, OpenSIPS can actively monitor the gateways (as availability), enable and disable them on the fly, and adjust the gateway routing only to the available gateways. The following figure shows OpenSIPS working as a SIP router:

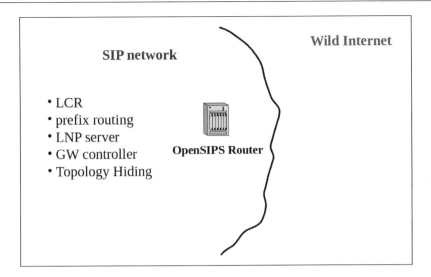

The dynamic routing engine in OpenSIPS provides extensions for advanced routing, such as quality-based routing. Based on the routed calls, OpenSIPS dynamically learns the quality of each gateway and adapts the routing to primarily send calls to the gateways providing better quality. The quality of a gateway can be given by statistics such as the following:

- **Answer Seizure Ratio (ASR)**
- **Average Call Duration (ACD)**
- **Post Dial Delay (PDD)**

The peering with the carriers can be subject to traffic limitation—certain carriers/gateways may accept a *maximum calling rate* or *maximum number of parallel calls*. OpenSIPS has the ability of calculating these values in real time in a per gateway manner and automatically rerouting the calls to a different gateway when the limits are reached.

The egress OpenSIPS may also be responsible for interacting with other third-party service providers for services such as **LNP** (number portability) or **CNAME** (Caller ID).

The interaction with such services can be done either at SIP level (using the SIP redirect mechanism) or via REST APIs. For SIP interfacing, you just need the OpenSIPS basic scripting, while for REST interfacing, OpenSIPS provides a REST client module to perform custom queries.

Similar to the ingress side, the egress side controls the IP and SIP layers of traffic, such as performing network bridging, SIP protocol conversion, NAT traversal, or media handling (pinning, transcoding, and recording).

Who's using OpenSIPS?

A wide range of SIP-oriented service providers choose OpenSIPS to power their platform, mainly because of its throughput, capabilities, and reliability as a stable and mature open source software project.

VoIP service providers take advantage of the rich feature set of OpenSIPS to build attractive and competitive services for residential or enterprise customers. The flexibility of OpenSIPS (in terms of service creation) and the fast releasing cycle gives them an advantage in creating cutting-edge services in the competitive VoIP markets.

The ability to pipe large amounts of traffic through OpenSIPS in a reliable and precise fashion allows providers for Trunking services, DID, or Termination services to scale and become more efficient. The dynamic nature of these services and interoperability concerns are key aspects that make OpenSIPS the perfect candidate for the job.

Currently, OpenSIPS has exceeded its original Class 4 status and is now able to offer Class 5 signaling features. So, Hosted/Virtual PBX providers use OpenSIPS as the core component to emulate PBX-like services. OpenSIPS is flexible enough to integrate all the complex Class 5 features and even more to interface with external SIP engines (media servers).

The ability of OpenSIPS to frontend existing platforms for the load balancing and clustering (even geodistribution) core components opens the markets populated by existing players who offer PBX Services or Termination Services. Such players can now take advantage of OpenSIPS too.

Besides calls, OpenSIPS provides presence and instant messaging capabilities, which are essential to build **Rich Communication Services (RCS)**.

In the area of advanced SIP services, LNP providers, CNAME providers, and Fraud Detection providers are relying on OpenSIPS skills to interface with various DB engines and handle huge amounts of data (typical for their services). OpenSIPS can offer both, an efficient SIP frontend and a powerful backend to connect to DBs and other external tools.

With the OpenSIPS evolution into the Class 5 area, new capabilities such as Back-to-Back User Agent and Call Queuing were exploited by Call Center Providers (inbound and outbound termination). As compared with the existing solutions, OpenSIPS-based call centers are able to handle large amounts of calls and offer, in a geodistributed fashion, an all-in-one platform: call queuing, DID management, PSTN routing, SIP peering, and others.

Nevertheless, being an open software, OpenSIPS offers a perfect study and research platform. Universities and research centers are using OpenSIPS to familiarize students with the VoIP/SIP world to build projects or research cases. It is important to mention here that this relation with universities and research institutes is for the benefit of both parties as the OpenSIPS project gets a lot of traction and expansions from these study/research projects.

The project manages a list of OpenSIPS users, which is continuously growing:
`http://www.opensips.org/About/WhoIsUsing`

The OpenSIPS design

Architecturally speaking, OpenSIPS is formed out of two logical components: the **core** and **modules**.

The core is the application itself and it provides the low-level functionalities of OpenSIPS, the definition of various interfaces, and some generic resources.

The modules are shared libraries, loaded on demand at the startup time. Each module implements a well-defined functionality for a specific routing algorithm or authentication method. There are mainly two types of modules in OpenSIPS:

- Modules providing functionalities and functions directly for the routing script
- Modules implementing a core-defined interface (such as a module implementing the SQL interface will become a backend to a certain SQL server)

The following is a figure showing the OpenSIPS architecture:

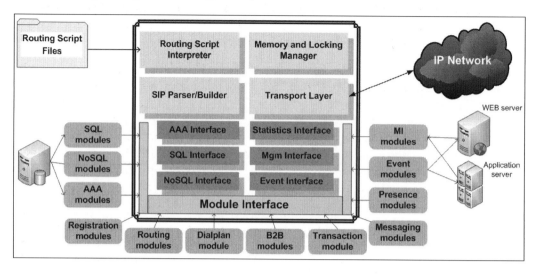

The OpenSIPS core

The OpenSIPS core is a minimal application. By itself, it is only able to proxy the SIP requests and replies in a stateless mode with very basic scripting capabilities. In most of the cases, the core is used in conjunction with several modules.

The OpenSIPS core provides the following features:

- The SIP transport layer
- The SIP factory — the message parser and builder
- The routing script parser and interpreter
- The memory and locking manager
- The core script functions and script variables
- The SQL interface definition (implementation provided by modules and not by the core itself)
- The NoSQL interface definition
- The AAA interface definition
- The management interface
- The events interface
- The statistics interface

The **SIP transport layer** implements various SIP transport protocols. Currently, OpenSIPS supports UDP, TCP, TLS, and WebSockets. Which transport protocols are to be used depends on the SIP listeners defined in the routing script. Multiple transport protocols can be used at the same time.

The **SIP factory layer** provides functions to parse and build SIP messages. OpenSIPS implements a lazy but efficient SIP parser, which means that the parsing is done on demand (OpenSIPS parses as far as requested) and is selective. (The header bodies are parsed only if requested; otherwise, only the header name is parsed.) The parsing process is transparent at the script level, each function (core or modules) doing its own parsing internally. When it comes to changing the message, it is very important to know that the changes you make from the script are not applied in real time to the message but stored and applied to all only when the message processing is done.

Due to this offline handling of changes, you are not able to see your own changes over the message. For example, if you add a new SIP header and test its presence, you will not find it, or if you remove a SIP header and look again for it, you will find it.

The **routing script parser and interpreter** loads and parses (to the memory) the routing script at the startup time; after this, the file is no longer needed. The routing script cannot be reloaded at runtime; OpenSIPS must be restarted in order to read the routing script again. Aside from various global settings, the routing script contains the routing logic; this logic is defined via a C/Shell language, custom to OpenSIPS. Configuring the routing logic in OpenSIPS is more like doing simple programming. This approach (writing your own program to route the traffic) gives OpenSIPS a tremendous flexibility when it comes to routing.

The **memory and locking manager** is a global resource in OpenSIPS. For performance reasons, OpenSIPS implements its own internal manager for memory allocation and locking operations. This part is not visible at the route scripting level, but it may be configured at compiling time. (OpenSIPS has several implementations for the memory and locking managers.)

The OpenSIPS core provides its own **script functions and script variables** to be used from the routing script. As compared with the functions and variables exported by the modules, the core set is quite limited in number and functionality. The online manual lists and documents all the functions and variables provided by the OpenSIPS core.

The **SQL interface** is defined by the core but not implemented. The definition is done here in the OpenSIPS core for standardization reasons. Modules can use the SQL services via the SQL interface without being aware of the undelaying SQL driver. Additionally, other modules may implement the SQL interface, offering drivers to various SQL DBs, such as MySQL, Postgre, Oracle, Berkeley, Unix odbc, and many others. (See all the modules starting with the db_ prefix.) Even if the SQL interface is for internal usage (between modules), it is partially exposed at the script level by the avpops module:

```
avp_db_query("select first_name, last_name from subscribers where
    username='$rU' and domain='$rd'", "$avp(fname);$avp(lname)");
```

Similar, the **NoSQL interface** is defined for the standardizing of the operations with the NoSQL databases. OpenSIPS modules currently implement drivers to Redis, CouchBase, Cassandra, MongoDB, Memcached, and other databases. (See all the modules starting with the cachedb_ prefix.) The NoSQL interface is directly exposed by the OpenSIPS core via a simple set of functions:

```
cache_store("redis:cluster1", "key1", "$var(my_val)", 1200);
cache_fetch("redis:cluster1", "key1", "$var(my_val)");
cache_remove("redis:cluster1", "key1");
```

The **AAA interface** defines the interfacing to AAA servers in a similar way. Currently, OpenSIPS supports the RADIUS driver for the AAA interface, the Diameter driver being under heavy rework at this time. The AAA interface is not exposed at all at the routing script level as it is exclusively used internally between modules.

The **Management Interface (MI)** is an OpenSIPS interface that allows external applications to trigger predefined commands in OpenSIPS. Such commands typically allow an external application/script to perform the following:

- Push data into OpenSIPS (such as setting the debug level, registering a contact, and so on)

- Fetch the data from OpenSIPS (see registered users, see ongoing calls, get statistics, and so on)

- Trigger an internal action in OpenSIPS (reloading the data, sending a message, and so on)

The MI commands are provided by the OpenSIPS core (See the online documentation at http://www.opensips.org/Documentation/Interface-CoreMI-2-1.) and also by the modules. (Check the online module documentation to see the commands provided by each module at http://www.opensips.org/Documentation/Modules-2-1.)

For MI, OpenSIPS supports the following drivers: XMLRPC, FIFO file, Datagrams, JSON RPC, and HTTP. (See all the modules starting with the `mi_` prefix.)

A simple example of interacting with OpenSIPS via the MI interfaces is using the `opensipsctl` utility; it uses the FIFO or XMLRPC protocols to push the MI commands into OpenSIPS. The `opensipsctl` utility allows you explicitly run an MI command via the FIFO file, as shown here:

```
opensipsctl fifo ps

opensipsctl fifo debug 4
```

A simple program in Python to trigger to run an MI command in OpenSIPS via the XMLRPC protocol is as follows:

```
#!/usr/bin/python
import xmlrpclib
opensips = xmlrpclib.ServerProxy('http://127.0.0.1:8080/RPC2')
print opensips.ps();
```

The **events interface** is an OpenSIPS interface that provides different ways to notify external applications about certain events triggered in OpenSIPS. In order to notify an external application about the OpenSIPS internal events, the event interface provides the following functions:

- Manages exported events
- Manages subscriptions from different applications
- Exports generic functions to raise an event (regardless of the transport protocol used)
- Communicates with different transport protocols to send the events

Events can be triggered by the core activities (See the online documentation at `http://www.opensips.org/Documentation/Interface-CoreEvents-2-1.`), module activities (See the *Exported Events* section in the module documentation at `http://www.opensips.org/Documentation/Modules-2-1.`), or explicitly from the routing script via the `raise_event()` function, as follows:

```
raise_event("E_SCRIPT_EVENT", $avp(attributes), $avp(values));
```

To deliver the events, OpenSIPS modules implement the following drivers: datagram, RabbitMQ, and XMLRPC. (See all the modules starting with the `event_` prefix.)

The **statistics interface** provides access to various internal statistics of OpenSIPS. It provides valuable information about what is going on in OpenSIPS. This can be used by external applications to monitor the purposes, load evaluation, and real-time integration with the other services. The values of the statistic variables are exclusively numerical. OpenSIPS provides two types of statistic variables:

- **counter like**: Variables that keep counting things that happened in OpenSIPS, such as received requests, processed dialogs, failed DB queries, and so on
- **computed values**: Variables that are calculated in real time, such as how much memory is used, the current load, active dialogs, active transactions, and so on

To know more about statistic variables, refer to `http://www.opensips.org/Documentation/Interface-Statistics-1-10`.

In OpenSIPS, the statistics variables are grouped in different sets depending on their purposes or how to provide them. For example, the OpenSIPS core provides the shmem, load, net, and other groups (refer `http://www.opensips.org/Documentation/Interface-CoreStatistics-2-1`), while each OpenSIPS module provides its own group. (Typically, the group has the same name as the module.)

The statistics can be easily queried via the MI with the `get_statistics` command, as shown here:

```
# get various statistic variables, by list of names
> opensipsctl fifo get_statistics rcv_requests inuse_transactions
> core:rcv_requests = 453
> tm:inuse_transactions = 10
```

The OpenSIPS modules

Each OpenSIPS module is a dynamic library that can be loaded on demand at the OpenSIPS startup, if instructed in the routing script.

The modules are identified by their names and they typically export various resources to be used in/from the routing script:

- A set of module parameters (optional): They allow the module to be configured at startup
- A set of script functions (optional): They are functions to be used from the routing script

- A set of asynchronous script functions (optional): They are functions to be used from the routing script but in an asynchronous way via a resume route (refer to *Chapter 14, Advanced Topics with OpenSIPS 2.1*)

- A set of variables (optional): They are variables that can be used from the routing script

- A set of statistics variables (optional): They are statistics specific to the module that can be read via the MI

- A set of MI commands (optional): They are commands specific to the module to be triggered via the MI from outside OpenSIPS

- A set of events (optional): They are events that can be triggered by the module and delivered by the event modules to external applications

Based on what they implement, there are three types of modules in OpenSIPS:

- Modules implementing the functionalities to be used from the routing script (that is, authentication methods, routing algorithms, registration handling, and so on).

- Modules implementing one of the interfaces defined by the core in order to provide a driver for a certain communication protocol (that is, a MySQL driver for the SQL interface, a RADIUS driver for the AAA interface).

- Modules implementing their own particular API; such an API is to be used directly (bypassing the core) by the other modules. This allows modules to use other modules, independent of the core. (Such modules are the `b2b_entities`, the dialog module, TM module, and others.)

We can conclude that even if most of the modules provide functionalities to the routing script, there are modules providing functionalities to other modules via the core interfaces or their own APIs.

Here are some examples of the modules:

- The `db_mysql` module implements the SQL interface defined by the core; the `auth_db` module using the SQL interface to perform the SQL operations can transparently use any module implementing the SQL interface

- The `b2b_entities` module defines and implements its own API (to manage SIP UASs and UACs); the `b2b_logic` module uses the API from the `b2b_entities` module directly in order to build even more complex functionalities (that are used later from the routing script)

This leads to the concept of module dependencies and an OpenSIPS module may depend on the following:

- An external library at linking time, that is, `b2b_logic` depends on the `xml2` library

- The core interface at startup time; if a module uses the SQL interface, you need to load one or more modules implementing a SQL driver

- The other modules; one module depends directly and explicitly on the other modules (that is, `b2b_logic` depends on `b2b_entities`)

The documentation of each module (the readme file) contains information on the module's dependencies, what functions or parameters are exposed, and what MI commands or events are available. See the online module documentations at `http://www.opensips.org/Documentation/Modules-2-1`.

Summary

In this chapter, you have been provided information to understand OpenSIPS in terms of what OpenSIPS is, how to acquire OpenSIPS knowledge, when to use OpenSIPS, and who is using OpenSIPS. From the internal perspective, you learned the design/structure of OpenSIPS, such as what are the OpenSIPS modules and what they can provide.

With this better understating of OpenSIPS, in the next chapter, we will focus on using OpenSIPS and the scripting language and routing concepts.

3
Installing OpenSIPS

In the previous chapter, you learned about SIP and OpenSIPS. Now, it is time for some hands-on experience. The installation is just the beginning of the work. It is very important to install OpenSIPS correctly from the source code or packages. You can install it much faster using the `apt-get` utility. However, the installation from the source code is more flexible allowing you to select the modules that will be compiled. This is why we won't use any shortcuts for the installation. We will use Debian for this book because it is the distribution that we are used to. You can safely use other distributions such as CentOS, Ubuntu, Red Hat, and SUSE, just to mention the most popular ones.

By the end of this chapter, you should be able to understand the following topics:

- Installing Linux for OpenSIPS
- Downloading OpenSIPS source and dependencies
- Compiling and installing OpenSIPS with MySQL support
- Starting and stopping OpenSIPS
- Configuring the Linux system to start OpenSIPS at boot time

Hardware and software requirements

There are no minimum hardware requirements for OpenSIPS. It can even run on an ordinary PC. On a server containing an Intel i7 920 @ 2.67GHz CPU with 6 GB of available RAM, OpenSIPS is capable of an astonishing 13,000 calls per second. The complete results can be found at `http://www.opensips.org/About/PerformanceTests-StressTests`.

The OpenSIPS software runs on a variety of Linux, BSD, and Solaris platforms. Some generic packages are available to a few varieties of Linux and Solaris. These packages can be downloaded from www.opensips.org/Resources/Downloads. The following packages are required to compile OpenSIPS:

- GCC (or any other C compiler such as suncc or icc)
- Bison or Yacc (Berkley yacc)
- Flex
- GNU make
- GNU tar
- GNU install
- libxml2-dev (if you are planning to use Presence)

Some modules such as MySQL, Postgres, RADIUS, dialplan, and others will require additional packages to compile. In the installation in this chapter, we will provide a string with all the modules required for this book. The module dependencies information is available in the module documentation (refer to http://www. opensips.org/Documentation/Modules-2-1).

Installing Linux for OpenSIPS

We recommend the usage of a virtual machine prepared using any hypervisor (VMware, VirtualBox, and so on) with the latest version of Debian installed (Version 7.7 at the time of writing this book). You can download it from http://cdimage. debian.org/debian-cd/.

Warning: The instructions for this lab formats the computer. Back up all the data on your PC in a virtual environment such as VMware or Xen before proceeding to follow these instructions.

Carry out the following steps to install Linux for OpenSIPS:

1. Insert the CD and boot the computer using Debian. Press *Enter* to start the installation:

In this screen, you can also select the boot and installation options. Sometimes, you will need to choose some hardware-specific parameters for your installation. Press *F1* for help if needed.

2. In the following **Select your location** screen, choose your location to be used in the installation process:

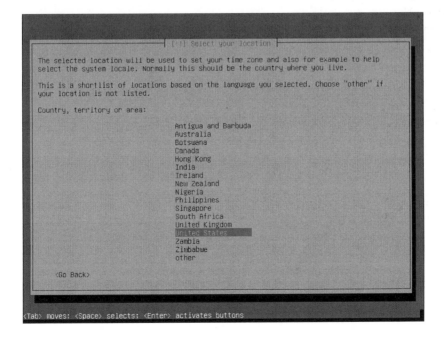

3. Choose the keyboard layout, as shown in the following screenshot:

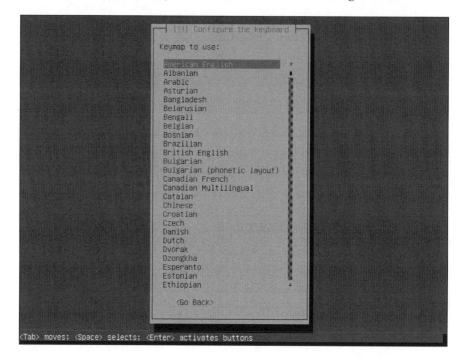

 It is very common to have to choose a keyboard layout, mainly in European and Asian countries.

4. Choose **Hostname**, as follows:

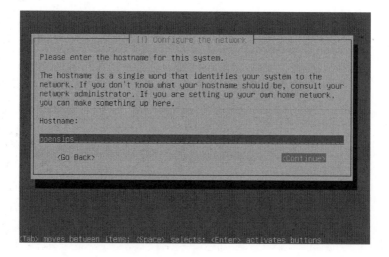

Choose the name of the server. It is important because you will need to use this name later to access the server.

5. Choose your **Domain name**, as shown in the following screenshot:

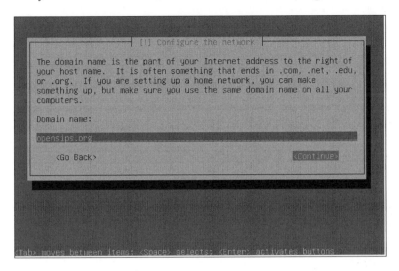

The domain name is obvious but important.

6. Choose a time zone, as shown here:

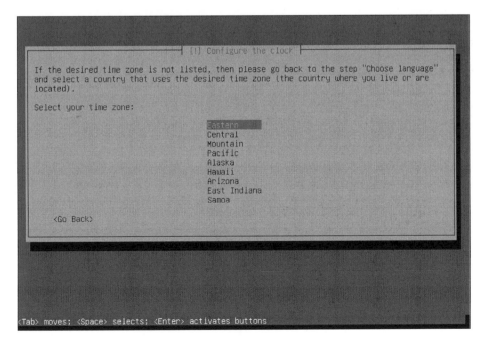

Select the time zone. It is important to have the correct time zone, mainly for reports. If you don't do it correctly, you will end up with voicemail messages with the wrong time.

7. Choose **Partitioning method**, as follows:

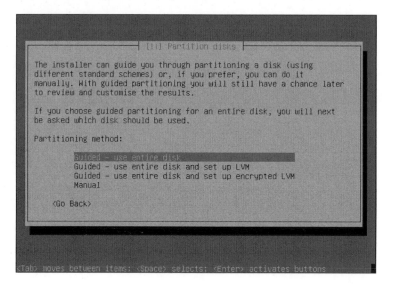

We could write a whole chapter about partitioning. Linux geeks will certainly use the manual option. For the purpose of learning, you can simply select the **Guided - use entire disk** option. Consult a Linux specialist for the best partitioning scheme for your server.

8. Next, select the **Select disk to partition** option, as shown in the following screenshot:

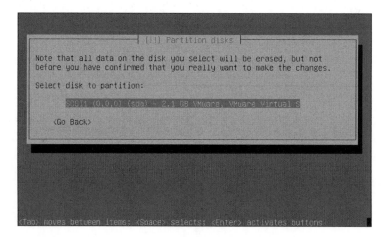

Now, just select the disk being used to install Linux.

9. In the following screen, select the **All files in one partition (recommended for new users)** option:

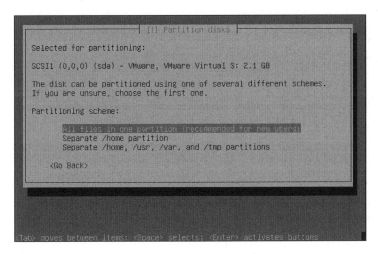

You can choose how to partition the system again. Let's stick with the default installation. Some advanced users may want to change it a bit.

10. Select the **Finish partitioning and write changes to disk** option, as follows:

Never select this option if you want to preserve your disk. After the partitioning, all the pre-existing contents of the disk will be erased. So do it wisely. I use VMware to test OpenSIPS as it is free and creates a virtual machine where I can

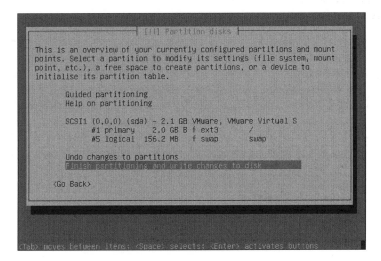

11. For the **Write the changes to disks?** option, select **Yes**, as shown here:

Now comes the scary part. Confirm that you want to *erase* all the contents of the disk. Well, think twice, or even three times, before saying yes.

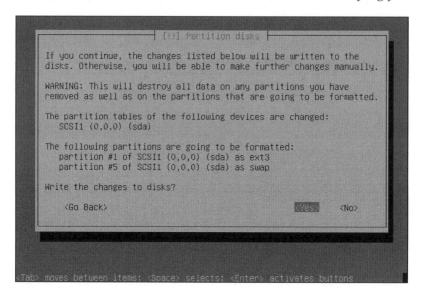

 Warning: All the data on the disk will be destroyed!

12. Set **Root password** to OpenSIPS, as follows:

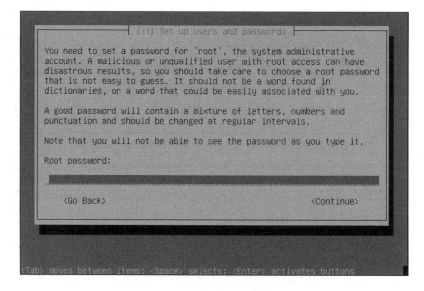

Choose a password for your root user. This is the most important password on the system.

13. Select the **Re-enter password to verify** option, as shown here:

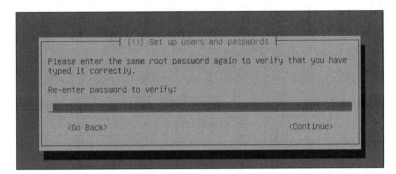

Re-enter the password for confirmation purposes. Try to use a password that is hard to crack (minimum eight characters, letters, numbers, and some kind of special characters, such as * or #).

14. Enter the full name for the user account as opensips, as shown in the following screenshot:

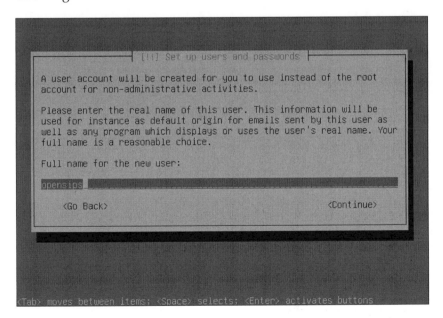

Some systems require you to create at least one user. Let's do it, starting with full user name.

15. Enter the name for the opensips user account:

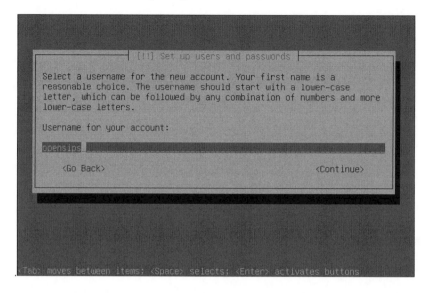

16. Enter the password for the opensips user account and re-enter to confirm:

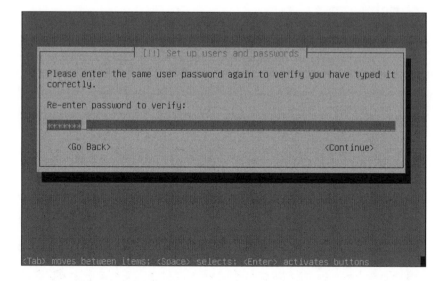

Enter the password and confirm it. Try to use a password that is hard to crack.

17. Next, you will be directed to the **Configure the package manager** screen, as follows:

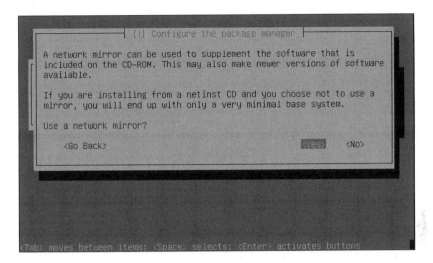

During the process of installation, we will use several packages distributed by Debian.

18. Select a mirror country, as shown in the following screenshot:

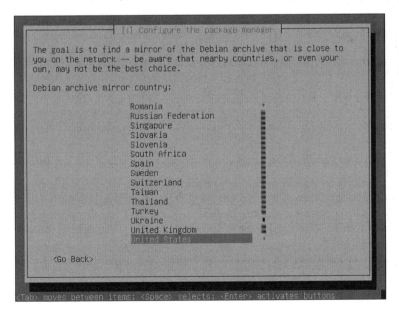

This screen will allow you to select from where you can download the packages.

19. Select **ftp.debian.org** or your preferred mirror. Select the nearest one to speed up the downloading of the packages:

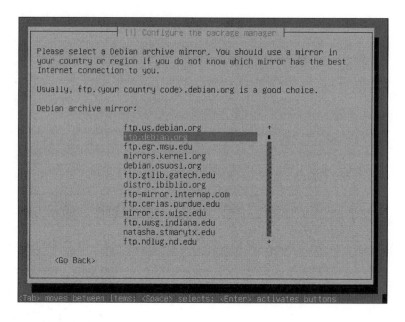

20. Leave the HTTP proxy blank or fill in with the appropriate parameters:

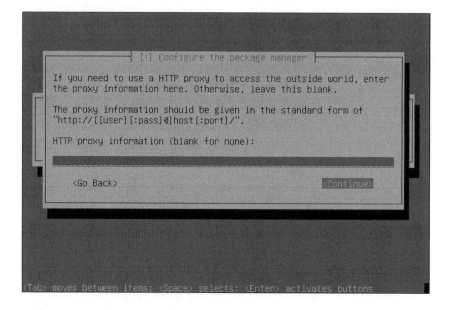

If you use an HTTP proxy such as Squid or Microsoft ISA server, fill in the appropriate parameters in order to allow Internet access for the downloads.

21. Select **No** for the package popularity survey:

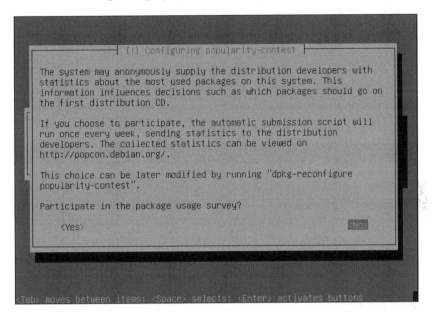

The package popularity survey generates statistics about the most downloaded packages.

22. Select **Standard system utilities** and **SSH server**:

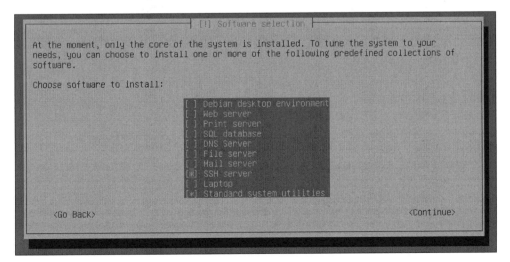

Debian comes in several predefined installations such as desktop. The desktop installations, for example, installs a GUI for Linux such as GNOME or KDE. We don't need this for our installation. So, choose **Standard system utilities** and **SSH server**. Later, we will manually install components such as the **Web server**, **Mail server**, and **SQL database**.

23. Select **Yes** to install the GRUB boot loader:

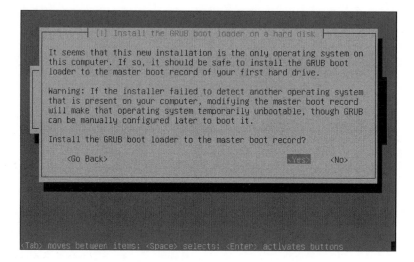

GRUB is a boot load manager for your server. It allows you to dual boot systems and to do some tricks during the boot process.

24. At last, you will see **Finish the installation** screen, as follows:

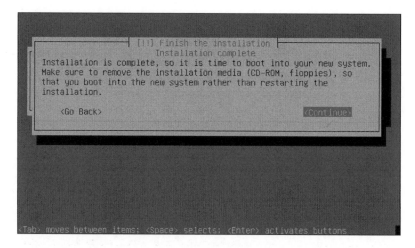

Finish the installation and boot the system.

Downloading and installing OpenSIPS v2.1.x

It is even easier to install OpenSIPS using the Debian packages. We will go through the compilation process. It is more flexible and we may need to recompile OpenSIPS a few times in this material to include other modules. The installation process is shown step by step as follows:

 Warning: Detailed instructions change very often. Check the OpenSIPS website for updates.

1. Update the operating system libraries by running the following command:

   ```
   apt-get update
   ```

2. Install the dependencies:

   ```
   apt-get install gcc bison flex make openssl
   libmysqlclient-dev perl libdbi-perl libdbd-mysql-perl
   libdbd-pg-perl libfrontier-rpc-perl libterm-readline-gnu-perl
   libberkeleydb-perl mysql-server ssh libxml2 libxml2-dev
   libxmlrpc-core-c3-dev libpcre3 libpcre3-dev subversion
   libncurses5-dev git ngrep libssl-dev
   ```

 The MySQL server is not really a dependency, but we will install it in order to use later.

3. Download the source code, as follows:

   ```
   cd /usr/src
   ```

   ```
   git clone https://github.com/OpenSIPS/opensips.git -b 2.1
   opensips_21
   ```

4. Compile and install the core and modules. Include the db_mysql and dialplan modules:

   ```
   cd opensips_21
   ```

   ```
   make menuconfig
   ```

5. Select **Configure Compile Options | Configure Excluded Modules** and select **dialplan** and **db_mysql**:

6. Select the **Compile And Install OpenSIPS** option:

7. Create the directory for the process identification file **Process Identifier (PID)**:

```
mkdir /var/run/opensips
```

Generating OpenSIPS scripts

One of the goals for the OpenSIPS project is to make the software simpler to use.
A great milestone in this direction was the script generator. Now, we can generate
scripts for several scenarios. This can save a lot of time in coding and reduce errors.
This book will use the **Residential Script** as the basis for most of the chapters. So,
let's generate a residential script to start with:

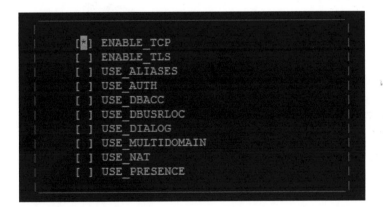

1. Navigate to **Generate OpenSIPS Script | Residential Script | Configure
   Residential Script**. For now, just enable TCP:

```
[*] ENABLE_TCP
[ ] ENABLE_TLS
[ ] USE_ALIASES
[ ] USE_AUTH
[ ] USE_DBACC
[ ] USE_DBUSRLOC
[ ] USE_DIALOG
[ ] USE_MULTIDOMAIN
[ ] USE_NAT
[ ] USE_PRESENCE
```

2. Generate the script and copy it to `/usr/local/etc/opensips` and change
   the specific date generated by your installation:

   ```
   cp /usr/src/opensips_210/etc/opensips_
   residential_2014-12-22_9\:25\:40.cfg  /etc/opensips/opensips.cfg
   ```

3. After generating the script, customize some lines of the code to your current
   IP address:

   ```
   listen=udp:127.0.0.1:5060    # CUSTOMIZE ME
   listen=tcp:127.0.0.1:5060    # CUSTOMIZE ME
   ```

Running OpenSIPS at the Linux boot time

Now, we will insert OpenSIPS at the Linux boot time to load the server whenever the server restarts:

1. Include OpenSIPS in the Linux boot:

    ```
    cd /usr/src/opensips_210/packaging/debian
    cp opensips.default /etc/default/opensips
    cp opensips.init /etc/init.d/opensips
    nano /etc/init.d/opensips
    PATH=/sbin:/bin:/usr/sbin:/usr/bin:/usr/local/sbin
    DAEMON=/usr/local/sbin/opensips
    chmod 755 /etc/init.d/opensips
    update-rc.d opensips defaults 99
    ```

2. Edit /etc/default/opensips and change the shared memory parameter to 128 MB, packaged memory to 4 MB, and RUN_OPENSIPS to yes. You can check the usage of the shared memory and package memory using the following commands:

    ```
    opensipsctl fifo get_statistics shmem:
    opensipsctl fifo get_statistics pkmem:
    ```

    It is hard to predict exactly how much memory your system will consume. It depends on the routing script, caching, and number of transactions and routes. You will probably be surprised on how low the memory requirements are.

3. To simplify the access, create a symbolic link to /usr/local/etc/opensips at /etc/opensips:

    ```
    ln -s /usr/local/etc/opensips /etc/opensips
    ```

4. Restart the computer to see if OpenSIPS starts. Confirm using the following command:

    ```
    ps-ef |grep opensips
    ```

 It is highly recommended that you change the username and group used to run OpenSIPS in the /etc/init.d/opensips file.

The OpenSIPS v2.1.x directory structure

After the installation, OpenSIPS will create a file structure. It is important to understand the file structure in order to locate the main folders where the system is stored. You will need this information to update or remove the software.

The configuration files

This is the directory of the configuration files with their respective samples:

```
opensips-1:/etc/opensips# ls -l
-rw------- 1 root root  6226 Dec 22 09:55 opensips.cfg
-rw------- 1 root staff 6078 Dec 22 10:05 opensips.cfg.sample
-rw-r--r-- 1 root staff 3696 Dec 22 09:41 opensipsctlrc
-rw-r--r-- 1 root staff 3696 Dec 22 10:05 opensipsctlrc.sample
-rw-r--r-- 1 root staff 3028 Dec 22 09:41 osipsconsolerc
-rw-r--r-- 1 root staff 3028 Dec 22 10:05 osipsconsolerc.sample
drwxr-sr-x 4 root staff 4096 Dec 22 10:05 tls
```

Modules

This is the directory for the modules. It is important to check if all the required modules are present after compilation:

```
opensips-1:/lib/opensips/modules# ls
root@bookosips:/usr/local/lib/opensips/modules# ls
acc.so              dialplan.so         mi_fifo.so            signaling.so
alias_db.so         dispatcher.so       mi_http.so            sipcapture.so
auth_aaa.so         diversion.so        mi_json.so            sipmsgops.so
auth_db.so          dns_cache.so        msilo.so              siptrace.so
auth_diameter.so    domainpolicy.so     nathelper.so          sl.so
auth.so             domain.so           nat_traversal.so      sms.so
avpops.so           drouting.so         options.so            speeddial.so
b2b_entities.so     enum.so             path.so               sst.so
b2b_sca.so          event_datagram.so   pdt.so                statistics.so
benchmark.so        event_route.so      peering.so            stun.so
cachedb_local.so    event_xmlrpc.so     permissions.so        textops.so
cachedb_sql.so      exec.so             pike.so               tm.so
call_center.so      fraud_detection.so  presence_callinfo.so  uac_auth.so
```

```
call_control.so    gflags.so         presence_xcapdiff.so  uac_redirect.
so                                                          so
cfgutils.so        group.so          qos.so                uac_
registrant.so
closeddial.so      imc.so            ratelimit.so          uac.so
db_cachedb.so      load_balancer.so  registrar.so          uri.so
db_flatstore.so    mangler.so        rr.so
userblacklist.so
db_mysql.so        mathops.so        rtpengine.so          usrloc.so
db_text.so         maxfwd.so         rtpproxy.so
db_virtual.so      mediaproxy.so     script_helper.so
dialog.so          mi_datagram.so    seas.so
Binaries   (/usr/local/sbin)
openips-1:/sbin# ls -l op*
total 2832
-rwxr-xr-x 1 root  staff 2594007 2009-10-09 17:04 opensips
-rwxr-xr-x 1 root  staff   52695 2009-10-09 17:04 opensipsctl
-rwxr-xr-x 1 root  staff    6270 2009-10-09 17:04 opensipsdbctl
-rwxr-xr-x 1 root  staff   13442 2009-10-09 17:04 opensipsunix
-rwxr-xr-x 1 root  staff  212692 2009-10-09 17:04 osipsconsole
```

Working with the log files

The initialization log can be seen at syslog (/var/log/syslog). You can redirect the log to a specific file such as opensips.log by changing the configuration of the rsyslog daemon. By default, OpenSIPS logs to the LOCAL_0 facility as defined in the opensips.cfg script:

```
log_facility=LOG_LOCAL0
```

To redirect log files to opensips.log, edit the /etc/rsyslog.conf file and add the following line to the rules section:

```
Local0.*                       -/var/log/opensips.log
```

Create the file and restart the daemon using the following command:

```
touch /var/log/opensips.log
/etc/init.d/rsyslog restart
```

After restarting OpenSIPS, you should see the following log. Logs are very important for this training. Whenever you have a problem, you should check the log files. You can see the log file in real time using the following command:

```
tail /var/log/opensips.log -f
```

You can also change the log level to a more or less verbose level dynamically:

```
opensipsctl fifo debug 3
```

A log example is shown here (with some lines suppressed):

```
tail /var/log/opensips.log -n 100
Dec 22 10:26:02 bookosips opensips: INFO:core:shm_mem_init: allocating
SHM block
Dec 22 10:26:02 bookosips opensips: INFO:core:fix_poll_method: using
epoll_lt as the IO watch method (auto detected)
Dec 22 10:26:02 bookosips /usr/local/sbin/opensips[22427]:
NOTICE:core:main: version: opensips 2.1.0dev-tls (i386/linux)
Dec 22 10:26:02 bookosips /usr/local/sbin/opensips[22427]:
INFO:core:main: using 128 Mb shared memory
Dec 22 10:26:02 bookosips /usr/local/sbin/opensips[22427]:

...

...

Dec 22 10:26:02 bookosips /usr/local/sbin/opensips[22427]:
INFO:usrloc:ul_init_locks: locks array size 512
Dec 22 10:26:02 bookosips /usr/local/sbin/opensips[22427]:
INFO:core:probe_max_sock_buff: using rcv buffer of 320 kb
Dec 22 10:26:02 bookosips /usr/local/sbin/opensips[22427]:
INFO:core:probe_max_sock_buff: using snd buffer of 320 kb
Dec 22 10:26:02 bookosips /usr/local/sbin/opensips[22427]:
INFO:core:init_sock_keepalive: -- TCP keepalive enabled on socket
Dec 22 10:26:02 bookosips opensips: INFO:core:daemonize: pre-daemon
process exiting with 0
Dec 22 10:26:02 bookosips /usr/local/sbin/opensips[22439]:
INFO:core:init_io_wait: using epoll_lt as the io watch method (auto
detected)
```

Startup options

OpenSIPS can be started using the `init` scripts or `opensipsctl` utility. If you start OpenSIPS using the `init` scripts, you can stop it using only the `init` scripts. The same is valid if you start using the `opensipsctl` utility.

Starting, stopping, and restarting OpenSIPS using the `init` scripts is shown here:

```
/etc/init.d/opensips start|stop|restart
```

Starting, stopping, and restarting OpenSIPS using the `opensipsctl` utility is as follows:

```
opensipsctl start|stop|restart
```

The OpenSIPS executable has several start up options. These options allow you to change the configuration of the daemon. Some of the most useful are as follows:

- `-C`: To check the configuration file.
- `-D -E -dddddd`: To check the module loading. Don't use for production as it binds the first interface only.

There are lots of others that allow you to fine-tune your configuration. Check the following help line:

```
version: opensips 2.1.0dev-tls (i386/linux)
Usage: opensips -l address [-l address ...] [options]
Options:
    -f file     Configuration file
    -c          Check configuration file for errors
    -C          Similar to '-c' but checks the flags of exported
                functions from included route blocks
    -l address Listen on the specified address/interface
  [proto:]addr[:port], where proto=udp|tcp and
                addr= host|ip_address|interface_name.
                -l udp:127.0.0.1:5080, -l eth0:5062.
   -n processes Number of child processes to fork per interface
                    (default: 8)
    -r          Use dns to check if is necessary to add a "received="
                field to a via
    -R          Same as `-r` but use reverse dns;
                (to use both use `-rR`)
```

```
-v          Turn on "via:" host checking when forwarding replies
-d          Debugging mode (multiple -d increase the level)
-D          Do not fork into daemon mode
-F          Daemon mode, but leave main process foreground
-E          Log to stderr
-T          Disable tcp
-N processes Number of tcp child processes
-W method   poll method
-V          Version number
-h          This help message
-b nr       Maximum receive buffer size
-m nr       Size of shared memory allocated in Megabytes
-M nr       Size of pkg memory allocated in Megabytes
-w dir      Change the working directory to "dir" (default "/")
-t dir      Chroot to "dir"
-u uid      Change uid
-g gid      Change gid
-P file     Create a pid file
-G file     Create a pgid file
```

Summary

In this chapter, you learned how to install and prepare Linux for the OpenSIPS installation. We downloaded and compiled OpenSIPS with RADIUS and MySQL modules. After the installation, we included the OpenSIPS `init` file to start OpenSIPS at boot time.

Now that OpenSIPS has been installed and is running, we will cover the basics of SIP routing and the language used to build the routing scripts in the next chapter.

4
OpenSIPS Language and Routing Concepts

In this chapter, you will learn about OpenSIPS routing. In the first part of the chapter, we will present the OpenSIPS configuration file—its structure, the types of routes, and how these routes are related to the SIP traffic. Going inside the routing script, we will see how to use functions, variables, transformations, and statements in order to create the actual script. In the second part of the chapter, you will learn about basic SIP routing concepts—how to do proper routing for the SIP sessions/dialogs in terms of how to route initial and sequential requests. After this, we will understand how the record routing mechanism works in SIP.

By the end of this chapter, you will learn the following concepts:

- How the OpenSIPS configuration file looks
- What are the types of routes available in the routing script
- How to use functions in the script
- How to use variables, transformations, flags, and operators
- How the scripting routes are triggered by the SIP traffic
- How to perform the proper routing of SIP dialogs with record routing

An overview of OpenSIPS scripting

If the SIP stack is considered to be the muscle responsible for handling large amounts of SIP traffic, then the routing script can be considered as the brain or intelligence deciding on how to handle the SIP traffic. The OpenSIPS routing script is a kind of program that tells OpenSIPS what to do with the SIP traffic — how to route the incoming traffic, how to forward the traffic, and how to generate new traffic.

The power to master OpenSIPS resides in the ability to write down and understand routing scripts. To do so, two kinds of knowledge on the scripting are required:

- An understanding of the scripting itself; how to use functions, how to use variables, and how to use various statements at the script level

- An understanding of the mapping between the routing script and flow of the SIP traffic, such as what part of the script is triggered when SIP messages are received or sent, how to forward or reply to SIP requests, or how a SIP dialog reflects over the routing script

The OpenSIPS configuration file

The OpenSIPS routing script (or configuration file) is a text file that is loaded by OpenSIPS at start up time. The content is parsed and loaded in memory so that the actual file on the disk is not used anymore at runtime.

OpenSIPS does not offer any mechanism to reload the routing script at runtime, so if you changed the configuration file, you need to restart OpenSIPS in order to apply the changes.

The text preprocessing built-in capabilities are limited in OpenSIPS; mainly reducing the ability to include other files via the `include_file` or `import_file` directives. The reason for this limitation is the presence of third-party text preprocessors, more powerful than we could develop in OpenSIPS, and the goal of OpenSIPS is in SIP processing, not text processing.

The **m4** macro preprocessor is a powerful third-party solution that perfectly helps OpenSIPS. This is very easy to integrate and is used to generate the configuration files (based on template and definition files) just before starting OpenSIPS.

The `menuconfig` utility provided by OpenSIPS to autogenerate configuration files (for different scenarios) also relies on the m4 text preprocessor to build the OpenSIPS configuration files.

As content, the OpenSIPS configuration file is a text-based file to set different parameters (global or per module parameters) and to script the routing logic.

This is a very short example of a simple OpenSIPS configuration file—it simply routes traffic based on the request URI:

```
####### Global Parameters #########
debug=3
log_stderror=no
fork=yes
children=4
listen=udp:127.0.0.1:5060


####### Modules Section ########

mpath="/usr/local/lib/opensips/modules/"
loadmodule "signaling.so"
loadmodule "sl.so"
loadmodule "tm.so"
loadmodule "rr.so"
loadmodule "uri.so"
loadmodule "sipmsgops.so"
modparam("rr", "append_fromtag", 0)


####### Routing Logic ########
route{
  if ( has_totag() ) {
    loose_route();
    route(relay);
  }

  if ( from_uri!=myself && uri!=myself ) {
    send_reply("403","Rely forbidden");
    exit;
  }

  record_route();

  route(relay);
}

route[relay] {
  if (is_method("INVITE"))
    t_on_failure("missed_call");
```

```
    t_relay();
    exit;
}

failure_route[missed_call] {
  if (t_check_status("486")) {
    $rd = "127.0.0.10";
    t_relay();
  }
}
```

Global parameters

The global parameters are parameters affecting the OpenSIPS core or affecting OpenSIPS globally (core and modules).

There is a rich set of global parameters, but the most important ones can be grouped by their functionality — by what part of OpenSIPS they control.

The *listening* parameters allow you to define the SIP listeners that can be used by OpenSIPS. Multiple listeners can be defined at the same time using different protocols, IPs, or ports:

```
listen=udp:127.0.0.1:5060
listen=tcp:192.168.1.5:5060 as 10.10.1.10:5060
listen=tls:192.168.1.5:5061
advertised_address=7.7.7.7 #global option, for all listeners
```

 Transport protocols such as TCP and UDP are provided by the OpenSIPS core, while transport protocols such as TLS or WS are provided by modules, which are not compiled by default; be sure that you compile such modules if you want to use the corresponding transport protocols.

Several *logging* parameters are provided to control the logging destination (`syslog` or `stderror`), logging level, logging facility, and other settings:

```
debug=2 # log level 2 (NOTICE)
log_stderror=0 #log to syslog
log_facility=LOG_LOCAL0
log_name="sbc"
```

An important set of parameters are the *parameters to control the number of SIP worker processes* created by OpenSIPS. All the processes are created by OpenSIPS at start up time—no processes are created or terminated at runtime—so you need to be very careful in dimensioning your OpenSIPS capacity as the number of processes.

There is no magic formula to determine how many processes OpenSIPS needs as this depends highly on how complex and heavy your routing script is. More available processes mean a higher level of parallelism in handling traffic (more SIP packages processed at the same time). However, too many processes may lead to performance penalties because of the process context switching (system time) and the internal synchronization and locking of OpenSIPS (user space time). So, you need to find the balance depending on your routing logic.

If your routing logic is mainly CPU-oriented (no I/O operations—DNS, **DataBase (DB)**, and HTTP), it should be sufficient to define as many processes as your server has cores. On the other hand, if your logic is I/O-intensive (rich in DB queries, DNS lookups, and so on), you need to create more processes for each core; you can roughly estimate the number of processes directly proportional with the following aspects:

- The average number of I/O operations per SIP message
- The average duration of the I/O operations

The parameters to control the number of SIP worker processes are as follows:

```
fork=yes  #create more than one SIP worker
children=4  #processes per UDP listener
tcp_children=12 #overall processes for TCP/TLS listeners
```

For UDP, you define the number of processes per listener, while for TCP, you define the overall number (independent of the number of listeners).

The *protocol control* parameters are used to enable or disable the support for certain SIP transport protocols:

```
disable_tcp = off
disable_tls = on
```

Note that the UDP transport protocol cannot be disabled; it is always on!

Actually, there is a very long and rich list of parameters provided by the OpenSIPS core. The full list, along with descriptions, can be found in the OpenSIPS online manual at `http://www.opensips.org/Documentation/Script-CoreParameters`.

The modules section

In this section, the script writer loads and configures (via parameters) the modules required by his routing script.

Each module provides various additional functions or scripting variables, so in order to use them, the module must be explicitly loaded. Setting parameters may be optional from module to module or use case to use case.

Modules can be loaded by specifying the full name (including the path to the object file):

```
loadmodules "/lib/opensips/modules/rr.so"
loadmodules "/lib/opensips/modules/tm.so"
```

You can do the same simply by name; in this case, you need to instruct OpenSIPS where the module object files are located (as a directory on the disk):

```
mpath="/lib/opensips/modules/"
loadmodules "rr.so"
loadmodules "tm.so"
```

Each module may accept an optional/variable number of parameters. For the module, a parameter may be optional or mandatory (depending on its meaning). A parameter may also take string or integer values. Some parameters may even accept multiple values.

 If a parameter does not accept multiple values (as most do), you might overwrite its value by setting the same parameter multiple times!

The full description of the parameters, which are mandatory, and what values they accept can be found in the module documentation refer to `http://www.opensips.org/Documentation/Modules-2-1` (either online or the README file provided by the module).

Scripting routes

The scripting routes section is the part containing the actual routing logic. The OpenSIPS routing script is a shell-like script (programming style) and is formatted in routes (or blocks) broken into sections.

There are basically two type of routes:

- Main routes
- Subroutes

The **main routes** are routes triggered by OpenSIPS when handling SIP messages. Depending on the type of traffic (inbound or outbound, requests or replies, received or locally generated messages), OpenSIPS provides multiple types of main routes:

- Request route
- Branch route
- Failure route
- Reply route
- Local route
- Start up route
- Timer route
- Event route
- Error route

Aside from the main routes, OpenSIPS defines **subroutes**. These routes are not internally triggered by OpenSIPS (they are not entry points in the script), but they are triggered by other routes from the script. They are mainly used for the structuring of the routing script, similar to calling functions in a script to organize and reuse blocks of code.

A subroute has a name; it can take parameters and return a value:

```
# request route
route {
    ......
  if (is_method("INVITE")) {
    route(check_hdrs,1);
    if ($rc<0) exit;
  }
```

```
     ......
}
# sub-route
route[check_hdrs] {
  if (!is_present_hf("Content-Type"))
    return(-1);
  if ( $param(1)==1 && !has_body() )
    return(-2);

  return(1);
}
```

In a subroute, you can fetch the pass parameters via the `$param(idx)` variable. The return code of a subroute or function can also be accessed via the `$rc` or `$retcode` variables.

 Do not use zero as the return value because this will completely break the script execution (all the way up to the main route).

The OpenSIPS routing script is mainly event-driven—different events (SIP-related or not, such as timers or start up) trigger the execution of a certain main route. In the next sections, you will learn about the types of main routes, when they are triggered, and what you can do there.

The request route

The request route is the only mandatory route in OpenSIPS and is the most important one; this route is the entry point of SIP requests in the OpenSIPS routing logic.

This route is on the inbound side of OpenSIPS. Each time a new SIP request is received from the network layer, the request route will be triggered. So, in the request route, you are handling a SIP request—the login there will tell OpenSIPS how to route and what to do with this SIP request.

 As the name of this main route says, this route is triggered only by incoming SIP requests. It is not triggered by SIP replies at all.

In the request route, you can take the following signaling action to the SIP requests:

- End a reply
- Forward the request
- Drop the request

The default behavior of the request route (in case you do not perform any signaling action) is to drop the requests; nothing here is done for you automatically.

Usually, in the request route, you inspect the incoming SIP request, do the routing (determine the next SIP destination), and perform the signaling operation:

```
# request route
route {
  # is it an OPTIONS request  ?
  if (is_method("OPTIONS")) {
    send_reply("200","OK");
    exit;
  }
  # is it a REGISTER request ?
  if (is_method("REGISTER")) {
    save("location");
    exit;
  }
  # is it a sequential request ?
  if (has_totag()) {
    loose_route();
    t_relay();
  }
  # initial request route based on registrations
  if (!lookup("location")) {
    send_reply("404","Not Found");
    exit;
  }
  # forward the request to the new destination
  t_relay();
}
```

The preceding code can be summarized in the following points:

- It is triggered by an incoming/inbound SIP request
- It processes the SIP request
- The default action is to drop the request

The branch route

The branch route is an outbound route to handle the SIP requests leaving OpenSIPS. It is not a signaling route (you cannot do any SIP signaling operations in this route), but it just inspects, modifies, or drops the SIP requests that are about to leave OpenSIPS.

The main purpose of the branch route is to be used in SIP forking scenarios — parallel or serial forking — where you have one incoming request that translates into multiple outgoing requests (forks or branches).

If you do not use forking, all your processing for the SIP requests can be done in the request route. However, in forking scenarios, you may want to do special handling on a per branch basis (add or remove headers). The branch route gives you individual access to each outgoing branch.

The branch route can be used only in conjunction with the TM module. While handling the request, you need to arm the branch route using the t_on_branch("name") function. This is just setting a trigger; it is not executing the branch route. Once the trigger is set, OpenSIPS will execute the branch route — one time for each branch of that request — when the request is about to be sent out (as a result of a signaling operation such as t_relay()). Setting a branch route is per request/transaction — you can define multiple branch routes in the script and use different branch routes for different requests. Note that only one should be triggered per request; multiple settings of the trigger will simply overwrite.

In the branch route, you handle a SIP request (an outgoing branch). You cannot do any signaling operations such as relaying or replying to the requests. By default, the route will allow the branch to be sent out on the network unless the drop() statement is used; this will discard the branch (not sent on the network).

Usually, in the branch route, you inspect the outgoing SIP branches and perform changes over the SIP request or even drop it, as follows:

```
# request route
route {
  ......
  # initial request route based on registrations;
  # a user registration lookup may return multiple
  # destination, if user is registered with multiple
  # devices.
  if (!lookup("location")) {
    send_reply("404","Not Found");
    exit;
  }
```

```
    # arm a branch route to be executed when
    # sending out the branches
    t_on_branch("nat_filter");
    # send out the request to all the destinations
    t_relay();
    # basically, the branch route is executed inside
    # the t_relay() function, which is the one sending
    # out the SIP branches on the network
}

branch_route[nat_filter]{
    # drop the branches going to natted destinations
    if ($rd=~"^10\." || $rd=~"^192\.168\.") {
       drop();
    } else {
       append_hf("X-NAT: clear \r\n");
    }
}
```

The preceding code can be summarized in the following points:

- It is triggered by an outbound/outgoing branch/fork
- It processes the SIP request
- The default action is sent out

The failure route

The failure route is triggered by a SIP failure, which means that a SIP transaction was completed with a negative non-2xx reply code. For a SIP transaction to fail, all its branches must have received non-2xx replies (>= 300).

 Note that the failure route does not execute due to an error but is about requests/transactions completing with non-2xx codes!

One of the failure route use cases is serial forking. Basically, after receiving a non-2xx reply from the destination(s) that you tried, the failure route gives you the opportunity to continue the processing of the original request and either create more branches to be sent out or override the received non-2xx reply by sending a different reply code to the caller.

The failure route can be used only in conjunction with the TM module. While handling the request, you need to arm the failure route by using the t_on_ failure("name") function. This is just setting a trigger; it is not executing the failure route. Once the trigger is set, OpenSIPS will execute the failure route when the request/transaction is completed with non-2xx replies (received or internally generated such as timeouts).

So, in the failure route, you continue the processing of the original SIP request (handled in the request route). You can do any signaling operations, add more branches and send them out via t_relay(), or override the current non-2xx reply with a different one via the t_reply() function. By default, the failure will allow the current non-2xx reply (from the UAS side) to be sent to the caller (UAC side).

Similar to the branch route, the failure route is per request/transaction, and you can have only one set for a certain request.

> Note that after each triggering, the failure route automatically resets itself. If you want to use a failure route again, you need to rearm it from another failure route.

Usually, in the failure route, you inspect why your request/transaction failed and create more branches (serial forking):

```
# request route
route {

......

   # initial request route based on registrations;
   if (!lookup("location")) {
     send_reply("404","Not Found");
     exit;
   }
   # arm a failure route to be executed in case
   # the transaction fails with non-2xx reply
   t_on_failure("vm_redirect");
   # send out the request
   t_relay();
}


failure_route[vm_redirects]{
   # check the reply code to see if we need
   # to redirect to voicemail system
   if ( t_check_status("(487)|(408)") ) {
     # change the destination to VM system
     $rd = "10.10.1.100";
```

```
   # send out the new branch
   t_relay();
} else {
   # replace all non-2xx replies from
   # end-users with 480
   t_reply("408","Unavailable");
}
}
```

The preceding code can be summarized in the following points:

- It is triggered by the failure of a request/transaction
- It processes the original SIP request
- The default action is to relay back the SIP reply that caused the failure

The reply route

The reply route is triggered by the SIP replies received from the network. This route is the only route in OpenSIPS that gives access to the SIP replies. The access is exclusively to inspect and change the SIP replies (as headers). There are no SIP signaling operations to be performed on the SIP replies as OpenSIPS automatically routes the replies back to UAC based on the Via header information.

 For provisional replies (between 100 and 199), you can use the `drop()` statement to instruct OpenSIPS to discard such replies.

The reply route can be used only in conjunction with the TM module. While handling the request, you need to arm the reply route by using the `t_on_reply("name")` function. This is just setting a trigger; it is not executing the reply route. Once the trigger is set, OpenSIPS will execute the reply route for each incoming reply (any code) for this request.

Similar to the branch route, the reply route is per request/transaction, and you can have only one set for a certain request.

Aside from the per request reply route (provided by the TM module), the OpenSIPS core provides you with a global reply route (with no name), which is triggered by any incoming reply to OpenSIPS.

Note that the global reply route does not have any transaction or dialog state as it is operated in a SIP stateless mode by OpenSIPS.

Usually, in the reply route, you inspect the incoming replies for the logging purposes or to apply changes over these replies:

```
# request route
route {
  ......
  # initial request route based on registrations;
  if (!lookup("location")) {
    send_reply("404","Not Found");
    exit;
  }
  # arm a reply route to see the
  # incoming replies
  t_on_reply("inspect_reply");
  # send out the request
  t_relay();
}

onreply_route[inspect_reply]{
  if ( t_check_status("1[0-9][0-9]") ) {
    xlog("provisional reply $T_reply_code received\n");
  } if ( t_check_status("2[0-9][0-9]") ) {
    xlog("successful reply $T_reply_code received\n");
    remove_hf("User-Agent");
  } else {
    xlog("non-2xx reply $T_reply_code received\n");
  }
}
```

The preceding code can be summarized as follows:

- It is triggered by an incoming/inbound SIP reply
- It processes the received SIP reply
- The default action is to relay back the SIP reply

The local route

The local route is triggered by OpenSIPS whenever there is an internally generated request to be sent out. Even if OpenSIPS is mainly proxying SIP requests, it is also able to generate requests by itself. Such requests do not trigger the request route as they are not received from the network, so the local route complements the request route for the locally/internally generated requests.

The script can have only one local route (optional) and it depends on the TM module. OpenSIPS can generate internal requests when the dialog module terminates a call from the middle (sending BYE requests in both directions), when using the t_uac_dlg **Management Interface (MI)** command, or when using the Presence server modules.

The local route provides the possibility of discarding the outgoing requests using the drop() function.

The local route is an outbound kind of route and its main usage is to inspect or modify the outgoing local requests; no SIP signaling is allowed in this route:

```
local_route {
  # look for internal BYEs
  if ( is_method("BYE") ) {
    acc_log_request("local BYE");
  } else if ( is_method("INVITE") ) {
    append_hf("X-Hint: local request\r\n");
  }
}
```

The preceding code has the following features:

- It is triggered by internal outbound requests (locally generated)
- It processes a SIP request
- The default action is to send the request to the network

The start up route

The start up route is executed only once when OpenSIPS starts up before it handles any kind of SIP traffic. There is only one optional start up route in the script.

As it is triggered by a non-SIP event, the start up route is not related to any SIP message. Due to this, no SIP signaling and SIP message processing is allowed in this route.

The main purpose of this route is to initialize data that you may use in the script or to populate some caches (loading data from DBs):

```
startup_route {
  # populate the local cache with the known gateways
  avp_db_query("select gw_ip from routing", "$avp(ip)");
  $var(i) = 0;
  while ($avp(ip)!=NULL) {
    cache_store("local","gw_ip_$var(i)"," $avp(ip)");
    $var(i) = $var(i) + 1; #increase counter
    $avp(ip) = NULL; #delete the top value
  }
}
```

The timer route

The timer route is a route to be periodically executed by OpenSIPS. The route definition specifies the interval (in seconds) for the triggering of the route. The OpenSIPS routing script may contain multiple timer routes.

Similar to the start up route, the timer route is not related to any SIP message, so no SIP signaling and SIP message processing is allowed in this route.

The main purpose of this route is to refresh the cached data, delete old data, and perform periodical tests or generic cleanups:

```
timer_route[gw_update, 120] {
  # update the local cache if signalized
  if ($shv(reload) == 1 ) {
    avp_db_query("select gwlist from routing where id=10",
                 "$avp(list)");
    cache_store("local","gwlist10"," $avp(list)");
  }
}
```

The event route

The event route is triggered by an event generated by OpenSIPS. Basically, an event route can be considered as a subscriber to a certain OpenSIPS event.

The OpenSIPS routing script may contain the definition of multiple event routes. In its definition, each route specifies what is the triggering event (by name).

Similar to the start up route, the event route is not related to any SIP message, so no SIP signaling and SIP message processing is allowed in this route.

The event route may be used to capture events generated by OpenSIPS and trigger further processing (logging, DB operations, or data updates):

```
event_route[E_DISPATCHER_STATUS] {
  # log each time a dispatcher destination
  # changes its status
  xlog("Dispatcher destination has new status \n");
}
```

The error route

The error route is automatically executed when a parsing error occurs over a SIP message handled in the OpenSIPS routing script. It is a kind of *try and catch* mechanism that allows a more efficient parsing error handling in the script. Instead of testing the return code of each script function in order to detect the parsing error, the error route is automatically triggered by the script interpreter when such a parsing error is reported by the OpenSIPS stack.

In the error route, depending on the reported error, you can decide what to do. Aside from logging or DB operations, the route allows SIP signaling such as sending a reply with the proper non-2xx code and reason.

In the error route, the following variables are available for more information on the error details:

- $(err.class): The class of the error (Now, class 1 is for parse errors)
- $(err.level): The severity level for the error
- $(err.info): The text describing the error
- $(err.rcode): The recommended reply code
- $(err.rreason): The recommended reply reason phrase

The following is an example on how to use error_route:

```
error_route {
xlog("$rm from $si:$sp  - error level=$(err.level),
  info=$(err.info)\n");
    sl_send_reply("$err.rcode", "$err.rreason");
    exit;
}
```

Scripting capabilities

Now that we understand the routes (or routing block), what they are good for, and how they are linked to the handling of the SIP traffic, it is time to look in the routes and see what the scripting capabilities offered by the OpenSIPS routing language are—capabilities in terms of functions, statements, variables, operators, and assignments.

The scripting functions

There are two types of functions available in the OpenSIPS routing blocks: functions provided by the OpenSIPS core and functions provided by the modules.

The functions provided by the core are typically simple functions and they have a very flexible prototype; they can have any number of parameters, they can be called from any type of route, and they can accept parameters as string or integer values. This flexibility is because the core functions are not limited (as prototypes) by the interface between the OpenSIPS core and modules.

The following OpenSIPS online manual contains a list of all the functions offered by the core along with their description:

http://www.opensips.org/Documentation/Script-CoreFunctions-2-1

The functions provided by the modules have a more rigorous prototype; they have up to maximum six parameters and they can take only string values (even if the parameter is an integer by nature, it must be passed as a string):

```
sl_send_reply("404","Not Found");
```

 The full list of functions provided by the modules can be found at http://www.opensips.org/Documentation/Function-Index-2-1.

The module functions may be restricted as usage only from certain types of routes. The allowed route types are always indicated in the module documentation and trying to use a function from a wrong route type will result in a start up failure.

All functions in OpenSIPS return an integer value as a result of their execution. This return value or return code is available after the execution of the function and can be tested. The return code can be read via the $rc variables.

Note that any sequential function call will rewrite the return code! The return code reflects the status of the latest executed functions all the time!

The values returned by functions are correlated with the meaning of true and false in the script tests:

- **Failure**: A strict negative value
- **Success**: A strict positive value

 Zero is never returned by the script functions.

The following is an example of a function call and return codes:

```
lookup("location");
#here the $rc holds the return code of the lookup
$var(n) = $rc;
xlog("The return code of lookup() is $var(n)\n");
#here the $rc holds the return code of the xlog function
switch ( $var(n) ) {
case -1:
  # no contacts found
  send_reply("404","Not Found");
  break;
case -2:
  # contacts found but method not supported
  send_reply("405","Method not supported");
  break;
case -3:
  # some error occurred
  send_reply("500","Server error");
  break;
default:
  xlog("registration found\n");
}
```

What is the meaning of the parameters and how the return code should be interpreted differs from function to function; this information is documented in the module README files.

The scripting variables

The scripting variables are one of the most powerful tools that you have in the OpenSIPS routing script. The variables are used to access information (from OpenSIPS or SIP messages) or hold custom information (at the script level).

Historically, OpenSIPS inherits some old-fashioned variables; actually, they are keywords used to get access to information from SIP messages. Such keywords can be tested against ordinary string or integer values or against predefined values:

```
if (proto==UDP && af==INET) {......}
if (src_port==5060) {......}
if (method=="INVITE") {......}
```

Note that these keywords have become obsolete and you should use variables instead!

OpenSIPS provides you with multiple types of variables to be used in the routing script. The difference between the types of variables is given as follows:

- The scope or visibility of the variable (when it is visible)
- The read-write status of the variable (some types of the variables are read only)
- The way in which the multiple values (for the same variable) are handled

All the OpenSIPS variables start with a $ sign. The complete syntax for a variable is as follows:

```
$(<context>type(name)[index]{transformation})
```

Only the name part is mandatory. The meaning of the fields is given here:

- `type`: This is the type of the variable, such as `ru`, `var`, or `avp`.
- `name`: This is the name of a certain variable instance (of the given type), such as `$avp(tmp)` or `$var(n)`.
- `index`: Similar to an array, certain variables can store more than one value (a list of values).You can access a certain value from the list with an index. You can also specify indexes with negative values, `-1` means the last inserted, `-2` means the value before the previous inserted one, and so on.
- `transformation`: A set of processing actions can be applied to the value of the variable (see the *Scripting transformations* section).

- `context`: This is the context in which the variable will be evaluated. OpenSIPS defines two contexts: `reply` and `request`. The `reply` context can be used in the failure route to ask a variable to be evaluated in the context of the reply message. The `request` context can be used in a reply route to evaluate the variable in the context of the request packet and not in the context of the reply packet.

The following are some usage examples:

- Only by `type`: `$ru`
- By `type` and `name`: `$hdr(Contact)`
- By `type` and `index`: `$(ct[0])`
- By `type`, `name`, and `index`: `$(avp(gw_ip)[2])`
- By `context`:
    - `$(<request>ru)`: In a reply route, it will return the request URI from the request
    - `$(<reply>hdr(Contact))`: Context can be used from the failure route to access information from the SIP reply

The types of variables provided by the OpenSIPS core are as follows:

- Information reference variables
- **Attribute Value Pair (AVP)** variables
- Script variables

There are many other types of variables provided by modules, such as dialog-persistent variables provided by the `dialog` module or global variables provided by the `cfgutils` module.

The reference variables

The information reference variables provide access to information from the processed SIP message (headers, RURI, transport level information, and so on) or from the OpenSIPS internals (time values, process PID, return code of a function, and others).

Depending on what information they provide, these variables are bound to either the message or to nothing (global). In order to choose what SIP message to refer to, you can use the variable context.

Most of these variables are read-only but some also allow write operations.

A variable may return several values or only one depending on the referred information (whether it can have multiple values or not). Most variables are read-only and return a single value (if not documented otherwise). You can read more about the variables at `http://www.opensips.org/Documentation/Script-CoreVar-2-1`.

Here a couple of examples:

- `$ru`: A reference to the SIP request URI
- `$hdr(from)`: A reference to the From header
- `$ci`: A reference to the SIP Call-ID
- `$Ts`: The current time as a Unix timestamp

Variables can be given as parameters to different script functions and they will be replaced with a value before the execution of the function.

The AVP variables

The **Attribute Value Pairs** (**AVPs**) are dynamic variables that can be created on demand.

The AVPs are linked to a particular message or transaction if stateful processing is used. A message or transaction will initially (when received or created) have an empty list of AVPs attached to it. During the routing script, you can create new AVPs that will automatically be attached to the current message/transaction directly via scripting or via the scripting functions.

The AVPs will be visible in all the routes where any message (reply or request) of that transaction will be processed—the branch route, failure route, and onreply route. For the onreply route, you need to enable the TM parameter, `onreply_avp_mode`.

AVPs are read-write and an existing AVP can even be deleted (removed). An AVP may contain multiple values; a new assignment (or write operation) will add a new value to the AVP. The values are kept in the **Last In, First Out** (**LIFO**) to be used order (stack).

More information on the AVP variables can be found here: `http://www.opensips.org/Documentation/Script-CoreVar-1-8`

Here are some examples of the variables:

- `$avp(my_ip)`: The last added value of the AVP `my_ip`
- `$(avp(my_ip)[-1])`: The first added value of the AVP `my_ip`
- `$(avp(ips)[*])`: All the values of the AVP `my_ip`

The AVPOPS module provides you with a rich set of functions to perform complex operations with AVPs including DB queries.

The script variables

As the name indicates, these variables are strictly bound to the scripting routes. The variables are visible only in the routing blocks and they have no persistency — when the route (with all its subroutes) ends, the variables are discarded.

Before using a script variable, be sure that you initialize it! The script variables do not have an initial value and they can have random bogus values (because of how they are implemented).

Script variables are read-write and they can have integer or string values. A script variable can have a single value only. A new assignment (or write operation) will overwrite the existing value. The following is an example on how to use script variables:

```
$var(uri) = "sip:"+$rU+"@sip.com";
$var(i) = $var(i) + 1;
```

Scripting transformations

A transformation is basically a function that is applied to a variable in order to process its value and get another resulting value from it. The value of the original variable is not altered.

The transformations are intended to facilitate access to different attributes of variables (such as the string length of a value, parts of a value, or substrings) or complete different value of variables (encoded in `hexa`, `md5` value, `escape`/`unescape` value for DB operations, and so on), as follows:

```
# the length of From URI ($fu is variable for From URI)
$(fu{s.len})
# get the 2 chars from position 5
$(var(x){s.substr,5,2})
# get the username part of a SIP URI like value
$(avp(my_uri){uri.user})
```

Several transformations can be chained at the same time to a variable:

```
# the length of escaped 'Test' header body
$(hdr(Test){s.escape.common}{s.len})
```

 Wherever you can use a variable, you can also include a set of transformations.

OpenSIPS offers a large set of transformations:

- **string-value-oriented transformation {s.xxxxx}**: The input is a generic string value and the transformation does a string-oriented operation:
    - `$(var(x){s.int})`: Converts to an integer
    - `$(fU{s.substr,0,2})`: Gets the first two characters of the From username

    For more information, refer to `http://www.opensips.org/Documentation/Script-Tran-2-1#toc1`.

- **URI-value-oriented transformation {uri.xxxxx}**: The input is a SIP URI-like string value and the transformation does a URI-oriented parsing:
    - `$(avp(uri){uri.host})`: The domain/host part of the URI held by the AVP
    - `$(fu{uri.param,transport})`: The value of the `transport` parameter of the From URI

    For more information, refer to `http://www.opensips.org/Documentation/Script-Tran-2-1#toc23`.

- **VIA-value-oriented transformation {via.xxxxx}**: The input is a SIP Via-like string value and the transformation does a Via-oriented parsing:

    ◦ `$(hdr(via){via.branch})`: The `branch` parameter of the first Via header

    For more information, refer to `http://www.opensips.org/Documentation/ Script-Tran-2-1#toc39`

- **parameter-list-value-oriented transformation {param.xxxxx}**: The input is a parameter list-like string value and the transformation does a parameter-oriented parsing:

    ◦ For example, `"a=1;b=2;c=3"{param.value,c} = "3"`

    For more information, refer to `http://www.opensips.org/Documentation/ Script-Tran-2-1#toc51`

- **name-address value-oriented transformation {nameaddr.xxxxx}**:

    ◦ For example, `'"test" <sip:test@opensips.org>;tag=dat43h' {nameaddr.param,tag} = dat43h`

    For more information, refer to `http://www.opensips.org/Documentation/ Script-Tran-2-1#toc57`

- **IP-value-oriented transformation {ip.xxxxx}**: The input is an IP-like string value and the transformation does an IP-oriented operation:

    ◦ For example, `"192.168.2.134" {ip.pton}{ip.family} = "INET"`

    For more information, refer to `http://www.opensips.org/Documentation/ Script-Tran-2-1#toc63`

- **CSV-value-oriented transformation {csv.xxxxx}**: The input is a CSV-like string value and the transformation does a CSV-oriented operation:

    ◦ For example, `"a,b,c" {csv.count} = 3`

    For more information, refer to `http://www.opensips.org/Documentation/ Script-Tran-2-1#toc69`

- **SDP-value-oriented transformation {sdp.xxxxx}**: The input is an SDP-like string value and the transformation does an SDP-oriented parsing:

    ◦ `$(rb{sdp.line,m})`: Gets the first `m` line from the SDP body

    For more information, refer to `http://www.opensips.org/Documentation/ Script-Tran-2-1#toc72`

- **RE-value-oriented transformation {re.xxxxx}**: The input is a Regular-Expression-like string value and the transformation does an RE-oriented operation:

  ○ For example, `"abc"{re.subst,/a/A/g}` = `"Abc"`

  For more information, refer to `http://www.opensips.org/Documentation/Script-Tran-2-1#toc74`

The following is an example of transformations:

The length of the value of the parameter at position `1` (Remember that `0` is the first position and `1` is the second position.) is as follows:

```
$var(x) = "a=1;b=22;c=333";
$(var(x){param.value,$(var(x){param.name,1})}{s.len}) = 2
Test if the request is an un-registerif(is_method("REGISTER") &&
    is_present_hf("Expires") && $(hdr(Expires){s.int})==0)
        xlog("This is an un-register message");
```

Scripting flags

The OpenSIPS script offers support to use binary state flags (on or off). Flags are a simple and easy-to-use mechanism to mark and remember something during your routing logic.

Depending on the scope (or what they are attached to), there are three types of flags in OpenSIPS:

- **Message flags (or transaction flags)**: These flags are transaction-persistent. They are visible in all the routes and contexts where the transaction is present.

- **Branch flags**: They are saved in the transaction but per branch. They will be saved in `usrloc` (per contact) as well. So, these flags will be registration-persistent and branch-persistent.

- **Script flags**: They are none-message-related flags—they are only script-persistent and you can use them strictly for the scripting. Once you exit a top-level route, they will be lost. These flags are useful and offer an option to free the message flags. Many flags have no need to be saved as they just reflect the scripting status.

For each type of flag, there are corresponding functions to set, reset, and test the value of a certain flag.

OpenSIPS allows you to use a maximum of 32 flags per type. A certain flag is referred to by its name (a string). There is no need to predefine the names of the flags; you have to simply use them, as shown in the following code:

```
if ($rd=="domain.sip")
  setflag(MY_DOMAIN);
if ( isflagset(MY_DOMAIN) )
  xlog("Domain in Request URI is domain.sip \n");
```

Each type of flag has a special behavior in relation to certain types of routes:

- **Message/transaction flags**: These flags will show up in all the routes where messages related to the initial request are processed. So, they will be visible and changeable in the branch, failure, and onreply routes. The flags will be visible in all the branch routes; if you change a flag in a branch route, the next branch route will inherit the change.

- **Branch flags**: These flags will show up in all the routes where messages related to the initial branch request are processed. So, in the branch route, you will see different sets of flags (as they are different branches); in the onreply route, you will see the branch flags corresponding to the branch that the reply belongs to; in the failure route, the branch flags corresponding to the branch that the winning reply belongs to will be visible. In the request route, you can have multiple branches (as a result of lookup(), enum query, append_branch(), and so on); the default branch is zero (corresponding to the RURI). In the reply routes, there will be only one branch, the zero. In the branch route, the default branch is the current process branch (having the index zero). In the failure route, initially there is only one branch (index zero) that is corresponding to the failed branch.

- **Script flags**: These flags are available only in a route and its subroutes and are reset after each top-level route execution (routes internally triggered by OpenSIPS). They will be persistent per main route, onreply route, branch route, and failure route. Note that they will be inherited in the routes called from other routes.

 For more information, refer to http://www.opensips.org/ Documentation/Script-Flags-2-1.

Scripting operators

Assignments and string and arithmetic operations can be done directly in the configuration file.

Assignments can be done in C, via the = (equal) operator. Note that not all the variables (from the script) can be written; some are read-only, as follows:

```
$var(a) = 123;
$ru = "sip:user@domain";
```

There is a special assign operator := (colon equal) that can be used with AVPs. If the right value is `null`, all AVPs with that name are deleted. If different, the new value will overwrite all the existing values for the AVPs with that name. (In other words, the existing AVPs with the same name will be deleted and a new one with the right-side value will be added.)

```
$avp(val) := 123;
```

For string operations, + is available to concatenate:

```
$var(a) = "test";
$var(b) = "sip:" + $var(a) + "@" + $fd;
```

For arithmetic and bitwise operations with numbers, you can use the following:

- +: Plus
- -: Minus
- /: Divide
- *: Multiply
- %: Modulo
- |: Bitwise OR
- &: Bitwise AND
- ^: Bitwise XOR
- ~: Bitwise NOT
- <<: Bitwise left shift
- >>: Bitwise right shift

Here is an example:

```
$var(a) = 4 + ( 7 & ( ~2 ) );
```

To ensure the priority of operands in expression evaluations, use parentheses.

Arithmetic expressions can be used in conditional expressions via the test operator [...]:

```
if( [ $var(a) & 4 ] )
    log("var a has third bit set\n");
```

Script statements

The OpenSIPS script offers classic programming statements such as `if`, `switch`, or `while`.

The logical operators that can be used in the logical expressions are as follows:

- `==`: Equal
- `!=`: Not equal
- `=~`: Regular expression matching
- `!~`: Regular expression not-matching
- `>`: Greater
- `>=`: Greater or equal
- `<`: Less
- `<=`: Less or equal
- `&&`: Logical AND
- `||`: Logical OR
- `!`: Logical NOT
- `[ ... ]`: Test operator; there can be any arithmetic expression inside this

Here is an example of a `while` loop:

```
$var(i) = 0;
while($var(i) < 10) {
   xlog("counter: $var(i)\n");
   $var(i) = $var(i) + 1;
}
```

To control the script execution, OpenSIPS provides you with a couple of termination statements:

- `exit()`: Terminates the whole script execution through all the levels of subroutes.

- `drop()`: Similar to `exit()`, but additionally instructs OpenSIPS that the current message/operation should be discarded.

- `return(n)`: Terminates the current route/subroute and returns to the parent one (if it exists). A return from a main route behaves exactly as an exit.

 Do not use `return(0)` as it has the same effect as `exit()`.

- `break`: This is to be used only inside a `while` or `switch` statement to exit from that statement.

SIP routing in OpenSIPS

The OpenSIPS routing script is tightly connected to the working of the SIP protocol. Without understanding SIP and how SIP transposes over OpenSIPS, you will never be able to fully understand and use OpenSIPS.

This chapter aims to explain more about the relation between the routing script and SIP protocol.

Mapping SIP traffic over the routing script

Each individual route type was explained in the previous chapters in terms of what event is triggering what route, what kind of SIP message can you handle in each route type, and what SIP signaling operations you can do.

Here, we try to put everything together in a graphical way in order to see how all the OpenSIPS routes map over the SIP traffic over a simple SIP transaction (a request and its replies) going through OpenSIPS.

The first example is of a call with serial forking, as shown in the following diagram:

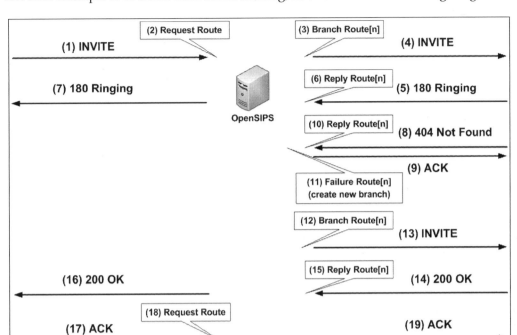

The steps are as follows:

1. An incoming **INVITE** is received from the network.
2. The request route is executed for the INVITE; the script does a relay to the request.
3. The branch route is triggered when the INVITE is sent out (in t_relay()).
4. The outbound **INVITE** is placed on the network.
5. A **180 Ringing** reply is received from the network.
6. An onreply route is executed for the incoming **180 Ringing**.
7. The **180 Ringing** reply is forwarded to the calling UAC.
8. A **404 Not Found** negative reply is received from the network.
9. The TM engine automatically sends back an **ACK** for the negative reply.
10. The onreply route is executed for the incoming **404 Not Found**.
11. The failure route is executed as the 404 reply completed the INVITE transaction with a negative code; here, our script creates a new branch by relaying the request to a new destination.

12. The branch route is triggered when the new INVITE is sent out (in `t_relay()`).

13. The new outbound **INVITE** is placed on the network.

14. A **200 OK** reply is received from the network (for the new **INVITE**).

15. The onreply route is executed for the incoming **200 OK**.

16. The **200 OK** reply is forwarded to the calling UAC.

17. The **ACK** for **200 OK** is received from the UAC.

18. The request route is triggered for the incoming **ACK** request; we also relay it at the script level.

19. The **ACK** is forwarded to the UAS—note that the branch route is not triggered for the ACK requests as the ACK requests do not form transactions.

The second example is of a call with parallel forking, as follows:

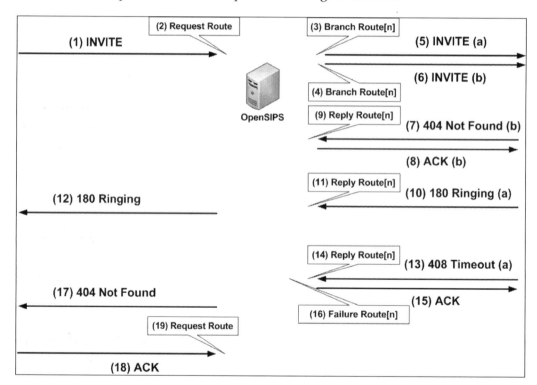

The steps are as follows:

1. An incoming **INVITE** is received from the network.

2. The request route is executed for the **INVITE**; the script does a relay of the request to two destinations, (a) and (b), and two branches are created.

3. The branch route is triggered for the **INVITE** branch **(a)** (in t_relay()).

4. The branch route is triggered for the **INVITE** branch **(b)** (in t_relay()).

5. The outbound **INVITE** branch **(a)** is placed on the network.

6. The outbound **INVITE** branch **(b)** is placed on the network.

7. A **404 Not Found** negative reply is received for branch **(b)** from the network.

8. The TM engine automatically sends back an **ACK** for the negative reply.

9. An onreply route is executed for the incoming **404 Not Found** branch **(b)**. Note that a failure route is not triggered here as the transaction has not yet been completed — branch (a) is still ongoing.

10. A **180 Ringing reply** is received for branch **(a)** from the network.

11. An onreply route is executed for the incoming **180 Ringing** branch **(a)**.

12. The **180 Ringing** reply is forwarded to the calling UAC.

13. A **408 Timeout** negative reply is received for branch **(a)** from the network.

14. An onreply route is executed for the incoming **408 Timeout** branch **(a)**. Note that a failure route is not triggered here as the transaction has not yet been completed — branch (a) is still ongoing.

15. The TM engine automatically sends back an **ACK** for the negative reply.

16. A failure route is executed as the 408 reply completes the INVITE transaction; this reply completes branch (a), while branch (b) is already completed, so the whole transaction is now complete. Here, we do not do any signaling (new branch or replying).

17. The **404 Not Found** final reply is the winner in the transaction and it is sent back to the calling UAC.

18. The **ACK** for **404 Not Found** is received from the UAC.

19. A request route is triggered for the incoming **ACK** request. We relay it at the script level as well, but TM simply absorbs this ACK — the ACK for negative replies is hop-by-hop and an ACK was already sent.

Stateless and stateful routing

From the SIP routing perspective, OpenSIPS can act as both a **stateless** proxy and **stateful** proxy; it is just a matter of what functions are used in the script for the SIP signaling.

In the **stateful mode**, OpenSIPS keeps the state of the SIP transactions in memory. A transaction is formed by a SIP request along with all the SIP replies to this request. So, in the stateful mode, OpenSIPS knows which reply belongs to which request (it matches the replies with the requests), it remembers where the request was sent, what was the last reply received, and what is the transaction state.

In the **stateless mode**, OpenSIPS keeps no information about the handled SIP messages. After processing and forwarding a SIP message, it simply forgets all the information on this message. So, there is no state of the transaction; each SIP request and SIP reply is an individual and unrelated SIP message in OpenSIPS.

The stateless processing requires fewer resources: it is faster as there are no SIP packets matching and does not use memory to keep transactions. However, stateless processing is very limited in terms of capabilities.

There are certain capabilities that are possible only in the stateful mode as they require a transaction state in order to remember what was done so far for a request. The capabilities are as follows:

- **Retransmission detection**: In order to detect and discard incoming retransmissions, you need to have transactions (to know which requests were already received).

 In the stateless mode, the retransmissions will end up being fully processed as any other request.

- **Performing retransmissions**: Based on the transaction information, OpenSIPS can do retransmissions for the last request or reply sent out (if the reply is expected to be confirmed).

- **Timeouts**: OpenSIPS can be instructed to wait for a certain amount of time for a transaction to get completed (to receive a final reply). If it does not, the transaction will time out and OpenSIPS will generate an internal 408 Timeout reply for the caller side. To control the transaction timeout (or waiting), see the $T_fr_timeout and $T_fr_inv_timeout variables in the TM module.

- **Parallel and serial forking**: A transaction is required to store all the information about the branches and the status of each branch; without such information, OpenSIPS will never be able to tell when a branch completes, remember what replies were received on each branch, and tell when the whole transaction is complete.

 Even if you create additional branches, they will simply be discarded if you use stateless SIP forwarding.

- **Script routes**: There are certain types of routes that work only in the stateful mode as they depend on storing information in the transaction and are triggered by transaction-related events. The branch route, failure route, onreply route, and local route depend on the transaction context and so they can be used only in the stateful mode.

The stateless handling is provided directly by the OpenSIPS core and **StateLess Module (SL)**, while the stateful mode is offered via the **Transaction Module (TM)**. In order to perform stateful SIP signaling, you need to load the TM module in your script.

You can see the following corresponding functions in stateless and stateful modes:

Operation	Stateless	Stateful
SIP forward	`forward()`	`t_relay()`
SIP replying	`sl_send_reply()`	`t_reply()`
Create transaction	n/a	`t_newtran()`
Match transaction	n/a	`t_check_trans()`

 The stateless or stateful mode can be selected in a per-request manner. For each request, you can decide in which mode it should be handled!

In the stateful mode, a transaction life cycle consists of the transaction creation, transaction matching, and transaction deletion.

A transaction can be created explicitly from the script via `t_newtran()` or using one of the stateful SIP signaling functions (`t_relay()` or `t_reply()`).

Note that the processing of a request starts in the stateless mode — there is no transaction created unless you create it from the script or a module implicitly creates it!

Once the transaction has been created, the following different kinds of SIP requests can match it:

- Retransmission of the original request: When detected, the script execution is automatically terminated
- ACK for negative replies (only for the INVITE transactions): When matched, the transaction state will be updated on ACK that is received without performing any further SIP signaling
- CANCEL request (only for the INVITE transactions)

All the stateful functions perform transaction matching before doing the actual operation. For explicit request matching, the TM module provides the t_check_trans() script function: this only performs matching without any other additional operations.

 To detect and get rid of retransmissions, do t_check_tran() or t_newtran() as soon as it makes sense in your request logic.

A particular case is the CANCEL request — according to RFC 3261, the CANCEL request must be routed to the same destination as INVITE with the same Via header and request URI as the INVITE that it tries to cancel.

OpenSIPS can do all this for you using the transaction information. Once the CANCEL matches the INVITE transaction, OpenSIPS has access to all the information on how the INVITE was handled so that it can send it out for you as the RFC requires. At the script level, all that you need to do is call the t_relay() function and OpenSIPS will take care of the rest:

```
if (is_method("CANCEL")) {
  # see if this CANCEL matches an INVITE,
  # if not, simply drop it
  if (!t_check_tran())
    exit;
  # if an INVITE transaction was matched,
  # let TM to do the job for us
  t_relay();
}
```

When it comes to reply matching, OpenSIPS automatically does it—there is nothing that you have to do at the script level. All the received SIP replies will be checked and matched against the existing transactions. If a reply does not match any transaction, it will be forwarded to the caller in the stateless mode.

> If the stateless forwarding function (forward()) is not used in the script, OpenSIPS will automatically drop any reply that does not match a transaction (it will not try to forward it stateless). The idea behind this logic is simple: if there was no request sent out in the stateless mode, you cannot receive stateless replies!

The transactions are deleted by OpenSIPS automatically upon termination. Transactions may terminate when they receive a final reply or on timeout.

In-dialog SIP routing

This chapter is more on SIP than OpenSIPS. Nevertheless, a better understanding of SIP leads to a better usage of OpenSIPS.

As SIP is about sessions, it is important to know how OpenSIPS routing should be done with regard to SIP sessions. Not all requests in a SIP session require the same approach when it comes to the routing logic.

The routing logic is different for two types of requests (relative to a SIP session):

- **Initial requests**: These are the requests that create a SIP session or dialog. All SIP dialogs have initial requests. INVITE is the initial dialog for call sessions, the SUBSCRIBE request for the presence subscription sessions, and others.

- **Sequential requests**: These are also called in-dialog requests; they are requests in an existing session that are used to modify or terminate a SIP session. For example, ACK, BYE, and re-INVITEs are sequential requests for call sessions, SUBSCRIBE and NOTIFY are sequential requests for the presence sessions, and so on.

How to distinguish between an initial and sequential request? As an initial request does not know the caller/B side, it is missing the tag parameter in the To header. This To header's tag parameter is populated in the messages after the B party was reached/discovered, so all the sequential requests will have this To header's tag parameter.

> Use the has_totag() script function to check whether a request has the tag parameter!

The initial requests are as follows:

- Discover the called endpoint. The initial requests go through different SIP servers that apply various routing logic (DNS-based, prefix, domain-based, ENUM, registration, and so on).

- Record the path on how to get from the caller to the callee; once the discovery is done, the initial requests have collected a set of SIP hops to be visited in order to get from A to B. Thanks to this, the path is known to the sequential requests and there is no need to apply any routing logic again.

The sequential requests are as follows:

- Simply follow the path recorded by the initial requests; no need for expensive discovery logic again.

The mechanism to record and later use the path between the caller and callee is called record routing (the recording) and loose routing (the usage).

When a SIP server/hop is visited by an initial SIP request, the SIP server may decide that it wants to stay in the middle of the signaling session in order to be visited by all the sequential requests of this session. There are countless reasons for this, as follows:

- Accounting purposes
- Keeping dialog states
- Performing network bridging
- Performing protocol conversion (for example, TLS to UDP)
- Firewall penetration

If the SIP server decides to be visited by the sequential requests, it must perform the record routing action over the initial request; this adds a new Record-Route header to the requests with the address of the server. When the initial SIP request reaches the callee/B side, it will carry a set of Route headers pointing to all the SIP servers that need to be visited by the sequential requests. This set of Route headers is mirrored to the caller/A side via the 200 OK reply. In this way, both the parties, A and B, learn about the intermediary SIP hops that need to be visited by the sequential requests.

When the transaction of the initial request is successfully completed, both parties can build what is called the route set. The route set is the full list of hops on how to get from A to B, including the endpoints.

The route set of each party is composed of the following:

- The intermediary servers that did the record routing (taken from the Record-Route headers)
- The contact IP of the other party (taken from the Contact header of the received message)

The following diagram shows how the record routing mechanism works for an initial request:

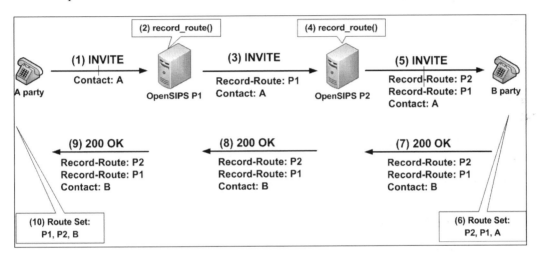

The steps are as follows:

1. A party sends the **INVITE** carrying its own IP in the Contact header.

2. The **P1** proxy does **record_route()** so that a Record-Route with the IP of P1 is added to the requests on top of any existing Record-Route headers.

3. The **P1** proxy does the routing logic and sends the **INVITE** to P2.

4. The **P2** proxy does **record_route()** so that a Record-Route with the IP of P2 is added to the requests on top of the existing Record-Route headers.

5. The **P2** proxy does the routing logic and sends the **INVITE** to the **B party**.

6. The **B party** computes its routing set as follows: first, all the intermediary hops from the Record-Route headers and then the other end party from the Contact header (the A party).

7. The B party accepts the calls and sends a **200 OK** reply mirroring all the received Record-Route headers (in the same order as received); the Contact header is populated with its own IP (the B party).

8. The **200 OK** is relayed to proxy P1 (based on the Via headers).

9. The **200 OK** is relayed to the A party (based on the Via headers).

10. The B party computes its routing set as follows: first, all the intermediary hops from Record-Route headers, in reverse order, and then the other end party from the Contact header (the B party).

After all these steps, each party knows exactly what steps need to be followed in order to get to the other endpoint (so no discovery mechanism is needed, just use the route set), as shown in the following image:

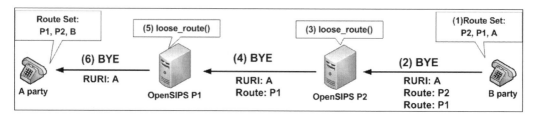

The steps are as follows:

1. Taking the existing route set (P2, P2, and A), the **B party** uses the final destination (the A party) as the request URI and the remaining hops are pushed as Route headers.

2. The routing algorithm (based on the Route headers) is to route to the first Route header in the message ignoring the RURI. So, the **BYE** request is sent to the P2 proxy.

3. The **P2** proxy performs the same loose routing algorithm (based on the Route headers), but first, it removes the top Route header as this one points to itself. (The Route header did its job.)

4. Based on the loose routing, the P2 proxy sends the request to the top Route header. So, the **BYE** is sent further to the P1 proxy.

5. The **P1** proxy performs the same loose routing as P2, so remove the Route P1 as it points to itself.

6. The P2 proxy tries to apply the loose routing, but there are no Route headers left in the request. The P2 proxy falls back to the default SIP routing based on RURI and sends the request to the **A party**.

As you can see, by applying a standard routing algorithm (the loose routing), the proxies can route sequential traffic between them and there is no need for custom routing for these sequential requests.

The conclusion is that, at the SIP level, the initial and sequential requests need to be routed differently. For the sequential requests, you can use the standard loose routing mechanism, while for the initial requests, you need to do the actual routing and service logic, which reflects the way your OpenSIPS needs to behave.

In routing scripts, simply deal with the sequential requests as soon as possible using the loose routing mechanism and concentrate on the custom routing for the initial requests only.

Summary

In this chapter, you learned all about the OpenSIPS configuration file, starting from its structure and types of routes all the way to using functions, variables, flags, and transformations. Soon, you will be able to put together a routing script, understand how the SIP traffic flows through the script, and what kind of routes are triggered for different SIP messages.

At this point, you have a better understanding of how SIP routing should be done. First, we saw the difference between stateful and stateless routing in terms of behavior, functions, and capabilities. Next, we saw the in-dialog routing and how to do proper SIP routing for the in-dialog requests. Here, you learned how to use the record routing and loose routing mechanisms in order to achieve correct and efficient SIP routing.

In the next chapter, we will see how to implement authentication; basically, how to use the database backends to process SIP requests and deal with calls.

5

Subscriber Management

In this chapter, you will learn how to use the database backends to authenticate the SIP requests and save data such as location and aliases tables. We will use MySQL as the reference database, but most examples can be easily adapted to any other supported database. This chapter is divided in two parts. In the first one, you will learn how to implement the authentication, and in the second one, you will learn how to deal with calls in each direction.

In this chapter, we will cover the following topics:

- Configuring MySQL for the authentication
- Using the `opensipsctl` utility for basic operations such as adding users
- Changing the `opensips.cfg` script to connect to a database
- Implementing the persistence for the location tables
- Implementing the aliases tables
- Using the group module and ACL to authorize resources
- Authenticating users by their IP addresses using the permissions module
- Restarting the server without losing the location records
- Dealing correctly with inbound and outbound foreign domains

At the moment, we are still focusing on the SIP proxy. However, we will include a new component, **Database**. OpenSIPS can use MySQL and PostgreSQL. For this book, we have chosen to work with MySQL. It is, by far, the most used database for OpenSIPS. The following is a figure for Learning Map:

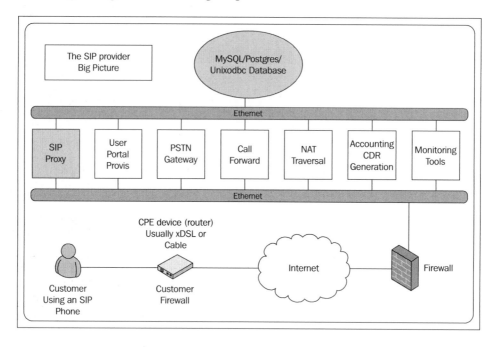

Modules

In this chapter, we will describe several modules. The first one is AUTH_DB, which is responsible for the authentication process from a database. DB_MYSQL is the driver for the database. The USRLOC module is used to maintain the user location table and exports several commands. REGISTRAR is used for the registration process. PERMISSIONS will be used for the IP authentication, ALIAS_DB for the alias translation, and finally, GROUP for the authorization process. For a complete list of all the functions and parameters exported by this module, you can check the documentation at http://www.opensips.org/html/docs/modules/2.1.x/.

The AUTH_DB module

The database authentication is performed by the AUTH_DB module. Other types of authentication such as RADIUS can be performed using AUTH_AAA. The AUTH_DB module works with database modules such as MySQL and Postgres. In the following table, we have some of the most important parameters:

Parameter	Default	Description
db_url	mysql://opensipsro:opensipsro@localhost/opensips	This is the URL of the database
user_column	username	This is the name of the column holding the names of users
domain_column	domain	This is the name of the column holding the domains of users
password column	ha1	This is the name of the column holding the passwords
password_column2	ha1b	This is the name of the column holding the precalculated HA1 strings, which were calculated including the domain in the username
calculate_ha1	0 (server assumes that HA1 strings are already calculated in the database)	This tells the server whether it should expect plain text passwords in the database or not
use_domain	0 (domains won't be checked when looking up in the subscriber database)	You can use this parameter set to one if you have a multidomain environment
load_credentials	rpid	This specifies the credentials to be fetched from the database when the authentication is performed; the load credentials will be stored in **Attribute Value Pair (AVP)**.

The AUTH_DB module exports two functions. The table parameter is the database table to look for subscribers; by default, subscriber. The realm parameter is usually the domain name. If you leave it blank, it authenticates any domain. The functions have been explained here:

- www_authorize(realm, table): This function is used for the registration authentication in accordance with RFC 2617.

- proxy_authorize(realm, table): This function verifies the credentials according to RFC 2617 (refer http://www.ietf.org/rfc/rfc2617.txt#_blank) for the non-REGISTER requests. If the credentials are verified successfully, the request will be marked as authorized.

You have to use `www_authorize` when your server is the endpoint of the request. Use `proxy_authorize` when the request's final destination is not your server, and you can forward the request to the next hop, which is actually working as a proxy.

The difference between when to use `www_authorize` and `proxy_authorize` is the final destination of the request. If the final destination is the proxy itself (for example, REGISTER), you should use the first one. If you are relaying the request to another endpoint, you should use the latter.

The REGISTER authentication sequence

The script should authenticate REGISTER and INVITE messages. Let's see how this happens before changing the `opensips.cfg` script. When OpenSIPS receives the REGISTER message, it checks for the existence of the Authorization header. If it is not found, it will challenge UAC for the credentials and exit.

After being challenged, the UAC should send a REGISTER message with an Authorization header field:

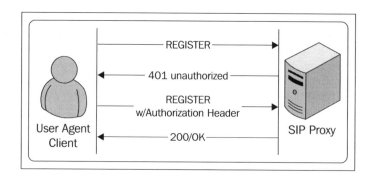

The REGISTER sequence

See the following registration process shown by these packets captured by the **ngrep** utility. The ngrep tool is a handy utility, easy to install on any Linux server. The ngrep command used to capture the packet is as follows:

`ngrep -p -q -W byline port 5060`

`U 192.168.1.119:29040 -> 192.168.1.155:5060`

`REGISTER sip:192.168.1.155 SIP/2.0.`

`Via: SIP/2.0/UDP 192.168.1.119:29040;branch=z9hG4bK-d87543-13517a5a8218ff45-1--d87543-;rport.`

`Max-Forwards: 70.`

Contact: <sip:1000@192.168.1.119:29040;rinstance=2286bddd834b3cfe>.

To: "1000"<sip:1000@192.168.1.155>.

From: "1000"<sip:1000@192.168.1.155>;tag=0d10cc75.

Call-ID: e0739d571d287264NjhiZjM2N2UyMjhmNDViYTgzY2I4ODMxYTVlZTY0NDc..

CSeq: 1 REGISTER.

Expires: 3600.

Allow: INVITE, ACK, CANCEL, OPTIONS, BYE, REFER, NOTIFY, MESSAGE, SUBSCRIBE, INFO.

User-Agent: X-Lite release 10031 stamp 30942.

Content-Length: 0.

U 192.168.1.155:5060 -> 192.168.1.119:29040

SIP/2.0 401 Unauthorized.

Via: SIP/2.0/UDP 192.168.1.119:29040;branch=z9hG4bK-d87543-13517a5a8218ff45-1--d87543-;rport=29040.

To: "1000"<sip:1000@192.168.1.155>;tag=329cfeaa6ded039da25ff8cbb8668bd2.41bb.

From: "1000"<sip:1000@192.168.1.155>;tag=0d10cc75.

Call-ID: e0739d571d287264NjhiZjM2N2UyMjhmNDViYTgzY2I4ODMxYTVlZTY0NDc..

CSeq: 1 REGISTER.

WWW-Authenticate: Digest realm="192.168.1.155", nonce="46263864b3abb96a423a7ccf052fa68d4ad5192f".

Server: Opensips (2.1-notls (i386/linux)).

Content-Length: 0.

U 192.168.1.119:29040 -> 192.168.1.155:5060

REGISTER sip:192.168.1.155 SIP/2.0.

Via: SIP/2.0/UDP 192.168.1.119:29040;branch=z9hG4bK-d87543-da776d09bd6fcb65-1--d87543-;rport.

Max-Forwards: 70.

Contact: <sip:1000@192.168.1.119:29040;rinstance=2286bddd834b3cfe>.

To: "1000"<sip:1000@192.168.1.155>.

From: "1000"<sip:1000@192.168.1.155>;tag=0d10cc75.

Call-ID: e0739d571d287264NjhiZjM2N2UyMjhmNDViYTgzY2I4ODMxYTVlZTY0NDc..

CSeq: 2 REGISTER.

Expires: 3600.

Allow: INVITE, ACK, CANCEL, OPTIONS, BYE, REFER, NOTIFY, MESSAGE, SUBSCRIBE, INFO.

User-Agent: X-Lite release 10031 stamp 30942.

Authorization: Digest username="1000",realm="192.168.1.155",nonce="462638 64b3abb96a423a7ccf052fa68d4ad5192f",uri="sip:192.168.1.155",response="d7b 33793a123a69ec12c8fc87abd4c03",algorithm=MD5.

Content-Length: 0.

U 192.168.1.155:5060 -> 192.168.1.119:29040

SIP/2.0 200 OK.

Via: SIP/2.0/UDP 192.168.1.119:29040;branch=z9hG4bK-d87543-da776d09bd6fcb65-1--d87543-;rport=29040.

To: "1000"<sip:1000@192.168.1.155>;tag=329cfeaa6ded039da25ff8cbb8668bd2.c577.

From: "1000"<sip:1000@192.168.1.155>;tag=0d10cc75.

Call-ID: e0739d571d287264NjhiZjM2N2UyMjhmNDViYTgzY2I4ODMxYTVlZTY0NDc..

CSeq: 2 REGISTER.

Contact: <sip:1000@192.168.1.119:29040;rinstance=2286bddd834b3cfe>;expires=3600.

Server: Opensips (2.1-notls (i386/linux)).

Content-Length: 0.

Let's see how this sequence is coded in the `opensips.cfg` script:

```
if (is_method("REGISTER"))
{
  # authenticate the REGISTER requests
  if (!www_authorize("", "subscriber"))
  {
    www_challenge("", "0");
    exit;
  }

  if (!db_check_to())
  {
    sl_send_reply("403","Forbidden auth ID");
    exit;
  }

  if (proto==TCP) setflag(TCP_PERSISTENT);

  if (!save("location"))
    sl_reply_error();

  exit;
}
```

In the preceding sequence, the REGISTER packet is not authenticated by the www_ authorize() function in the first pass. Then, the www_challenge() function is invoked. It sends the **401 Unauthorized** packet, which contains the authentication challenge, according to the Digest authentication scheme. In the second pass, UAC sends the REGISTER packet with the correct Authorization header field and then save("location") is invoked to save **Address of Record (AOR)** in the MySQL location table. The flags are saved in the location table, such as the TCP_PERSISTENT table, and are responsible for keeping the TCP connection alive.

The db_check_to() function is part of the URI module. It checks the user part of the URI present in the To header. It prevents the registration from a subscriber using the credentials from another one.

The INVITE authentication sequence

Here is the INVITE authentication sequence of an ordinary call. The proxy server always answers the first INVITE message with a reply containing the **407 Proxy Authentication Required** message. This message has the Authorization header field, which contains information about the Digest authentication, such as realm and nonce (nonce is a number used once in the authentication process and it prevents replay attacks). Once received by UAC, this message is replied with a new INVITE. Now, the Authorize header field contains the Digest calculated using the username, password, realm, and nonce with the MD5 algorithm. If a match exists between the Digest informed in the request and the one calculated in the server using the same parameters, the INVITE request is authenticated. The INVITE authentication sequence is as follows:

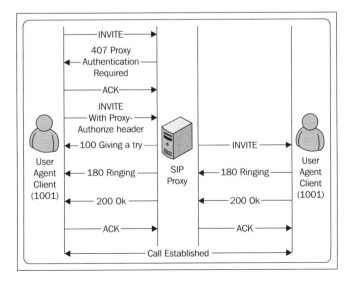

The INVITE sequence packet capture

We captured an INVITE authentication sequence using ngrep. This sequence will help you understand the preceding figure. The SDP headers were stripped off to avoid a long list.

```
U 192.168.1.169:5060 -> 192.168.1.155:5060

INVITE sip:1000@192.168.1.155 SIP/2.0.

Via: SIP/2.0/UDP 192.168.1.169;branch=z9hG4bKf45d977e65cf40e0.

From: <sip:1001@192.168.1.155>;tag=a83bebd75be1d88e.

To: <sip:1000@192.168.1.155>.

Contact: <sip:1001@192.168.1.169>.

Supported: replaces.

Call-ID: 8acb7ed7fc07c369@192.168.1.169.

CSeq: 39392 INVITE.

User-Agent: TMS320V5000 TI50002.0.8.3.

Max-Forwards: 70.

Allow: INVITE,ACK,CANCEL,BYE,NOTIFY,REFER,OPTIONS,INFO,SUBSCRIBE.

Content-Type: application/sdp.

Content-Length: 386.

(sdp body striped off).


U 192.168.1.155:5060 -> 192.168.1.169:5060

SIP/2.0 407 Proxy Authentication Required.

Via: SIP/2.0/UDP 192.168.1.169;branch=z9hG4bKf45d977e65cf40e0.

From: <sip:1001@192.168.1.155>;tag=a83bebd75be1d88e.

To: <sip:1000@192.168.1.155>;tag=329cfeaa6ded039da25ff8cbb8668bd2.b550.

Call-ID: 8acb7ed7fc07c369@192.168.1.169.

CSeq: 39392 INVITE.

Proxy-Authenticate: Digest realm="192.168.1.155", nonce="4626420b4b162ef8
4a1a1d3966704d380194bb78".

Server: Opensips (2.1-notls(i386/linux)).

Content-Length: 0.


U 192.168.1.169:5060 -> 192.168.1.155:5060

ACK sip:1000@192.168.1.155 SIP/2.0.

Via: SIP/2.0/UDP 192.168.1.169;branch=z9hG4bKf45d977e65cf40e0.

From: <sip:1001@192.168.1.155>;tag=a83bebd75be1d88e.
```

```
To: <sip:1000@192.168.1.155>;tag=329cfeaa6ded039da25ff8cbb8668bd2.b550.

Contact: <sip:1001@192.168.1.169>.

Call-ID: 8acb7ed7fc07c369@192.168.1.169.

CSeq: 39392 ACK.

User-Agent: TMS320V5000 TI50002.0.8.3.

Max-Forwards: 70.

Allow: INVITE,ACK,CANCEL,BYE,NOTIFY,REFER,OPTIONS,INFO,SUBSCRIBE.

Content-Length: 0.


U 192.168.1.169:5060 -> 192.168.1.155:5060

INVITE sip:1000@192.168.1.155 SIP/2.0.

Via: SIP/2.0/UDP 192.168.1.169;branch=z9hG4bKcdb4add5db72d493.

From: <sip:1001@192.168.1.155>;tag=a83bebd75be1d88e.

To: <sip:1000@192.168.1.155>.

Contact: <sip:1001@192.168.1.169>.

Supported: replaces.

Proxy-Authorization: Digest username="1001", realm="192.168.1.155",
algorithm=MD5, uri="sip:1000@192.168.1.155", nonce="4626420b4b162ef84a1a1
d3966704d380194bb78", response="06736c6d7631858bb1cbb0c86fb939d9".

Call-ID: 8acb7ed7fc07c369@192.168.1.169.

CSeq: 39393 INVITE.

User-Agent: TMS320V5000 TI50002.0.8.3.

Max-Forwards: 70.

Allow: INVITE,ACK,CANCEL,BYE,NOTIFY,REFER,OPTIONS,INFO,SUBSCRIBE.

Content-Type: application/sdp.

Content-Length: 386.

(sdp header striped off)
```

The INVITE code snippet

In the following code, the SIP proxy will challenge the user for credentials on
any request different from REGISTER. After authentication, we will consume the
credentials; in other words, we will remove the Authorize header from the request—
for security reasons—in order to avoid sending the encrypted material ahead:

```
if (!proxy_authorize("","subscriber")) {
  proxy_challenge("","0");
  exit;
};
```

```
consume_credentials();


# native SIP destinations are handled using our USRLOC DB
if (!lookup("location")) {
  sl_send_reply("404", "Not Found");
  exit;
};
route(relay);
```

Digest authentication

The Digest authentication is based on RFC 2617, **HTTP Basic** and **Digest Access Authentication**. Our objective in this chapter is to show the basics of a system with Digest authentication. It is not an answer to all the possible security problems with SIP, but it is certainly a good method to protect names and passwords traversing the network. The following figure shows how digest authentication works:

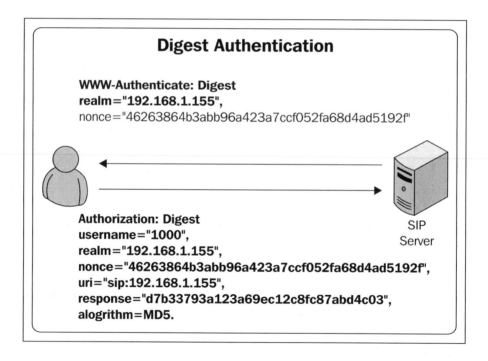

The Digest scheme is a simple challenge-response mechanism. It challenges UA using a **nonce** value. A valid response includes a checksum of all the parameters. Thus, the password is never transmitted as simple text.

The authorization request header

If a server receives a REGISTER or an INVITE request and a valid Authorize header field is not sent, the server replies **401 unauthorized** with a header field, **WWW-Authenticate**. This header contains a realm and nonce.

The client is expected to try again, now passing the Authorize header field. It contains the username, realm, nonce (passed by the server), URI, a hexadecimal answer with 32 digits, and an algorithm method of authentication (in this case, MD5). This answer is the checksum generated by the client using the referred algorithm:

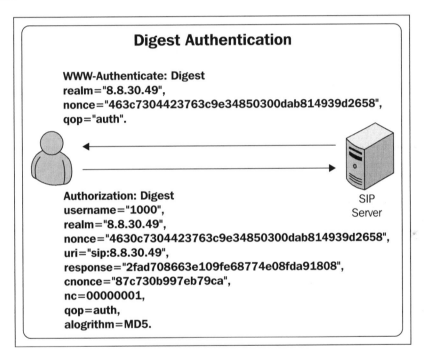

Quality of protection

The **Quality Of Protection (QOP)** parameter indicates the quality of protection that the client has applied to the message.

You can configure the QOP parameter on both function calls, `www_challenge(realm,qop)` and `proxy_challenge(realm,qop)`. If configured to one, the server will ask for the QOP parameter. Always use `qop=1` (enabled); it will help you to avoid *replay* attacks. However, some clients can be incompatible with QOP. A detailed description of the Digest authentication can be found in RFC 2617.

Plaintext or prehashed passwords

You can store passwords in clear text or as a hash. Storing passwords as hashes is safer. Text or hash passwords are controlled by the opensipsctlrc and opensips. cfg files. The opensipsctlrc file controls the opensipsctl and osipsconsole utilities. It will store the password in plaintext in the password column if the STORE_PLAINTEXT_PW parameter is set to 1 or the HA1 value in the ha1 column is set to 0 (HA1 is a hash, the MD5 computation of user, realm, and password). The calculate_ha1 parameter defines whether MD5 will be computed on the fly or not. When set to 1, it tells the server to use the plaintext passwords from the password column and calculate HA1 on the fly. On the other hand, if set to 0, it tells the server to expect the HA1 strings directly from the HA1 column, and it won't need to calculate them because they are already precalculated. There are two password columns, password_column and password_column_2; the latter is used to store the HA1 hash, including the domain. Some user agents include the domain in the user credentials. So, to use plaintext passwords, perform the following commands:

- In the opensips.cfg file, set the following command:

  ```
  modparam("auth_db", "calculate_ha1", 1)
  modparam("auth_db", "password_column", "password")
  ```

- In the opensipsctlrc file, set the following command:

  ```
  STORE_PLAINTEXT_PW=1
  ```

To use hash passwords, perform the following commands:

- In the opensips.cfg file, set as follows:

  ```
  modparam("auth_db", "calculate_ha1", 0 )
  modparam("auth_db", "password_column", "ha1")
  ```

- In the opensipsctlrc file, set the following:

  ```
  STORE_PLAINTEXT_PW=0
  ```

Installing MySQL support

To save the users and location information in a database, OpenSIPS will need to be configured with a database such as MySQL. Before you proceed, it is important to verify that you have MySQL installed and the opensips-mysql module compiled and installed.

In *Chapter 3, Installing OpenSIPS*, we compiled OpenSIPS with MySQL support. Check the lib directory for the db_mysql.so module.

Some additional tasks have to be done before you can use OpenSIPS with MySQL.

The following are the step-by-step instructions to create a database using the `opensipsdbctl` command and change the `opensips.cfg` file to allow the authentication of the REGISTER and INVITE requests:

1. Verify the existence of the `db_mysql.so` module in the directory:

    For 32 bit:

    ```
    ls /lib/opensips/modules/db_mysql.so
    ```

    For 64 bit:

    ```
    ls /lib64/opensips/modules/db_mysql.so
    ```

    If the module does not exist, compile OpenSIPS with MySQL support. The path depends on the installation prefix. For 64-bit systems, check lib64 instead of lib.

2. Edit the `opensipsctlrc` file before creating the database and change the following attributes:

    ```
    SIP_DOMAIN=192.168.11.138 #Please, CUSTOMIZE to your own address
    DBENGINE=MYSQL
    DBHOST=localhost
    DBNAME=opensips
    DBRWUSER=opensips
    DBRWPW="opensipsrw"
    DBROUSER=opensipsro
    DBROPW=opensipsro
    ALIASES_TYPE="DB"
    OSIPS_FIFO="/tmp/opensips_fifo"
    PID_FILE=/var/run/opensips/opensips.pid
    ```

3. Create MySQL tables using the `opensipsdbctl` shell script. The syntax for this utility is as follows:

    ```
    opensipsdbctl create <db name or db_path, optional>
    ```

4. Run the script with the following command line:

    ```
    opensipsdbctl create
    ```

    The output of the command would be as follows:

    ```
    Opensips:~# opensipsdbctl create
    MySQL password for root:
    INFO: test server charset
    INFO: creating database opensips ...
    ```

```
INFO: Core Opensips tables succesfully created.
Install presence related tables? (y/n): y
INFO: creating presence tables into opensips ...
INFO: Presence tables succesfully created.
Install tables for imc cpl siptrace domainpolicy carrierroute?
(y/n): y
```

A password will be solicited to access the database. The password is empty at this moment. The script will ask for the password twice; press *Enter* in both.

The `opensipsdbctl` utility has several options, such as `drop`, `reinit`, `backup`, `restore`, `copy`, and install extra tables for `presence` and the other modules. Check the help screen of the utility by running it without any parameters.

5. Generate the script with authentication support.

   In this book, we will generate scripts and analyze them.

   To generate the reference script for this chapter, follow these instructions:

   ```
   cd /usr/src/opensips_21
   make menuconfig
   ```

   Navigate to **Generate OpenSIPS Script | Residential Script | Configure Residential Script**.

   Select **USE_ALIASES, USE_AUTH,** and **USE_DBUSRLOC**:

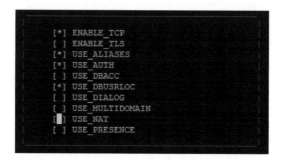

The scripts will be generated at `/usr/src/opensips_21/etc/`. Copy the script that is generated to `/etc/opensips/opensips.cfg`:

```
cp opensips_residential_2014-12-23_6\:49\:56.cfg /etc/opensips/
opensips.cfg
```

 Don't forget to change the IP address in the generated script from `127.0.0.1` to your own IP address.

Analysis of the opensips.cfg file

Now the configuration is ready to authenticate the REGISTER transactions. We can save the AOR in the location table to achieve persistence. This allows us to restart the server without losing the AOR records and affecting UACs. The configuration file will show the modules that have been loaded, their respective parameters, and the main sections of the code related to this chapter.

To make the authentication work, it is necessary to load the following modules:

```
loadmodule "db_mysql.so"
loadmodule "auth.so"
loadmodule "auth_db.so"
```

The MySQL support is added easily by including db_mysql.so in the list of loaded modules. MySQL should be loaded before the other modules. The authentication capability is provided by the auth.so and auth_db.so modules. These modules are required to enable the authentication functionality:

```
modparam("auth_db", "calculate_ha1", 1)
modparam("usrloc", "db_mode", 2)
```

The calculate_ha1 parameter tells the auth_db module to use plaintext passwords. We will use this setting for compatibility with the OpenSIPS control panel.

The db_mode parameter tells the usrloc module to store and retrieve the AOR records in the MySQL database.

The REGISTER requests

In the following code snippet, we will check the authentication for the REGISTER method:

```
if (is_method("REGISTER"))
{
  # authenticate the REGISTER requests
  if (!www_authorize("", "subscriber"))
  {
    www_challenge("", "0");
    exit;
  }

  if (!db_check_to())
  {
    sl_send_reply("403","Forbidden auth ID");
    exit;
```

```
    }

    if ( proto==TCP) setflag(TCP_PERSISTENT);

    if (!save("location"))
      sl_reply_error();

    exit;
  }
```

If the method is REGISTER and the credentials are correct, www_authorize returns
true. After the authentication, the system saves the location data for this UAC. The
first parameter specifies the realm where the user will be authenticated. The realm is
usually the domain name or hostname. The second parameter tells OpenSIPS which
MySQL table to look for:

```
    www_challenge("","0");
```

If the packet does not have an Authorize header field, we will send a **401
unauthorized** message to the UAC. This tells the UAC to retransmit the request
with the included Digest credentials. The www_challenge() command receives
two parameters. The first one is the realm that the UAC should use to compute the
Digest. The second parameter affects the inclusion of the QOP parameter in the
challenge. Using 1 will include the QOP in the Digest. Some phones do not support
QOP. You can try 0 in these circumstances.

The non-REGISTER requests

All SIP requests, except for CANCEL and ACK, are usually authenticated. For
requests traversing the SIP proxy, we will use the proxy_authorize() function
instead of www_authorize():

```
  if (!(is_method("REGISTER")))
  {
    if (from_uri==myself)
    {
      # authenticate if from local subscribers
      #(domain in FROM URI is local)
      if (!proxy_authorize("", "subscriber")) {
        proxy_challenge("", "0");
        exit;
      }

      if (!db_check_from()) {
        sl_send_reply("403","Forbidden auth ID");
```

```
        exit;
    }
    consume_credentials();
    # caller authenticated

  } else {
    # if caller is not local
    if (!uri==myself) {
        send_reply("403","Relay forbidden");
        exit;
    }
  }
}
```

It doesn't make sense to authenticate requests to the external domains. So, to make sure that we are handling a domain served by our proxy, we will use the following line:

```
if (from_uri==myself)
```

By default, OpenSIPS uses an `auto_aliases` parameter for doing a reverse lookup on the IP address to discover its own domain. You can disable the `auto_aliases` parameter and manually set the local domain using the following core commands:

```
auto_aliases=no
alias=opensips.org
```

When starting OpenSIPS, you can see the local domains in the output:

```
Restarting opensips: opensips Listening on
            udp: 192.168.255.131 [192.168.255.131]:5060
            tcp: 192.168.255.131 [192.168.255.131]:5060
Aliases:
            *: opensips.org:*
```

The sequence for the INVITE authentication is very similar to the REGISTER. If the request does not have a valid Authorization header, the proxy will send a challenge in the **407 Proxy Authentication Required** message to the UAC. The UAC will then retransmit the request, which now contains the `Authorization:` header. Some commands that deserve to be mentioned are as follows:

- `consume_credentials()`: We want to avoid sending the authentication credentials to the destination servers. We will use the `consume_credentials()` function to remove the Authorize header field from the request before relaying.

- `if (!proxy_authorize("","subscriber")) {:` We will use the `proxy_authorize()` function to check for the authentication headers. If we didn't check the credentials, we would be considered an open relay. The arguments are similar to `www_authorize`.

- `db_check_from():` When operating a SIP proxy, you should guarantee that a valid account won't be used by non-authenticated users. The `db_check_to()` and `db_check_from()` functions are used to map the SIP users with the authentication user. The SIP user is in the From and To header fields and the `auth` user is only used for authentication (Authorize header field) and has its own password. In the current example, the function verifies that a SIP user and `auth` user is the same. This is to ensure that a user A does not use the credentials of user B. These functions are enabled by the `URI` module.

The opensipsctl shell script

The `opensipsctl` utility is a shell script installed in `/sbin`. (The path depends on the installation prefix.) It is used to manage OpensSIPS from the command line. It can be used to perform the following functions:

- Start, stop, and restart OpenSIPS

- Show, grant, and revoke ACLs

- Add, remove, and list aliases

- Add, remove, and configure an AVP

- Manage a **Low Cost Route (LCR)**

- Manage a **Remote Party Identity (RPID)**

- Add, remove, and list subscribers

- Add, remove, and show the `usrloc` table in-**Random Access Memory (RAM)**

- Monitor OpenSIPS

We will learn several of its options in the next chapters. The following is the output of the `opensipsctl` help command:

```
opensips:~# opensipsctl -help
/sbin/opensipsctl $Revision: 4448 $

Existing commands:

 -- command 'start|stop|restart'

restart .......................... restart OpenSIPS
start ............................ start OpenSIPS
stop ............................. stop OpenSIPS


 -- command 'acl' - manage access control lists (acl)

acl show [<username>] ............. show user membership
acl grant <username> <group> ....... grant user membership (*)
acl revoke <username> [<group>] .... grant user membership(s) (*)


 -- command 'lcr' - manage least cost routes (lcr)

   * IP addresses must be entered in dotted quad format e.g. 1.2.3.4 *
   * <uri_scheme> and <transport> must be entered in integer or text,*
   * e.g. transport '2' is identical to transport 'tcp'.            *
   *    scheme: 1=sip, 2=sips;   transport: 1=udp, 2=tcp, 3=tls     *
   * Examples:  lcr addgw level3 1.2.3.4 5080 sip tcp 1            *
   *            lcr addroute +1 '' 1 1                             *
```

Configuring the opensipsctl utility

To configure `opensipsctl`, you have to edit the resource file, `opensipsctlrc`. This script is found in `/etc/opensips`. It is parsed by the `opensipsctl` utility to configure the database authentication and communication parameters. Usually, it uses the FIFO mechanism to send commands to the OpenSIPS daemon.

> For security reasons, it is important to change the default user and password used for database access.

To edit the file, use the `vi` text editor or any other of your preference:

```
vi opensipsctlrc
# $Id: opensipsctlrc 4331 2008-06-06 14:36:01Z anca_vamanu $
#
# The OpenSIPS configuration file for the control tools.
#
```

Here you can set variables used in the opensipsctl and opensipsdbctl setup

scripts. Per default all variables here are commented out, the control tools

will use their internal default values.

your SIP domain

SIP_DOMAIN=192.168.11.138

chrooted directory

$CHROOT_DIR="/path/to/chrooted/directory"

database type: MYSQL, PGSQL, ORACLE, DB_BERKELEY, or DBTEXT, by default none is loaded

If you want to setup a database with opensipsdbctl, you must at least specify

this parameter.

DBENGINE=MYSQL

database host

DBHOST=localhost

database name (for ORACLE this is TNS name)

DBNAME=opensips

database path used by dbtext or db_berkeley

DB_PATH="/usr/local/etc/opensips/dbtext"

database read/write user

DBRWUSER=opensips

password for database read/write user

DBRWPW="opensipsrw"

database read only user

DBROUSER=opensipsro

```
## password for database read only user
DBROPW=opensipsro

## database super user (for ORACLE this is 'scheme-creator' user)
DBROOTUSER="root"

# user name column
# USERCOL="username"

# SQL definitions
# If you change this definitions here, then you must change them
# in db/schema/entities.xml too.
# FIXME

# FOREVER="2020-05-28 21:32:15"
# DEFAULT_ALIASES_EXPIRES=$FOREVER
# DEFAULT_Q="1.0"
# DEFAULT_CALLID="Default-Call-ID"
# DEFAULT_CSEQ="13"
# DEFAULT_LOCATION_EXPIRES=$FOREVER

# Program to calculate a message-digest fingerprint
# MD5="md5sum"

# awk tool
# AWK="awk"

# grep tool
# GREP="grep"

# sed tool
# SED="sed"

# Describe what additional tables to install. Valid values for the
variables
```

```
# below are yes/no/ask. With ask (default) it will interactively ask the
user
# for an answer, while yes/no allow for automated, unassisted installs.
#


# If to install tables for the modules in the EXTRA_MODULES variable.
# INSTALL_EXTRA_TABLES=ask


# If to install presence related tables.
# INSTALL_PRESENCE_TABLES=ask


# Define what module tables should be installed.
# If you use the postgres database and want to change the installed
tables, then you
# must also adjust the STANDARD_TABLES or EXTRA_TABLES variable
accordingly in the
# opensipsdbctl.base script.


# opensips standard modules
# STANDARD_MODULES="standard acc lcr domain group permissions registrar
usrloc msilo
#                      alias_db uri speeddial avpops auth_db pdt dialog
dispatcher
#                      dialplan"


# opensips extra modules
# EXTRA_MODULES="imc cpl siptrace domainpolicy carrierroute
userblacklist"


## type of aliases used: DB - database aliases; UL - usrloc aliases
## - default: none
ALIASES_TYPE="DB"


## control engine: FIFO or UNIXSOCK
## - default FIFO
# CTLENGINE=xmlrpc


## path to FIFO file
```

```
OSIPS_FIFO="/tmp/opensips_fifo"

## MI_CONNECTOR control engine: FIFO, UNIXSOCK, UDP, XMLRPC
# MI_CONNECTOR=FIFO:/tmp/opensips_fifo
# MI_CONNECTOR=UNIXSOCK:/tmp/opensips.sock
# MI_CONNECTOR=UDP:192.168.2.133:8000
# MI_CONNECTOR=XMLRPC:192.168.2.133:8000

## check ACL names; default on (1); off (0)
# VERIFY_ACL=1

## ACL names - if VERIFY_ACL is set, only the ACL names from below list
## are accepted
# ACL_GROUPS="local ld int voicemail free-pstn"

## verbose - debug purposes - default '0'
# VERBOSE=1

## do (1) or don't (0) store plaintext passwords
## in the subscriber table - default '1'
# STORE_PLAINTEXT_PW=0

## OPENSIPS START Options
## PID file path - default is: /var/run/opensips.pid
# PID_FILE=/var/run/opensips.pid

## Extra start options - default is: not set
# example: start opensips with 64MB share memory: STARTOPTIONS="-m 64"
# STARTOPTIONS=
```

Using OpenSIPS with authentication

Now, let's implement the authentication in a practical way:

1. Use the residential script generated with the authentication.

2. Configure `opensipsctlrc` with the default parameters used with
   `opensipsctl`:

   SIP_DOMAIN=your-sip-domain

   DBENGINE=MYSQL

   DBHOST=localhost

   DBNAME=opensips

   DBRWUSER=opensips

   DBROUSER=opensipsro

   DBROPW=opensipsro

   DBROOTUSER="root"

   ALIASES_TYPE="DB"

   CTLENGINE="FIFO"

   OSIPS_FIFO="/tmp/opensips_fifo"

   VERIFY_ACL=1

   ACL_GROUPS="local ld int voicemail free-pstn"

   VERBOSE=1

   #STORE_PLAINTEXT_PW=0

3. Configure two user accounts using the `opensipsctl` utility:

   /sbin/opensipsctl add 1000@opensips.org password

   /sbin/opensipsctl add 1001@opensips.org password

When asked for the password, use `opensipsrw`

You can remove users using `opensipsctl rm` and change a
password using `opensipscl passwd`.

4. Restart OpenSIPS with `/etc/init.d/opensips restart`.

5. Use the `ngrep` utility to see the SIP messages:

   ngrep -p -q -W byline port 5060 >register.pkt

6. Register both the phones now using the name and password.

   The following is a configuration example of a softphone. (I'm using Bria
   from Counterpath, but there are dozens of free softphones available on the
   Internet.) The parameters are similar:

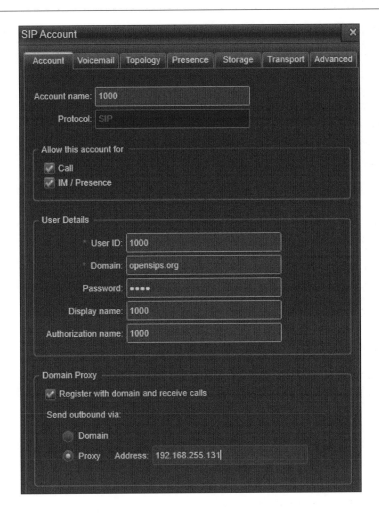

Note that I'm filling the domain and a proxy address. If your domain is resolving to the correct IP address, you don't need to provide a proxy address. In this case, I'm using the **opensips.org** domain in a test virtual machine. You can also use an IP address as a domain for simplicity.

7. Verify that the phones are registered using the following command:

```
#opensipsctl ul show
Domain:: location table=512 records=1
  AOR:: 1000
  Contact::sip:1000@192.168.255.1:61307;transport=tcp;
    ...
```

8. You can find out the users that are online using the following command:

   `#opensipsctl online`

9. You can ping a client as follows:

   `#opensipsctl ping 1000`

10. Verify the authentication messages using the ngrep utilty and save them to a file named `register.pkt`.

11. Make a call from one phone to another.

12. Verify the authentication in the `register.pkt` file using the following:

    `#pg register.pkt`

The registration process

A critical process that you have to understand is the location process. Whenever a client is registered, it is saved to the `location` table. You can see the `location` table in the cache using the following command:

```
opensipsctl ul show
root@bookosips:/etc/opensips# opensipsctl ul show
Domain:: location table=512 records=1
  AOR:: 1000
  Contact::sip:1000@192.168.255.1:61307;transport=tcp;
  rinstance=905a1f57627c7abf
  Expires:: 3565
  Callid:: ZDZjNjYxOWUxOGYxYzY5NjA5OWVjNjc3NjA0ODkwZTA
  Cseq:: 4
  User-agent:: Bria 3 release 3.5.5  stamp 71238
  State:: CS_SYNC
  Flags:: 0
  Cflags::
  Socket:: tcp:192.168.255.131:5060
  Methods:: 5951
```

The AOR is the actual user defined in the subscriber table. In our case, we are not differentiating records by domain; we will see multidomain environments later. The `Contact:` field has the actual IP address and transport of the SIP device. The `State:` field can be `CS_NEW` when the record is not synchronized with the location table and `CS_SYNC` when it is. `Flags` and `Cflags` show the flags associated with the record. Lastly, the `Socket:` file is also important. In systems with more than one interface, this file will define the interface from where the packet will be sent.

Whenever you call from one phone to another, you are going to pass through the following snippet of code. I have added the `xlog` lines to show you what happens to the request URI after the `lookup("location")` command:

```
# do lookup with method filtering
xlog("L_INFO","Request URI before lookup location $ru");
if (!lookup("location","m")) {
  if (!db_does_uri_exist()) {
    send_reply("420","Bad Extension");
    exit;
  }

  t_newtran();
  t_reply("404", "Not Found");
  exit;
}
xlog("L_INFO","Request URI after lookup location $ru");
```

Calling from the phone 1001 to the phone 1000 will produce the following results:

```
Request URI BEFORE lookup location sip:1000@opensips.org;transport=UDP
Request URI AFTER lookup location sip:1000@192.168.255.1:19052;rinstan
ce=09802e0c5257ca3a
```

The lookup process replaces the IP address in the original request to a URI with the real IP location of the SIP device.

Enhancing the opensips.cfg routing script

Besides authentication, it is important to check the source and destination of your message. We will see how to handle the incoming and outgoing calls to different domains:

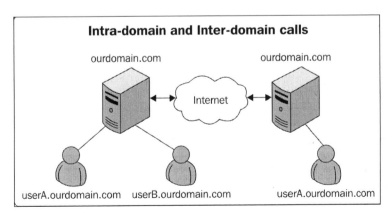

The calls handled by the SIP proxy can be classified as follows:

- Intra-domain
- Outbound inter-domain
- Inbound inter-domain
- Outbound to outbound

The default residential script uses the `from_uri==myself` statement to identify if the From header of the request belongs to one of the domains served in this computer. The domains served by this computer are defined by the global parameter, `alias=`. There are two ways to populate the domains served. The first is to create one line of `alias` for each domain and another is to allow the automated discovery of the alias using reverse DNS. The first one is, in my opinion, the easiest and safest one.

If the method is different than REGISTER and the `uri` present in the `From:` header belongs to one of the domains being served, the script will authenticate the request. On the other hand, if a request comes from an unknown domain, it will bypass the authentication if the destination is local (the domain is one of the aliases defined in the globals section). Later in the script, you will find the following:

```
if (!uri==myself) {
  append_hf("P-hint: outbound\r\n");

  route(relay);
}
```

During the authentication process, the system will send an error message if the source and destination is not local:

```
} else {
# if caller is not local, then called number must be local
  if (!uri==myself) {
    send_reply("403","Relay forbidden");
    exit;
  }
}
```

So, the script generated is handling the inter-domain and intra-domain calls using the following logic:

- From URI local, Request URI foreign: Action: Authenticate and Route
- From URI local, Request URI local: Action: Authenticate and Route
- From URI foreign, Request URI local: Action: Route
- From URI foreign, Request URI foreign: Action: Send a reply 403 Relay Forbidden

Managing multiple domains

Until now, we authenticated the requests using the username part of the URI only. To manage multiple domains, it is *not* required to change the behavior of some functions to consider the domain part of the URI using the use_domain parameter. In the OpenSIPS version 1.6, the use_domain parameter was removed and all the functions by default consider the whole uri. To use the old behavior, you have to append a d flag after the function that requires the domain name. To allow multidomain operations, you will need to load the domain.so module and replace some functions in your script. The domains will have to be inserted in the domain table of our database before being used. The following are the modules and parameters required:

```
loadmodule "domain.so"

# ----- domain params -----
modparam("domain", "db_url", "mysql://opensips:opensipsrw@localhost/
opensips")
modparam("domain", "db_mode", 1)    # Use caching
```

We used to verify the requests using the instruction, uri==myself. However, this instruction verifies the local names and addresses only. If we need to manage multiple domains, we will have to use the domain module and their respective functions, is_from_local() and is_uri_host_local(). The is_from_local() function verifies that the From header field contains one of the domains managed by our proxy. The second function, is_uri_host_local(), replaces the uri==myself instruction. The advantage of the domain-exported functions is that they check the domain on a MySQL table (domain). Then, you can handle multiple domains in your configuration.

> This function requires that all the served domains be inserted in the database.
>
> A fairly common mistake for users of this material is to forget to insert the domains in the MySQL database before they start registering the phones!

To insert a domain in the database, you can use the following command:

opensipsctl domain add domain

After inserting a new domain, it is necessary to reload the domain database:

opensipsctl domain reload

Using aliases

In some cases, you want to allow a user to have several addresses, such as the phone number associated to a main address. You can use aliases for this purpose.

You can add an alias as follows:

```
#opensipsctl alias_db add flavio@opensips.org 1000@opensips.org
```

The output for the preceding command is as follows:

```
database engine 'MYSQL' loaded
Control engine 'FIFO' loaded
MySql password for user 'opensips@localhost':
```

There are two different implementations of the alias functionality. The first one is the alias database. In this modality, you use the function, `lookup("aliases")`. This function goes to the aliases table, checks the existence of the alias, and replaces the RURI with the canonical form of the alias. Recently, a new module called `ALIAS_DB` has been created as an alternative for the user aliases via `usrloc`. The main feature is that it does not store all the adjacent data for the user location and always uses a database to search; it does not use memory caching and thus is much easier to provision. Aliases are often used for DID redirection.

Before you can use an alias, you will need to load the modules and related parameters:

```
loadmodule "alias_db.so"

# ----- alias_db params -----
modparam("alias_db", "db_url",
        "mysql://opensips:opensipsrw@localhost/opensips")
```

To search the aliases and replace the RURI with the results, use the following command:

```
alias_db_lookup("dbaliases");
```

The `alias_db_lookup("dbaliases")` function checks the `dbaliases` table in the database, and if a record is found, it translates it to the canonical address (the one in the subscriber's table).

Handling the CANCEL requests and retransmissions

A CANCEL method is used to cancel a request in the early state. According to RFC 3261, CANCEL requests need to be routed in the same way as INVITE requests. The following script checks whether CANCEL matches an existing INVITE transaction and takes care of all the necessary routing. Sometimes, we have retransmissions associated with an existing transaction. If a retransmission is detected while the system is still processing the original request, the t_check_trans() function will discard it.

```
#CANCEL processing
if (is_method("CANCEL"))
{
  if (t_check_trans())
    t_relay();
  exit;
}

t_check_trans();
```

Lab – multidomain support

Follow these steps for multidomain support:

1. Try to register your phone with the new configuration. You will probably note an error in your phone registration.

2. The preceding configuration now requires the module, domain.so. Now, to authenticate, the domain has to be in the domain table in the MySQL database.

   To add a domain, use the opensipsctl utility:

   opensipsctl domain add your-ip-address

   opensipsctl domain add your-domain

   Repeat the process for every domain.

   Don't forget to reload the module using the following command:

   opensipsctl domain reload

3. Try again to register the phone. Probably, now the register process will work fine.

Lab – using aliases

Follow these steps to use aliases:

1. Add an alias to the subscriber 1000:

    ```
    #opensipsctl alias_db add john@youripordomain 1000@youripordomain
    ```

    The output for the preceding command is:

    ```
    database engine 'MYSQL' loaded
    Control engine 'FIFO' loaded
    MySql password for user 'opensips@localhost':
    ```

    > Use opensipsrw as the password

2. From the softphone registered as 1001, dial John.

The call was completed. Why? Yes, because now, John is translated to 1000 before the script check to the user location table.

IP authentication

There are cases where you would prefer to authenticate by the IP instead of the name and password. Some examples are gateways that are not capable of doing Digest authentication and high-volume customers such as call centers. At high rates such as 100 calls per second, two additional messages (407) can make a difference.

The permissions module has a lot of functions; here, we will focus only on the check_address() function and address database. The syntax for the command is as follows:

```
check_address(group_id, ip, port, proto [, context_info [, pattern]])
```

In this command, the following points are explained as follows:

*   The group_id argument is the group to be matched in the address table. The group_id argument of value 0 means any group.
*   The ip argument is the source IP address to be matched.
*   The port argument is the source port to be matched. The value 0 means any port.
*   The proto argument is the protocol to be matched. The options are UDP, TCP, TLS, SCTP, and ANY.

- The `context_info` argument will be loaded in an AVP after the IP match. This field can be used to include identity information such as the username and domain.

- The `pattern` argument will be matched against the `pattern` field in the address table. A very common use for this field is the authentication by the IP and tech prefix. If you specify `$rU` (user in the request URI) in this field, you can match the dialed number against a pattern defined in the address table.

An example of a record in the address table is given as follows:

```
id: 72
grp: 9000
ip: 201.63.XXX.YYY
mask: 32
port: 0
proto: any
pattern: 2233#*
context_info: username=flavio;domain=opensips.org
```

The command is as follows:

```
check_address("0","$si", "$sp","$oP","$avp(context)","$rU")
```

In the preceding code, we are checking the source address for all the groups (0), the parameters to check are `$si`, which is the source address, `$sp`, which is the source port, and `$oP`, which is the protocol. The context defined in the database will be saved in AVP `$avp(context)`, and the pattern `2233#*` defined in the database would have to be matched against the dialed number, `$rU`, along with any number of digits.

In other words, a call coming from `201.63.XXX.YYY` with any port and protocol with the dialed number starting with `2233#*` would make the function return 1 (`true`).

To apply the IP authentication, you can include an if clause before the Digest authentication for INVITE requests. IP authentication usually does not make sense for REGISTER requests.

```
loadmodule "permissions.so"
modparam("permissions", "db_url", "mysql://opensips:opensipsrw@
localhost/opensips")

if (!is_method("REGISTER") && from_uri==myself) {
  ## Authorize by digest only if IP does not match
  if(!check_address("0","$si",
    "$sp","$oP","$avp(context)","$rU")){
    if (!proxy_authorize("", "subscriber")) {
```

```
        proxy_challenge("", "0");
        exit;
      }
   }
 }
```

To fill the address table, you have two options. You can insert the record using the `opensipsctl` utility or the opensips control panel GUI as we will see in the next chapter. The commands to add addresses in the database is as follows:

```
address show: show db content
address dump: show cache content
address reload: reload db table into cache
address add <grp> <ip> <mask> <port> <proto> [<context_info>]
[<pattern>]: add a new entry (from_pattern and tag are optional
arguments)
address rm <grp> <ip> <mask> <port>: remove all entries for the given
grp ip mask port
```

Following are the examples to add addresses in the database:

`opensipsctl address add 0 1.1.1.1 32 0 any`

This adds the address, `1.1.1.1`, for any port and protocol in the database. Pay attention to the mask; `32` means 255.255.255.255 or only this address. If you incorrectly set this parameter to `0`, it means that all the users will be associated with this entry.

The address table is cached for performance reasons. Whenever you change it, reload the cache:

`opensipsctl address reload`

Summary

In this chapter, you learned how to integrate MySQL with OpenSIPS. Now, our script is authenticating users, checking the To and From header fields, and handling the inbound and outbound calls. It's important to remember that domains have to be inserted in the database in order to support multiple domain support. If you change your domain or IP addresses, remember to reload your database.

In the next chapter, we will cover the web interface. Instead of creating users in the command line, we will use a web interface.

6
OpenSIPS Control Panel

In the previous chapter, you learned how to manage subscribers using a MySQL database. Now, we will need a tool to help users and administrators. Obviously, this tool has to be easier than opensipsctl. It is hard to manually manage thousands of users, so a user provisioning tool becomes very important for our process. In this chapter, we will see one of these tools called **OpenSIPS control panel**. We will see how to use some control panel modules in the next chapters when it is relevant.

In this chapter, we will cover the following topics:

- Identifying why you need a user portal for administration
- Installing the OpenSIPS control panel and its dependencies
- Integrating the OpenSIPS control panel into **Monit**
- Integrating a control panel to OpenSIPS using a FIFO file
- Configuring administrator and module access
- Adding and removing domains
- Managing subscribers
- Managing aliases
- Managing the **Access Control Lists (ACLs)**
- Managing permissions and IP authentication
- Using **OpenSIPS-CP** to send commands to the management interface

The OpenSIPS control panel

A graphical user interface is key to any project. People tend not to recognize a product without a GUI. On the other hand, sophisticated modules such as `dialplan` and `routing` were simply too complicated to be managed by `opensipsctl` and now can be easily provisioned by **Control Panel (CP)**. This tool, also known as **OpenSIPS-CP**, is the new graphical user interface for the SIP proxy. It was designed to be the primary tool to provision the user and system parameters for OpenSIPS modules in the database. The following screenshot shows you the tools available for the OpenSIPS-CP:

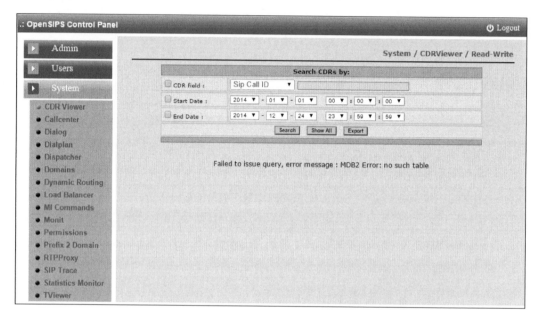

The tool is focused on the provisioning of the user and system parameters. The OpenSIPS-CP tools are categorized as **Admin**, **System**, and **Users**:

- Admin
    - Add Admin
    - List Admins

- Users
    - ACL Management
    - Alias Management
    - User Management

- System

  - ○ CDRviewer
  - ○ Call Center
  - ○ Dialog
  - ○ Dialplan
  - ○ Domains
  - ○ Dispatcher
  - ○ Dynamic Routing
  - ○ Load balancer
  - ○ MI Commands
  - ○ Monit
  - ○ Permissions
  - ○ Prefix 2 Domain
  - ○ RTPProxy
  - ○ Siptrace
  - ○ Statistics Viewer
  - ○ TMonitor

Installation of OpenSIPS-CP

The step-by-step instructions to install OpenSIPS-CP are as follows:

1. Install Apache and PHP:

   ```
   apt-get install apache2 php5
   ```

2. Install the php5-mysql and php5-xmlrpc packages and set the right parameters in the php.ini file:

   ```
   apt-get install php5-mysql php5-xmlrpc php-pear
   ```

3. Download opensips-cp and untar the file:

   ```
   cd /var/www
   svn checkout svn://svn.code.sf.net/p/opensips-cp
     /code/trunk opensips-cp
   chown -R www-data:www-data /var/www/opensips-cp
   ```

4. Install MDB2:

```
pear install MDB2
pear install MDB2#mysql
pear install log
```

5. Configure Apache for the OpenSIPS control panel. Edit the `apache2.conf` file:

```
vi /etc/apache2/apache2.conf
```

Include the following line in the last line:

```
Alias /cp "/var/www/opensips-cp/web"
nano /etc/php5/cli/php.ini
# Change short_open_tag = Off to short_open_tag = On
```

6. Install the `cdrs` table schema:

```
cd /var/www/opensips-cp/config/tools/system/cdrviewer
mysql -D opensips -p < opensips_cdrs.mysql
mysql -D opensips -p < cdrs.mysql
```

7. Edit the `cron_job/generate-cdrs.sh` file and change the `mysql` connection data (hostname, username, password, and database):

```
cd /var/www/opensips-cp/cron_job
vi generate_cdrs_mysql.sh
```

Edit the `/etc/crontab` file with the following command:

```
vi /etc/crontab
```

Add the following line for a three-minute interval:

```
*/3 * * * * root /var/www/opensips-cp/cron_job/
  generate-cdrs_mysql.sh
```

8. For the `smonitor` module, you must add two tables to the OpenSIPS database:

```
cd /var/www/opensips-cp/config/tools/system/smonitor
mysql -p opensips <tables.sql
```

9. Add a cron job that collects the data from the OpenSIPS machine(s). Here is a cron job that collects the data at one-minute intervals. Note that this interval is not arbitrary; it must be set at one minute by design:

```
vi /etc/crontab
```

```
* * * * * root php /var/www/opensips-cp/
  cron_job/get_opensips_stats.php > /dev/null
```

The cron jobs do not need to run as root, you might want to change the user.

10. Restart OpenSIPS and Apache.

/etc/init.d/apache2 restart

/etc/init.d/opensips restart

The installation instructions change very often. Check the OpenSIPS-CP project's website, http://opensips-cp.sourceforge.net/, for updates.

The instructions here are valid for systems based on Debian and Ubuntu. For other Linux systems, check how to install Linux, Apache, PHP, and MySQL.

Configuring the OpenSIPS-CP

In the previous section, you learned how to install the control panel. However, it is not ready to be used. We need to configure the access to the database and some files to make it work in your environment. Perform the following steps:

1. Configure the database access parameters. Edit the db.inc.php file used for all modules. You can change the DB parameters for a single module in the module configuration:

    cd /var/www/opensips-cp/config

    vi db.inc.php

    //database host

    $config->db_host = "localhost";

    //database port - leave empty for default

    $config->db_port = "";

    //database connection user

    $config->db_user = "opensips";

    //database connection password

    $config->db_pass = "opensipsrw";

```
//database name
$config->db_name = "opensips";

if ($config->db_port != "")$config->db_host=
  $config->db_host":" $config->db_port;
```

2. Configure the FIFO access in the `boxes.global.inc.php` file:

```
cd /var/www/opensips-cp/config/
vi boxes.global.inc.php

$box_id=0;

// options: fifo:/path/to/fifo_file | xmlrpc:host:port |
udp:host:port | json:json_url
$boxes[$box_id]['mi']['conn']="fifo:/tmp/opensips_fifo";

// monit host:port
$boxes[$box_id]['monit']['conn']="127.0.0.1:2812";
$boxes[$box_id]['monit']['user']="admin";
$boxes[$box_id]['monit']['pass']="monit";
$boxes[$box_id]['monit']['has_ssl']=0;
// description (appears in mi , monit )
$boxes[$box_id]['desc']="SIP Server #1";
```

3. Create the administrator privileges and the administrator itself:

```
cd /var/www/opensips-cp/config/tools/admin/add_admin
mysql -D opensips -p < ocp_admin_privileges.mysql
mysql -u root -p
mysql> INSERT INTO opensips.ocp_admin_privileges
  (username,password,ha1,available_tools,permissions)
  values ('admin','admin',md5('admin:admin'),'all','all');
mysql> quit
```

4. Use a browser to go to `http://server_ip_address/cp` and log in with the username as `admin` and password as `admin` and check each module for the correct functionality:

Installing Monit

Monit is a system monitoring utility, which allows an administrator to easily monitor files, processes, directories, or devices on your system. It can also be used for automatic maintenance/repairs by executing particular commands when errors arise. Monit is beyond the scope of this book, but we will provide installation instructions to avoid errors when you select the Monit tool. It is an excellent tool to restart a server when you have a software failure:

1. To install Monit on your server, simply use `apt-get`:

    ```
    apt-get install monit
    ```

2. Once installed, you'll find the main configuration file:

    ```
    vi /etc/monit/monitrc

    set daemon  120

    set logfile syslog facility log_daemon

    set alert root@localhost #Please customize your e-mail here

    set httpd port 2812 and

    use address yourdomain.com

    allow localhost       # allow localhost to connect to the
       server and

    allow youripaddress   # allow 192.168.1.2 to connect to
       the server,

                          # You can give only one per entry
    ```

```
allow admin:monit                # user name and password for
   authentication.


check process opensips with pidfile
/var/run/opensips/opensips.pid


   #Below is actions taken by monit when service got stuck.
   start program = "/etc/init.d/opensips start"
   stop program  = "/etc/init.d/opensips stop"


   # Admin will notify by mail if below of the condition
      satisfied.
   if cpu is greater than 70% for 2 cycles then alert
   if cpu > 90% for 5 cycles then restart
```

3. After modifying the configuration file, you should check for the syntax to make sure that they are correct:

   ```
   # monit -t
   ```

4. Start Monit using the following command:

   ```
   /etc/init.d/monit start
   ```

5. If everything went right, you should now see the following screen when you select **Monit** in the OpenSIPS-CP menu:

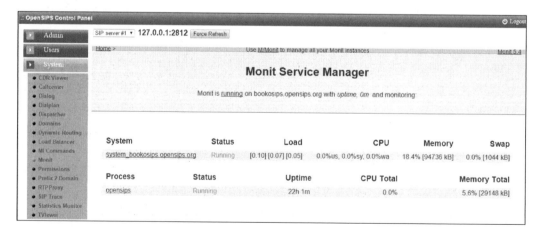

Configuring administrators

In the **Admin** section, you can add and list admins. Start listing admins as shown here:

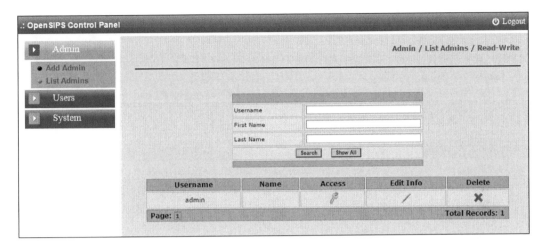

You can also give read-write or read only permissions for each module by clicking on the Access key icon:

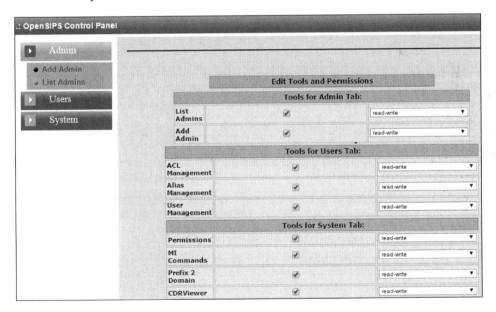

Adding and removing domains

To add and remove domains, select **System | Domains**. Now add the `opensips.org` domain by clicking on the **Add Domain** button. It is very simple and intuitive.

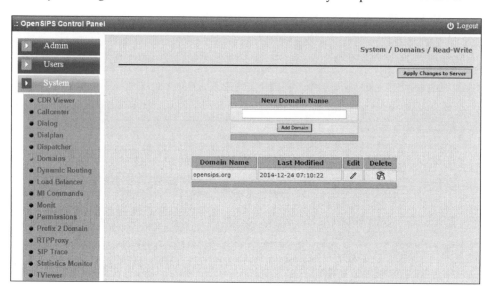

Manage the access control lists or groups

OpenSIPS subscribers can be members of groups. There is a module called `Group`. This module implements a table called `grp`. It is also possible to use regular expression groups, but this is beyond the scope of the tool. In the OpenSIPS script, you can check whether a user is a member of a group or not using the `db_is_user_in(uri,group)` function. This mechanism is often used to implement ACLs limiting the destinations dialed by a specific user. You will see more of this in *Chapter 7, Dialplan and Routing*. For now, let's just understand how to make the subscribers members of a group.

Let's configure the groups that we will use in the training:

Group	Description
VoIP	Makes calls only to VoIP destinations
LOCAL	Makes calls to local destinations
LD	Makes calls to long-distance destinations
INT	Makes calls to international destinations

To create these groups, let's edit the configuration file for the CP and add the groups:

1. Edit the configuration file for the tool:

   ```
   vi /var/www/opensips-cp/config/
     tools/users/acl_management/local.inc.php
   ```

   Edit the following line:

   ```
   $config->grps = array("voip","local","ld","int");
   ```

2. Add the user `1000` to all the groups and `1001` only to `local` and `voip`. We will use these ACLs later in *Chapter 7, Dialplan and Routing*. Select **Users | ACL Management** and add the ACLs, one by one:

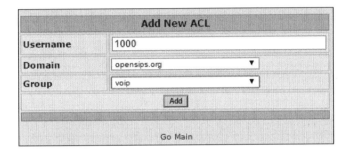

Managing aliases

Aliases are often used to give an alternative number to a subscriber to dial. Let's suppose that I'm using a hard phone and the SIP address for Bogdan is `bogdan@opensips.org`. It won't be possible or practical to dial alphanumeric addresses from IP phones. The solution is to add an alias such as `9000@opensips.org`. Another frequent case for aliases is **Direct Inward Dialing (DID)**. You can assign as many numbers as you want to a subscriber using aliases. To add an alias, use the **Alias Management** submenu under the **Users** menu:

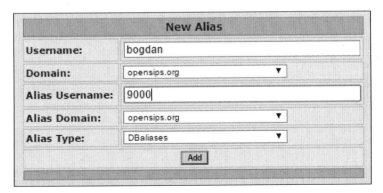

Managing subscribers

After adding aliases and ACLs, it is now easy to add new subscribers. Let's use the **User Management** submenu of the **Users** menu to add users. Add the users, John Doe and Jane Doe, to the system. Add the users to all the groups and create the aliases 1003 and 1004 pointing to these users, respectively. See the following example:

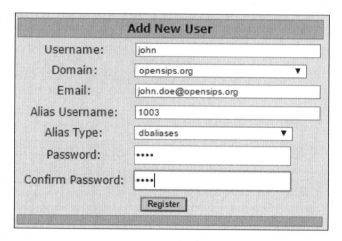

Add the ACLs to the users by clicking the Group icon in the users listing:

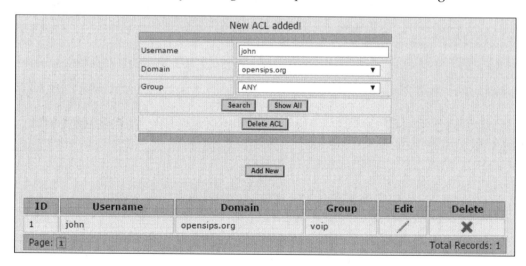

Verifying the subscriber registration

In many cases, it is important to check whether a user is registered. You can check the user's contacts in the **User Management** submenu:

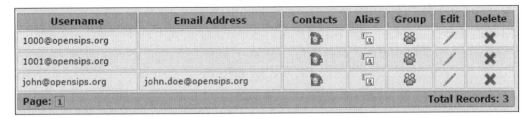

Username	Email Address	Contacts	Alias	Group	Edit	Delete
1000@opensips.org						
1001@opensips.org						
john@opensips.org	john.doe@opensips.org					

Page: 1 — Total Records: 3

Click on the Contacts icon to show the user's contacts. The user is registered when it has a contact and is not expired. You cannot register an alias.

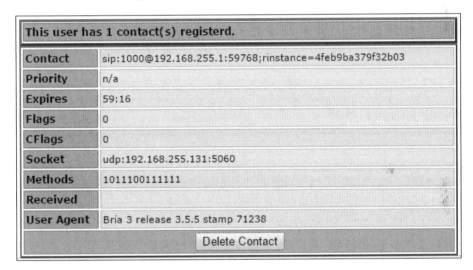

This user has 1 contact(s) registerd.	
Contact	sip:1000@192.168.255.1:59768;rinstance=4feb9ba379f32b03
Priority	n/a
Expires	59:16
Flags	0
CFlags	0
Socket	udp:192.168.255.131:5060
Methods	1011100111111
Received	
User Agent	Bria 3 release 3.5.5 stamp 71238
Delete Contact	

Managing permissions and IP authentication

There are scenarios where you will be required to authenticate by the source IP and not by username and password. Some gateways are not capable to authenticate. In some cases, you can choose to alleviate the burden of the additional messages required for challenge authentication. An example of this case is when you are serving a call center sending more than fifty calls per second. The challenge authentication is bypassed using the `check_source_address()` function as seen in the previous chapter. Pay attention that UDP is not connection-oriented as TCP; thus, it is susceptible to IP spoofing. If someone sends a request with a spoofed IP authorized in the address table, a 200 OK reply will be sent and the call is still payable. Whenever you use the IP authentication with UDP, we strongly recommend the use of a `tech` prefix as an additional measure of protection. Tech prefixes are four to five digit patterns added to the pattern field and checked in the script against the request URI. Even if the attacker would know one of the IP addresses that is allowed in the table, it would be harder to match the IP address to the `tech` prefix:

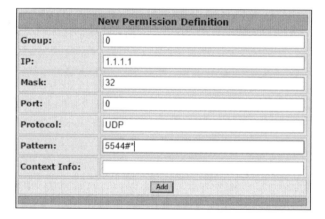

New Permission Definition	
Group:	0
IP:	1.1.1.1
Mask:	32
Port:	0
Protocol:	UDP
Pattern:	5544#*
Context Info:	
	Add

Pay attention to the **Mask** field. If you incorrectly set the mask to 0, it will authorize any IP, no matter what IP you have set in the **IP** field. Port 0 means any port.

Sending commands to the management interface

The control panel can send commands to the management interface. The communication to the OpenSIPS **Management Interface**, from now on called **MI**, is done using xmlrpc, FIFO files, datagram, or the new mi_json interface. The first step that we will take is show all the MI commands available using a which command:

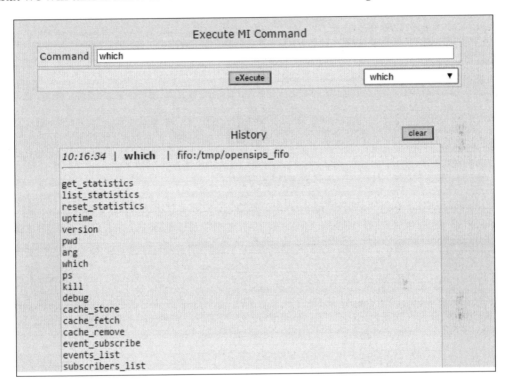

Now, you can see that all the commands made available by the core and modules are loaded on OpenSIPS. Some daily tasks that you could perform are increasing the debug level using debug 3 as an example. The command output is shown here:

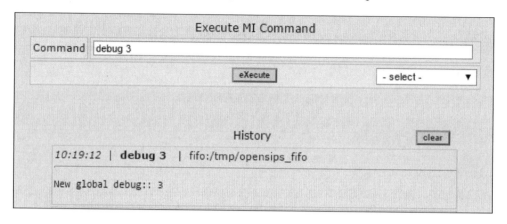

A generic table viewer

Using the control panel, it is also possible to add a new table to the interface. This is important when you construct a new feature using a new table on the system. In the following example, we have modified the configuration file located at /var/www/opensips-cp/config/tools/system/tviewer/local.inc.php.

This file was modified to show the table called version. The version table checks the schema of the database against the module's version. We used this table just as an example. The configuration file is shown here. I have removed some comments to reduce the size and the lines effectively changed are highlighted.

```php
<?php

//this is a very important parameter
$module_id = "tviewer";
$custom_config[$module_id] = array ();

// a custom global name for the tool
$custom_config[$module_id]['custom_name'] = "TViewer";

/* config for each submenu item */

$custom_config[$module_id][0]['custom_table'] = "version";
$custom_config[$module_id][0]['custom_table_primary_key'] =
    "table_name";
```

```
$custom_config[$module_id][0]['custom_table_order_by'] =
  "table_name";
$custom_config[$module_id][0]['per_page'] = 10;
$custom_config[$module_id][0]['page_range'] = 2;


$custom_config[$module_id][0]['custom_table_column_defs'] =

array ("table_name" => array (
"header"                    => "table_name",
"type"                      => "text",
"key"                       => "PRI",
"validation_regex"      => "",
"validation_err"        => "Invalid name",
"show_in_add_form"      => true,
"show_in_edit_form"     => true,
"searchable"            => true,
"disabled"                  => false,
"readonly"                  => false,
"default_value"         => NULL
),

"table_version" => array (
"header"                    => "table_version",
"type"                      => "int",
"key"                       => "UNI",
"validation_regex"      => "",
"validation_regex"      => "",
"validation_err"        => "Invalid version",
"show_in_add_form"      => true,
"show_in_edit_form"     => true,
"searchable"            => true,
"disabled"                  => false,
"readonly"                  => false,
"default_value"         => NULL
)
);

//need to reload 0 or 1
$custom_config[$module_id][0]['reload'] = 0;

//if you need reload please specify the MI command to be ran
$custom_config[$module_id][0]['custom_mi_command'] = "";
```

```
// what system to talk to for MI functions
$talk_to_this_assoc_id = 1 ;

$custom_config[$module_id][0]['custom_search'] =         array (
   "enabled" => true,
"action_script" => "custom_actions/search.php"
) ;

$custom_config[$module_id][0]['custom_action_columns'] =
array (
"0"       =>        array(
"header"                        => "Edit",
"show_header"            => false,
"type"                          => "link",
"action"                        => "edit",
"icon"                          => "images/edit.png",
"action_script"         => "custom_actions/edit.php",
"action_template"       => "template/custom_templates/edit.php"

),

"1"       =>        array(
"header"                        => "Delete",
"show_header"            => false,
"type"                          => "link",
"action"                        => "delete",
"icon"                          => "images/delete.png",
"action_script"         => "custom_actions/delete.php",
"action_template"       => "template/custom_templates/delete.php"
)
                                                        ) ;
$custom_config[$module_id][0]['custom_action_buttons'] = array (
"0"                 =>        array(
"text"                          => "Add",
"action"                        => "add",
"color"                         => "red",
"action_script"         => "custom_actions/add.php",
"action_template"       => "template/custom_templates/add.php"
)
) ;
```

After making these changes, you can now see the version table in the control panel as shown in the following image. You can now add, edit, and remove any record in the table. This can be very useful to customize the control panel according to your needs.

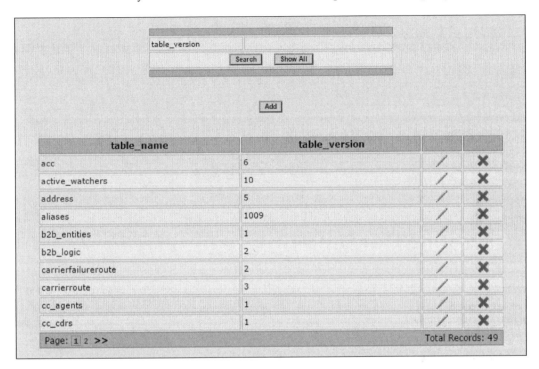

Summary

In this chapter, you learned why it is important to have a user and administrator portal. It is a piece of software that you should pay a lot of attention to. Some VoIP providers fail to allocate the time and resources to the important task of building the portal. OpenSIPS is an amazing SIP proxy, but a SIP proxy is just one of the components in a VoIP solution. Without good administrator and user interfaces, a VoIP provider project may easily fail. You learned how to install and manage users and domains and how to customize their appearance. For now, we can only call the registered subscribers. In the next chapter, we will learn how to send and receive calls to the PSTN.

7
Dialplan and Routing

In the previous chapter, you learned how to use OpenSIPS to route calls between SIP users, provision such users, and authenticate them using a database backend. However, you still cannot send calls to ordinary phones because you are not connected to the **Public Switched Telephone Network (PSTN)**. The challenge now is to route calls from and to the PSTN, as shown in the following figure:

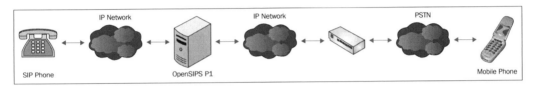

This PSTN interconnection comes with special needs such as advanced number matching and manipulation (dialplans), IP-based authentication, and dynamic routing (based on the prefix, priority, location, or time of day).

Unless you have a SIP trunk to interconnect calls with the PSTN, you will need a device called SIP PSTN gateway. There are several manufacturers for these devices in the market, such as Cisco™, AudioCodes™, and others. You can also use open source software such as **FreeSWITCH** or **Asterisk private branch exchange (PBX)** for this task. SIP trunks are becoming more popular and should replace all the existing **time-division multiplexing (TDM)** links in the future. Although you can connect a SIP trunk directly in OpenSIPS, I recommend that you use a **Session Border Controller (SBC)** or the **Back-to-Back User Agent (B2BUA)** module. When you traverse several proxies, they add new headers to your SIP request. It is very common to exceed the limit size for a UDP packet without fragmentation. Thus, an SBC can start a new leg without the additional headers. You can address an SBC in exactly the same way as you would address a gateway. Many SBCs are simply gateways with SIP trunks.

By the end of this chapter, you should be able to perform the following functions:

- Interconnect OpenSIPS to a SIP gateway
- Authorize and handle the incoming PSTN calls
- Use **Access Control Lists** (**ACLs**) to protect the PSTN gateway from unauthorized use
- Use the `dialplan` module to build dynamic dialplans
- Use the **Dynamic Routing** (**drouting**) module to route your calls

We will introduce four new modules (`drouting`, `dialplan`, `permissions`, and `group`) that will help you to route and secure calls from and to PSTN. It is important to understand a little about regular expressions because they are going to be used to route the calls. It is very easy to find a tutorial for **regular expressions** (**regexps**) on the Internet.

 If you are not familiar with regexps, this quick reference card may help you: `http://www.visibone.com/regular-expressions/`

The dialplan module

For dialplan-related capabilities, OpenSIPS provides you with the `dialplan` module. This module does not offer any routing capabilities, but it is a very powerful tool when it comes to matching (identifying) and manipulating (translating) strings. Such strings can be the dialed number, caller ID, or other strings that may appear in the SIP messages.

The `dialplan` module allows you to define various rules on how to match and translate these strings via **database** (**DB**). The rules are loaded from DB at the startup and cached to the OpenSIPS memory for runtime usage. If there is a need to refresh the cached data from DB, the module exposes the `dp_reload` **Management Interface** (**MI**) command.

Rules can be grouped into different sets for different purposes; for example, one set for dialplan rules to handle the dialed number, another set for dialplan rules to detect the media-oriented services, and so on.

The OpenSIPS control panel provisioning interface provides a tool to handle the dialplan data in relation to DB (add, edit, and remove rules) and OpenSIPS (perform reloads via the MI interface).

The dialplan function has a very simple usage. It takes a mandatory input string and can return an optional string (as the result). What the function does is shown in the following points:

1. It finds the rule to be used; this is done based on the input string—this string is tested against the matching expression of each rule. This matching expression can be a regular expression or simple matching string. Only the first matched rule will be used to process the input.

2. Once a rule is found, and if there is a translating part, this will be evaluated in order to provide an output string (for the dialplan function). The output can be a simple static string configured in the rule or some dynamic function of the input string. This is done via a regular expression in a sed-like replacement (`https://www.gnu.org/software/sed/`).

> The `dialplan` module can be used for match and transform operations and also for match-only operations (with no translation/transformation and no output).

The `dialplan` module provides a single function named `dp_translate()`. This function translates any variables according to a list of regular expressions. It is very useful to normalize dialed numbers and caller IDs and select different types of routing services.

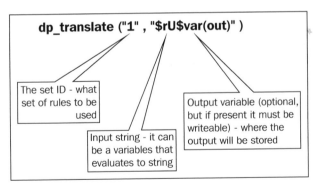

The online module documentation is available at `http://www.opensips.org/html/docs/modules/2.1.x/dialplan.html`.

During this chapter, we will use the `dialplan` module in different and multiple ways. In each case, examples of data (rules) and usage are provided.

PSTN routing

In this section, we will cover how to receive and send calls to PSTN. We will start with explaining how to receive calls.

Receiving calls from PSTN

The handling of the calls from the PSTN side can be split into the following steps:

1. Trusting and authenticating the gateways/carriers sending you the calls coming from the PSTN side.

2. Identifying the called party; as a call from PSTN will target a PSTN number, we have to translate it to a local subscriber.

Gateway authentication

The inbound PSTN gateways (often provided by **Direct Inward Dialing (DID)** providers) are, from an IP perspective, static devices. (They do not change their IP addresses.) At the same time, such gateways usually do not implement digest authentication; such a mechanism is intended to authenticate dynamic end users rather than static infrastructure devices.

Such gateways are usually authenticated based on their IP location—IP-based authentication—where you authenticate the sending device based on the source IP of the traffic.

Such known source IP addresses should be recognized and skipped from regular digest authentication in your script.

You can do this in a static way by hardcoding the IP addresses directly in your script:

```
{
..
  if ( ($si=="10.10.10.5" && $sp==5060 && $proto=="UDP") ||
    ($si=="10.10.10.9" && $sp==5060 && $proto=="UDP") ) {
    # trusted GW, skip digest authentication
  } else if (!proxy_authorize("", "subscriber")) {
    proxy_challenge("", "0");
    exit;
  }
..
}
```

This approach has the following important limitations:

- You have to change your configuration file and restart OpenSIPS each time you want to change one of the IP addresses
- There is no way to provision the IP addresses via a provisioning tool
- Static IP authentication does not scale as it will be a hard task to manage hundreds of IP addresses in the script

The `permissions` module can solve these issues.

The permissions module

This module allows you to manage large sets of IP addresses (or ranges of IP addresses). The addresses can be grouped by sets for different purposes, such as a set of IP addresses defining the inbound **gateways (GW)**, another set defining the addresses of your media servers, or another one defining your edge proxies.

The IP addresses are stored in the database via the `address` table. The content is loaded and cached in the OpenSIPS memory at startup. You can reload the data during runtime via the `address_reload` MI command.

The OpenSIPS control panel has a dedicated tool to provision IP addresses in the `address` table and trigger reload commands in OpenSIPS.

The equivalent of the preceding script, but using the `permissions` module, is as follows:

```
loadmodule "permissions.so"
modparam("permissions","db_url",
  "mysql://user:pwd@localhost/opensips")⌧
{
..
  if ( check_source_address("1") ) {
    # trusted GW
  } else if (!proxy_authorize("", "subscriber")) {
    proxy_challenge("", "0");
    exit;
  }
..
}
```

The `permissions` module provides you with a more flexible function named `check_address(group, IP, port, proto)` that can receive the IP, port, and protocol as parameters rather than automatically using the network source information.

The IP addresses can be easily added to the `address` table using the **opensipsctl** tool:

```
opensipsctl address  add  1  192.168.1.192  255.255.255.255  5060
  udp
opensipsctl address  reload
```

The full description of all the functions and parameters can be found in the online module documentation at `http://www.opensips.org/html/docs/modules/2.1.x/permissions.html`.

Caller identification

The calls received from inbound gateways will carry a PSTN number as a dialed string. This number must be mapped over a local subscriber or service; basically, we need to translate this PSTN number to a SIP address that can be recognized and processed by our SIP server.

Depending on the gateway, the dialed PSTN number can be delivered in different formats, such as national, international, E.164, among others. So, the first thing after authentication of a gateway call is to normalize the dialed numbers. This means that you bring all the formats to a single agreed one (which one you prefer is up to your script logic and service).

This normalization can be hardcoded in your configuration file:

```
{
..

  if ( check_source_address("1") ) {
    # trusted GW, normalize to E.164
    if ( $rU=~"^00" ) { # international 00 format
      strip(2);
    } else if ( $rU=~"^\+" ) { # international + format
      strip(1);
    } else if ( $rU=~"^0" ) { # national format
      strip(1);
      prefix("44"); # add the UK international prefix
    }
  }
..
}
```

You can also use a dialplan set for this:

```
loadmodule "dialplan.so"
modparam("dialplan","db_url",
  "mysql://user:pwd@localhost/opensips")☒
{
..
  if ( check_source_address("1") ) {
    # trusted GW, normalize to E.164
    if ( !dp_translate("10","$rU/$rU") ) {
      send_reply("404","Bad PSTN number");
      exit;
    }
  }
..
}
```

The corresponding DB content is as follows:

Set ID	Match operator	Match exp	Subst exp	Replace exp
10	1	`"^00[1-9][0-9]+$"`	`"^00(.*)$"`	`"\1"`
10	1	`"^\+[1-9][0-9]+$"`	`"^\+(.*)$"`	`"\1"`
10	1	`"^[1-9][0-9]+$"`	`"^(.*)$"`	`"44\1"`

Once the dialed number is determined, the next and last step is to look up the local subscriber or service that owns this PSTN number.

For this purpose, we can use the aliasing system, considering that the PSTN numbers are kind of aliases to the actual subscribers/services:

```
loadmodule "alias_db.so"
modparam("alias_db","db_url",
  "mysql://user:pwd@localhost/opensips")☒
{
..
  if ( check_source_address("1") ) {
    # trusted GW, normalize to E.164
    if ( !dp_translate("10","$rU/$rU") ) {
      send_reply("404","Bad PSTN number");
      exit;
    }
```

```
        # use the "dids" aliases table and do not
        # use the domain part when looking up for alias
        if ( alias_db_lookup("dids","d") ) {
          send_reply("404","DID not found");
          exit;
        }
      }
    ..
    }
```

Note that the `alias_db` module is performing runtime DB queries as it is not caching any kind of DB data. If you are going to run a very large list of numbers, you should consider caching the answers using the cached interface.

Other OpenSIPS modules can be used to match the DIDs to the subscribers SIP URI, such as the `drouting` module, which can also do caching.

Sending calls to PSTN

The handling of the calls towards the PSTN side can be split into the following steps:

1. Identifying and normalizing the dialed number.
2. Authorizing the PSTN gateway usage.
3. Presenting the proper caller ID for the PSTN side.
4. Routing the appropriate PSTN gateway.

Of course, before all these steps, the caller side must be authenticated using the appropriate mechanism: if our callers are end users, we use digest authentication; if our callers are call centers or trunks, we use IP authentication.

Identifying PSTN calls

An important decision is which calls have to be sent to a PSTN gateway. This means that whatever number the end user dialed, we need to process it and figure out whether it targets a PSTN number (and not a SIP URI using a number as a username).

Usually, it is much easier to do it the other way around, that is, to identify numbers that do not have to be sent to PSTN, such as numbers identifying services, numbers being used as subscriber IDs, or even your own DIDs. Whatever number you do not recognize can be considered as a potential PSTN number and subject to further format testing and filtering.

The identification can be hardcoded in the script. In this example, we have a setup where eight-digit numbers are used as subscriber IDs and five-digit numbers starting with number 4 are service numbers:

```
if ( !($rU=~"^[1-9][0-9]{7}$" || $rU=~"^4[0-9]{4}$") ) {
  # forward to the PSTN GW
}
```

This approach faces the known problems of reloading the script, manual provisioning, and lack of scaling.

The equivalent dynamic approach based on dialplan looks as follows:

```
if ( !dp_translate("2","$rU") ) {
  # forward to the PSTN GW
}
```

The following is the corresponding DB content:

Set ID	Match operator	Match exp	Subst exp	Replace exp
2	1	"^[1-9][0-9]{7}$"		
2	1	"^4[0-9]{4}$"		

Note that we do not use the transformation fields (Subst exp and Replace exp) as we are interested only in identifying the strings.

Of course, depending on your overall dialplan (distribution of numbers to services/subscribers), in some cases, it may be much easier to directly identify the PSTN calls by the international dialing format.

The corresponding DB content is as follows:

Set ID	Match operator	Match exp	Subst exp	Replace exp
2	1	"^00[1-9][0-9]"		
2	1	"^\+[1-9][0-9]"		

Authorizing PSTN calls

Before allowing a call to be forwarded to a PSTN gateway, you need to be sure that the caller has the permission to access the PSTN service. Note that any authorization (checking permissions) must be done each time after the call was authenticated.

An authorization without authentication is completely useless.

The authorization system must be designed to be fast and reliable. Depending on your system, you may consider opting for an authorization mechanism that can offer multilevel access to the resource (versus a simple binary yes or no access).

OpenSIPS offers multiple ways of implementing authorization mechanisms. Some of them are directly packed as modules and some mechanisms are implemented by direct scripting in the configuration file:

- Group-based authorization (yes or no access via the group module)
- ACL authorization (multilevel access via scripting)

The group module

The group module implements a Unix user-like authorization mechanism. For a user to have access to a specific resource or service, he must belong to the corresponding group. This approach offers a binary yes or no authorization mechanism (no multilevel access).

This module checks whether a user belongs to a group or not. The module performs the following checking:

- Against a SQL database (script functions are db_-prefixed)
- Against an **authentication, authorization, and accounting (AAA) (Remote Authentication Dial-In User Service (RADIUS))** server (script functions are aaa_-prefixed)

The module has two options, Strict membership checking and Regular Expression based checking. With strict membership DB, there is no caching, while with regular expressions, due to performance reasons, caching is available. For strict membership checking, we will use the following function:

```
db_is_user_in(URI, group)
```

Here is an example:

```
db_is_user_in("credentials", "ld") #Use digest credential to
    verify
```

In this chapter, we will use strict checking because it is usually faster than regular express matching. Check the reference documentation if you prefer to use regular expression matching and the db_get_user_groups() function. For strict membership checking, this module exports the db_is_user_in("credentials", "group") function to check whether a user belongs to a specified group.

In the following example, we have created two groups, ld for national and int for international calls. In the preceding script, we used regular expressions to check whether the call belongs to some of these groups:

```
loadmodule "group.so"
modparam("group",
   "db_url","mysql://user:pwd@localhost/opensips")
{
 ..

   if ( is_method("INVITE")) {
     if ($rU=~"^00[1-9][0-9]+") {
       if (!db_is_user_in("From", "int")) {
         send_reply("403", "Forbidden");
         exit;
       }
     } else if ($rU=~"^0[1-9][0-9]+") {
       if (!db_is_user_in("From", "ld")) {
         send_reply("403", "Forbidden");
         exit;
       }
     } else {
       send_reply("404", "Unknown number");
       exit;

     }
   }
 ..
}
```

You have to insert the groups in the MySQL table called group before using it. You can easily insert, remove, and show group membership using the following commands:

```
opensipsctl acl show [<username>]

opensipsctl acl grant <username> <group>

opensipsctl acl revoke  <username> [<group>]
```

Access Control Lists

With OpenSIPS scripting, you can implement various ACL mechanisms.

For example, we propose here an ACL mechanism based on strings. Each permission (access to a service or resource) has a fixed position allocated in the string. The position holds the access level for this permission.

Let's consider the following example with a three-digit encoding in the ACL string:

- First digit: Access control to the PSTN calls with the following values:
  - **0**: No access at all
  - **1**: Access to national calls
  - **2**: Access to international calls

- Second digit: Voicemail permissions with the following values:
  - **0**: No voicemail
  - **1**: Voicemail allowed
  - **2**: Voicemail enabled

- Third digit: Account status with the following values:
  - **0**: Account disabled
  - **1**: Incoming calls only
  - **2**: In and out calls

Such an ACL string can be explicitly loaded in the script via the AVPops module:

```
loadmodule "avpops.so"
modparam("avpops",
  "db_url","mysql://user:pwd@localhost/opensips")▯
..
avp_db_query("select acl_string from subscriber where
  username='$fU' and domain='$fd' ", "$avp(acl)");
```

You can also load the ACL string during digest authentication via the load_credentials statement from the auth_db module:

```
modparam("auth_db","load_credentials","$avp(acl)=acl_string")▯
```

Once the ACL value is loaded, its testing is a simple script operation:

```
....
$avp(acl_status) = $(avp(acl_string){s.substr,2,1}{s.int})⊠;
$avp(acl_pstn) = $(avp(acl_string){s.substr,0,1}{s.int})⊠;
if ( $avp(acl_status) < 2) {
  send_reply("403", "No permission to make calls");
  exit;
}
....
if ( is_method("INVITE") ) {
  if ($rU=~"^00[1-9][0-9]+") {
    if ( $avp(acl_pstn)<2 ){
      send_reply("403", "Forbidden");
      exit;
    }
  } else if ($rU=~"^0[1-9][0-9]+") {
    if ( $avp(acl_pstn)<1 ) {
      send_reply("403", "Forbidden");
      exit;
    }
  } else {
    send_reply("404", "Unknown number");
    exit;

  }
}
```

Caller ID in PSTN calls

As the SIP identities (SIP URIs) are not compatible with the PSTN identities (numbers), when a SIP user is making a call to PSTN, he must present a PSTN identity on top of his SIP identity.

As we know, the SIP identity is typically carried by the **From** SIP header. For the additional PSTN identity, SIP offers the following headers:

- **Remote-Party-ID** header
- **P-Asserted-Identity** header
- **Privacy** header

From the OpenSIPS perspective, it is just about adding these new headers with the proper information on the PSTN identity and its status (anonymous or not).

What if the PSTN identity and its status can be obtained in a different way? It can be explicitly loaded (for the caller party) from the local database or the `load_credentials` mechanism can be used (as you learned for ACLs fetching).

Assuming that we have the PSTN identity number in `$avp(pstn_id)` and the privacy status in `$avp(pstn_priv)`, adding the relevant headers looks as follows:

```
if ( $avp(pstn_priv)!=0  ) {
  # PAI headers
  append_hf("P-Asserted-Identity: Anonymous
    <sip:$var(rpid)@domain>\r\n");
  append_hf("Privacy: id\r\n");
  # RPID header
  append_hf("Remote-Party-ID: <sip:$var(rpid)@domain;user=phone>;
  privacy=full;screen=yes\r\n");
} else {
  # PAI headers
  append_hf("P-Asserted-Identity: $var(rpid)
    <sip:$var(rpid)@domain>\r\n");
  # RPID header
  append_hf("Remote-Party-ID: $var(rpid)
    <sip:$var(rpid)@domain;user=phone>;
  privacy=off;screen=yes\r\n");
}
```

Routing to PSTN GWs

In most of the cases, the routing to the PSTN gateways (selecting a gateway to be used for call termination in PSTN) is done by the prefix of the dialed number. Of course, there are cases where other policies are used in order to select the termination gateway for a call (cost, quality, load balancing, or others).

Such prefix-based routing can be hardcoded very quickly in the OpenSIPS script, as shown in the following code:

```
# dialled string is E.164 normalized
if ( $rU~="^44" ) {
  # UK destination
  $rd = "10.10.2.100";
} else if ( $rU~="^1" ) {
  # US destination
  $rd = "10.10.2.211";
} else if ( $rU~="^34" ) {
```

```
  # Spain destination
  $rd = "10.10.2.5";
} else {
  # default destination
  $rd = "10.10.2.111";
}
```

Of course, this approach has the following major problems:

- It does not scale: Some PSTN carriers may provide tens of thousands of prefix rules and hundreds of gateways

- It cannot be provisioned: There is no tool to allow you to provision directly into the OpenSIPS configuration file

- It will require a restart each time you change something in the GW or route's setting

The preceding script is fine if you have just a few gateways. However, VoIP providers usually have hundreds or thousands of routes. As an answer to all these problems, OpenSIPS provides you with the dynamic routing module.

The dynamic routing module

The drouting module is intended for prefix-based routing to a set of gateways (destinations).

The following are the dynamic routing features:

- Routing rule selection:
  - Prefix-based
  - Caller/group-based
  - Time-based
  - Priority-based

- Call processing:
  - Stripping and prefixing
  - Default routing rules
  - Inbound and outbound call processing
  - Script route triggering

- MultiGW handling:
  - ○ Failover with serial forking
  - ○ Weight/random-based GW balancing
  - ○ Carrier concept

 The **Least Cost Routing (LCR)** is a particular case of dynamic routing, where under a certain prefix, the possible gateways are order-based on cost.

In the dynamic routing module, the routing data (destinations, rules, and carriers) is stored in a database and cached in the memory at start up time. Besides simple caching, the routing prefixes are reorganized in a search tree, so the search time does not depend on the number of rules but on the maximum length of the prefixes. This data can be reloaded at runtime via the `dr_reload` MI command.

As you can define multiple gateways in a rule (for a prefix), the module can do load balancing or random selection of the gateways (from a given set) with or without weight support.

The module also provides good routing script integration. Variables are supported in script function calls. However, the most important thing is that the module allows you to set the scripting route that is to be triggered when certain rules are matched. This gives you the possibility to do custom actions such as adding SIP headers over the **SIP INVITE** when a rule is selected.

Even though the module is primarily designed to route to gateways, it offers bidirectional support in terms of handling traffic. It can do inbound and outbound processing (strip and prefixing when sending and receiving from a gateway). Even more, the module can be used to perform IP authentication for calls originated from the gateways.

One of the most important aspects of the dynamic routing module is the fact that it was designed with the performance aspect at the top, as follows:

- It is able to handle large volume of routing info, even more than 50 million rules

- It is very fast in searching through the rules as the searching time does not depend on the number of rules

- Low memory consumption is guaranteed as the module internally restructures all the data loaded from the DB

Routing entities

In order to understand how the dynamic routing module does the routing, let's first understand what are the entities defined and used by the module:

- The gateways are the end SIP entities where the traffic actually needs to be sent after routing. The gateways definition is stored in the table called dr_gateways and they are uniquely identified via a gateway ID.

- The carrier concept is used if you need to group gateways in order to have a better control over how the gateways will be used by the routing rules, such as in what order the gateways will be used.

Basically, a carrier is a set of gateways that has its own sorting algorithm and attribute string. They are by default defined in the dr_carriers table.

The routing rules are the actual rules that control the prefix-based routing. Using different criteria (prefix, time, priority, and so on), they will decide to which set of gateways the call will be sent.

The default name for the table storing the rule definitions is dr_rules. Each rule may be part of one or more sets of rules. The sets (of rules) are used to group and use only some specific routing rules for some specific purposes. For example, in your routing rules, you can have a set of rules to implement best-effort quality routing and other set of rules doing premium quality routing. (The rules will use different gateways providing different qualities.)

 A full description of the DB schema can be found on the OpenSIPS website: http://www.opensips.org/Documentation/Install-DBSchema-2-1#AEN4535

The following figure shows the relation between all the dynamic routing entities:

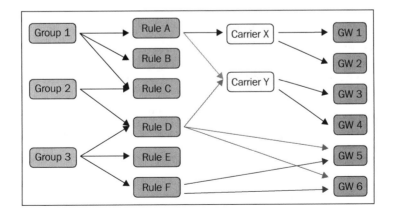

The selection algorithm

In order to take full advantage of the capabilities of the dynamic routing module, you need to understand how the module works in terms of how it does the routing, selects the routing rule, and selects the gateways from the rule.

In this section, we will explain step by step the entire selection process coupled with some examples for a better understanding. Let's consider the following sample rules:

Rule ID	Set	Prefix	Time	Priority	GW list
1	3	004021	NULL	0	5
2	3,1	0040	20150101T083000 | 10H | weekly | | | MO,TU, WE,TH,FR	1	4,5
3	3,4	0040	NULL	0	5,4
4	2,1	0044	NULL	0	3

First of all, the module has to discover the routing set/group of the calling user. This group may be provided from the script level as a parameter to the `do_routing()` function. If not provided, the module will attempt to perform a DB query in the `dr_groups` table in order to find the group based on the From header SIP URI.

Assuming that we want to use group 3, we will end up with the following:

Rule ID	Set	Prefix	Time	Priority	GW list
1	3	004021	NULL	0	5
2	3,1	0040	20150101T083000 | 10H | weekly | | | MO,TU, WE,TH,FR	1	4,5
3	3,4	0040	NULL	0	5,4

Once the group is known, the next step is to perform the prefix matching. This means to search (in the subset of the rules for this group) for the rules that match the destination based on the **Prefix** column. The set of rules with the longest prefix is chosen. If no digit from the prefix matches, the default rules are used (rules with no prefix defined).

Assuming that the dialed number is `0040246222222`, we will end up with the following:

Rule ID	Set	Prefix	Time	Priority	GW list
2	3,1	0040	20150101T083000|10H|weekly|||MO,TU,WE,TH,FR	1	4,5
3	3,4	0040	NULL	0	5,4

The next step is to do the time matching. The existing set of rules is narrowed down by discarding the rules that do not match the time criteria. The rules with no time expression are not subject to this filtering. (They will be considered as passed.)

The time constraint is defined based on RFC 2445 and its definition is as follows:

```
<dtstart>|<duration>|<freq>|<until>|<interval>|<byday>|
    <bymonthday>|<byyearday>|<byweekno>|<bymonth>
```

This means that the `20150101T083000|10H|weekly|||MO,TU,WE,TH,FR` time constraint translates into starting from 1st of Jan, 2015, 8:30 a.m., with a duration of 10 hours, repeating weekly but only from Monday to Friday. So, basically, it means from 8:30 a.m. to 6:30 p.m. during working days.

If we assume that the current time is 8:00 p.m., only **Rule ID 3** will match (no time definition matches any time). However, if the time is 5:00 p.m., both the rules will match, as follows:

Rule ID	Set	Prefix	Time	Priority	GW list
2	3,1	0040	20040101T083000|10H|weekly|||MO,TU,WE,TH,FR	1	4,5
3	3,4	0040	NULL	0	5,4

The last step is the priority sorting. From the existing set of rules, the rule with the highest priority is selected to drive the routing.

The winning rule is **Rule ID 2** as it has the highest priority:

Rule ID	Set	Prefix	Time	Priority	GW list
2	3,1	0040	20040101T083000|10H|weekly|||MO,TU,WE,TH,FR	1	4,5

Actually, rules **2** and **3** implement an on-peak and off-peak kind of routing. During peak hours (by matching both the rules and having **2** with a higher priority), we will use first gateway **4** and then **5**, while in off-peak hours (by matching only rule **3**), we will use first gateway **5** and then **4**.

Note that at the end of the rule matching algorithm, none or maximum one rule will be selected. The selected rule contains a set of gateways and/or carriers. The module will try to deliver the call to one of the gateway in the set provided by the rule. Which gateway is selected and in which order they are tried (for failover purposes) depends on your settings.

Once a rule is selected, the dynamic routing module will select and consume the gateways listed in the winning rule.

Before consuming, the list of the gateways needs to be ordered. There are two algorithms to order the gateways from a list:

- Given order (no rearranging)
- Weight-based reordering (covers random ordering as well)

There are two kinds of lists to be reordered:

- The list of destinations from the routing rule, which can contain gateways or carriers; the ordering is given by the W flag used when calling do_routing() from the script
- The list of gateways in a carrier; ordering is done based on the flags from the carrier definition

Here are some examples on how the ordering of the gateways is done. This is the first example:

```
CarrierA - GW1=25, GW2=75 (using weights)
CarrierB - GW3,GW4 (no weights)
Rule for prefix 4021 (no W flag) : #CarrierA,#CarrierB, GW5
Results:
  GW1, GW2,  GW3, GW4,   GW5
  GW2, GW1,  GW3, GW4,   GW5
```

Note how the GWs pushed by CarrierA may have a different order due to the weight-based reordering, while the GWs pushed by CarrierB have the same order all the time. In the rule as well, the order is the same all the time.

This is the second example:

```
CarrierA - GW1,GW2 (no weights)
CarrierB - GW3,GW4 (no weights)
Rule for prefix 4021 (with W flag) : #CarrierA=50,#CarrierB=50
Results:
  GW1, GW2,   GW3, GW4
  GW3, GW4,   GW1, GW2
```

Note how the GWs pushed by `CarrierA` and `CarrierB` do not change their order (relative to the carrier), but at the rule level, the two carriers can be reordered due to their weights.

Using the weight-based reordering with different weights distribution (equal or not), you can implement different ways of selecting the gateways to be used in a rule.

Once the gateways are ordered, they are pushed to the script, one by one, for usage. If a gateway fails (no answer or server error reply), you can do serial forking via the failure route and try the next available gateway from the selected rule.

Probing and disabling gateways

The module has the capability to monitor the status of the destinations by doing SIP probing (sending SIP requests such as OPTIONS).

For each destination, you can configure what kind of probing should be done (the `probe_mode` column):

- `(0)`: No probing at all.
- `(1)`: Probing only when the destination is in the disabled mode (disabling via the MI command will completely stop the probing as well). The destination will be automatically re-enabled when the probing will succeed the next time.
- `(2)`: Probing all the time. If disabled, the destination will be automatically re-enabled when the probing will succeed the next time.

A destination can become disabled in the following two ways:

- **Script detection**: By calling the `dr_disable()` function from the script after trying the destination. In this case, if the probing mode for the destination is `(1)` or `(2)`, the destination will be automatically re-enabled when the probing will succeed.

- **MI command**: By calling the `dr_gw_status` MI command to disable (on demand) the destination. If so, the probing and re-enabling of this destination will be completely disabled until you re-enable it again via the MI command—this is designed to allow controlled and complete disabling of a destination during maintenance.

Advanced features

The dynamic module has many other features that can be used in order to achieve more complex scenarios or address different other scenarios:

- **Data partitioning**: You can define multiple sets of tables (other sets of groups, rules, carriers, and gateways table) and have the module work with any of these partitions. Each partition is completely independent and can be separately reloaded. This is very useful if you want to use the dynamic routing module for multiple purposes in your script: PSTN routing, billing purposes, DID matching purposes, and others. See the `use_partitions`, `db_partitions_url`, and `db_partitions_table` module parameters.

- **Attributes**: All the dynamic routing entities (rules, carriers, and gateways) can have an attributes string attached. These attributes are not internally used by the module but simply pushed to the script level (via variables) whenever this entity is to be used. (If the rule matches, a certain carrier or gateway is used.) These attributes are usually used to store custom information (for scripting purposes only). See the `rule_attrs_pvar`, `carrier_attrs_pvar`, and `gw_attrs_pvar` optional parameters for the `do_routing()` function.

- **Blacklists**: The module can dynamically create destination blacklists based on gateways that you defined in the module. This is very handy because you can avoid attacks such as registration poisoning and DNS poisoning by applying blacklists generated dynamically. See the `define_blacklist` module parameter and the Preventing DNS and registration poisoning section of *Chapter 13, OpenSIPS Security* for further explanation.

- **Rule fallback**: Normally, the module uses a single rule to route a call. By enabling this option, the module will fall back and use rules with a lower priority or shorter prefix when all the destinations from the current rules fail. See the F flag for the `do_routing()` function.

- **Prefix matching only**: This only checks whether the dialed number matches any routing rule without loading/applying any routing information. (If no gateways/carriers are set, the RURI is not altered.) This feature is useful if you want to implement number detection/recognition without any routing. See the C flag for the `do_routing()` function.

- **Full number matching**: This does strict length matching over the prefix. Actually, the module will do full number matching and not prefix matching anymore. This is a useful feature if you want to implement DID matching with the dynamic routing module. See the L flag for the do_routing() function.

- **Direct routing**: Instead of doing routing based on the routing rules, you can force the module to do routing directly to a given carrier or gateway (identified by their IDs). See the route_to_carrier() and route_to_gw() functions.

Script samples

Here, we will see relevant scripting to implement inbound and outbound PSTN routing in your OpenSIPS script. We will use the dynamic routing and dialplan modules.

The script for the dynamic routing module is as follows:

- Gateway type 1 for inbound gateways (DID providers sending calls to us)
- Gateway type 2 for outbound gateways (PSTN carriers)
- Rules group 10 for DID matching; the attribute will hold the SIP username behind this DID
- Rules group 20 for prefix-based routing to gateways

The following is the dr_gateways table:

GW ID	Type	Address	Strip	PriPrefix	Attributes	Probing
"DID_UK"	1	sip:10.1.10.1:5060	0	""	""	0
"DID_US"	1	sip:10.24.3.4:5060	0	""	""	0
"OUT_UK"	2	sip:192.168.1.3:5060	0	""	""	1
"OUT_US1"	2	sip:192.168.1.8:5060	0	33224	""	1
"OUT_US2"	2	sip:192.168.1.9:5060	0	""	""	1

The `dr_rules` table is as follows:

Rule ID	Set	Prefix	Time	Priority	Attributes	GW list
1	10	44123123123	NULL	0	"bob"	""
2	10	1525345234	NULL	0	"alice"	""
3	20	44	NULL	0		"OUT_UK"
4	20	1	NULL	0		"OUT_US1=25,OUT_US2=75"

The script for the `dialplan` module is as follows:

- Group 1 to normalize the in and out PSTN numbers in the E.164 format

The following is the `dialplan` table:

Set ID	Match operator	Match exp	Subst exp	Replace exp
1	1	`"^00[1-9][0-9]+$"`	`"^00(.*)$"`	`"\1"`
1	1	`"^\+[1-9][0-9]+$"`	`"^\+(.*)$"`	`"\1"`
1	1	`"^[1-9][0-9]+$"`	`"^(.*)$"`	`"44\1"`

Here we have the scripted PSTN inbound sections:

```
....
# we have here only initial request !

# handle inbound traffic - first check if it comes
# from our DID providers (use IP auth with DRouting)
if ( is_from_gw("1") ) {
  # trusted inbound GW, normalize to E.164
  if ( !dp_translate("1","$rU/$rU") ) {
    send_reply("404","Bad PSTN number");
    exit;
  }
  # use DR to match DIDs- full number matching, no routing
  if ( !do_routing("10","LC",,"$avp(username)") ) {
    send_reply("404","DID not found");
    exit;
  }
```

```
   # set the new URI based on DID translation
   $rU = $avp(username);

} else if (!proxy_authorize("", "subscriber")) {
   proxy_challenge("", "0");
   exit;
}
```

These are the scripted PSTN outbound sections:

```
....
# we have here only initial request !

# here we decide how to route further the call

# is it a call for PSTN ?
if ( dp_translate("1","$rU/$rU") ) {
   # recognized and normalized to E.164

   # use DR to route with weights
   if ( !do_routing("20","W") ) {
      send_reply("503","No route found");
      exit;
   }
   xlog ("first gateway is $ru \n");
   # arm failure route to catch bad GWs
   t_on_failure("dr");

   t_relay();
   exit;
}
.....

failure_route[dr] {
   if (t_was_cancelled()) {
      exit;
   }
   # a gateway failure is only for 5xx and 6xx replies
   # or for a local timeout (no reply was received)
   if ( !(t_check_status("[56][0-9][0-9]") ||
      (t_check_status("408") && t_local_replied("all")) ) )
      exit;
```

```
if (use_next_gw()) {
  xlog ("next gateway is $ru \n");
  t_on_failure("dr");
  t_relay();
  exit;
} else {
  t_reply("503", "Service not available");
  exit;
}
}
```

Summary

In this chapter, you learned how to configure OpenSIPS to forward calls to a gateway. It is important to take care of the security. Using the `permissions` module, you can allow the gateways to bypass the digest authentication and get access by validating its IP address only. The `group` module is important to control the access from the UACs, and in order to route your calls to the PSTN gateways, the dynamic routing module is a very powerful and flexible tool. You should also prevent subscribers from sending a **REFER** method to the PSTN gateways to avoid fraud.

From the point you connect to PSTN, take a lot of care about toll fraud. I recommend that you have a security specialist verifying your environment periodically. Often, analyze your call detail records to detect abnormal activity.

In the next chapter, we will cover the `dialog` module. Here, you will learn how to control the dialogs, count calls per user, disconnect calls exceeding a timeout, and more.

8
Managing Dialogs

Initially, most SIP proxies were only transaction-aware—they had only the information regarding requests and replies. However, in many cases, this was a problem for solution developers. If we cannot control a dialog, it is not even possible to know how many simultaneous calls the system is handling. To supersede these limitations, we have the `dialog` module. This module is extremely important in applications such as prepaid billing, calling cards, and limiting of simultaneous calls per user, gateway, and route. Whenever you need to count, disconnect, and display active calls, you should use this module. In this chapter, we will cover the following topics:

- Enabling the dialog module
- Creating a dialog
- Describing and controlling the dialog matching process
- Listing the dialog states
- Setting a default timeout for established calls
- Discussing dialog variables and flags
- Profiling a dialog
- Disconnecting calls using the MI interface
- Using topology hiding based on the dialog module
- Validating a dialog and fixing broken dialogs
- Displaying the dialog statistics
- Enabling SIP session timers

Enabling the dialog module

To enable the dialog module, simply load it. You can integrate the dialog module into a database. The db_mode parameter defines how the system will update the records in the database.

The following list shows the available DB mode's parameters:

- 0: Dialogs in the memory are not flushed to the DB (No Database)
- 1: Changes will be inserted immediately in the database (Real time)
- 2: Flushed to the DB periodically and the timer is configurable (Delayed)
- 3: Flushed to the DB at shutdown (Shutdown)

Consider the following snippet:

```
#### Dialog Module
loadmodule "dialog.so"
modparam("dialog", "db_url",
   "dbdriver://username:password@dbhost/dbname")
modparam("dialog", "db_mode", 2)
modparam("dialog", "db_update_period", 120)
```

Creating a dialog

To create a dialog, you have to call the create_dialog() function in the initial request. You don't need to call this function again in sequential requests. The function has three parameters:

- P sends periodical in-dialog pings to the caller.
- p sends periodical in-dialog pings to the callee.
- B disconnects the call sending a BYE in both directions when the dialog times out. We call this feature BYE on timeout.

You should be careful while using in-dialog pings. This feature works fine with well-behaved end devices such as IP phones, analog terminal adapters, and gateways. However, avoid it when using clients such as dialers or softswitches that possibly will not answer an OPTIONS request. In this case, if the server does not receive an answer or if it receives an answer with the code 481 Call leg does not exist, the call is disconnected. You can control the ping interval by the following parameter:

```
modparam("dialog", "ping_interval", 20)
```

Dialog matching

OpenSIPS has to match all the sequential requests to a specific dialog. To perform this task, it usually applies a cookie (DID). This cookie is present in the Record-Route headers for initial requests and the Route headers for sequential requests. Let's take a look at the following example for an INVITE and its corresponding sequential request, BYE:

- Initial request:

```
INVITE sip:5551212@1.1.1.1:5060 SIP/2.0
Record-Route: <sip:2.2.2.2:5060;lr;did=0db.28e94f74>
```

- Sequential request:

```
BYE sip:5551212@2.2.2.2:5060 SIP/2.0
Route: <sip:1.1.1.1:5060;lr; did=0db.28e94f74>
```

If, for some reason, the client is broken and does not insert the Route headers correctly with cookies, you will have to fall back to a pure SIP dialog matching based on call-id, from-tag, and to-tag. You can control the dialog match using the following parameter:

```
modparam("dialog", "dlg_match_mode", 1)
```

The following Match modes are available:

- 0: Match exclusively based on DID
- 1: Match first on DID; if not present, fall back to SIP matching
- 2: Match exclusively on SIP elements (call-id, from-tag, and to-tag)

The default is **0**, DID only.

Dialog states

A dialog can assume several states. The dialog state is present in the $DLG_status variable. The values can be as follows:

- NULL: Not found
- 1: Unconfirmed (INVITE sent but no reply received)
- 2: Early state (INVITE sent and provisional reply received, 100,180,183)
- 3: Confirmed (INVITE sent, 200 OK received, no ACK)
- 4: Established (INVITE sent, 200 OK received, ACK confirmed)
- 5: Ended (BYE received)

It is very useful to check the dialog state before taking any action such as reading dialog variables. If the dialog is NULL, a dialog variable and/or flag is not readable.

Dialog timeout and call disconnection

One important feature for prepaid billing is the capability to set a timeout for calls. The dialog module has many ways to handle timeouts. We will see several ways on how to disconnect a call on timeout. When you create a dialog using the parameter, B, the call disconnects on timeout. To set a timeout, there are two ways:

- Specify the default timeout
- Set the timeout in the routing script

To specify a default timeout, you can set a module parameter to a specific value or to an **Attribute Value Pairs (AVP)**:

```
modparam("dialog", "default_timeout", 21600)
```

You can also set a new timeout by changing a **pseudo-variable (PV)**, $DLG_lifetime. You have to set this timeout in the initial request after creating a dialog or in a sequential request before any dialog matching commands, such as loose_route() or match_dialog().

Dialog variables and flags

OpenSIPS has several types of variables and vectors. Each type of variable has a different scope. Note that PV has the scope of a process and AVP has the scope of a transaction. Thus, if you need a variable that is capable to persist the whole duration of the call from the first INVITE to the end BYE, you will need dialog variables. You can also use flags, which are simpler.

There are strict rules with regard to the dialog variables. You can set a dialog variable after creating a dialog in the initial request. You can only read a dialog variable after a dialog matching command such as loose_route() or match_dialog().

Setting and reading the dialog variables

To attach a value to a dialog, you can use the `store_dlg_value(name,val)` function or directly set the variable using `$dlg_val(name)`. See the following examples:

```
store_dlg_value("type","residential");
# or
$dlg_val(type) = "residential";
```

To recover and/or set a dialog variable, you can again use the `fetch_dlg_value(name,pvar)` function or directly set the variable using `$dlg_val(name)`. See the following examples:

```
fetch_dlg_value("type","$avp(dlgtype)");
# or
$avp(dlgtype) = $dlg_val(type);
```

Setting and reading the dialog flags

The rules for the dialog variables also apply to the dialog flags. You have a few functions to set and test the flags. These functions are shown as follows:

- `set_dlg_flag(idx)`
- `test_and_set_dlg_flag(idx, value)`
- `reset_dlg_flag(idx)`
- `is_dlg_flag_set(idx)`

The following are some examples on how to use them:

```
set_dlg_flag("15");
test_and_set_dlg_flag("15", "0") #Values may be "0" or "1";
reset_dlg_flag("15");
is_dlg_flag_set("15")
```

One function deserving a bit of explanation is `test_and_set_dlg_flag()`. This function checks whether the dialog flag is equal to value. When true, it changes the value to the opposite one.

Profiling a dialog

There are many cases where you need to sort, count, and limit specific calls. It is very useful to count calls per subscriber, gateway, and route. In this section, we will learn how to set a profile for a specific call and count how many calls belong to a profile.

You have to define the profiles before using them. There are two types of profiles, profiles with value and profiles with no value:

- **Profiles with no value**: The dialog receives a simple description such as inbound, outbound, PSTN, local, or VoIP
- **Profiles with value**: The dialog is associated with a profile such as caller and the value is the name of the caller

You can verify the profiles for a specific call using the MI command:

```
opensipsctl fifo dlg_list_ctx
```

The output of the command is shown in the following example:

```
dialog::  hash=2405:1072531375
        state:: 4
        ...
        context::
                value:: rtpproxyset = 1
                profile:: caller = 8590@opensips.org
                profile:: inbound =
                profile:: domain = opensips.org
```

In the preceding case, we have two profiles with a value (`caller` and `domain`) and one profile with no value (inbound). You can now check whether a call belongs or not to a profile using the following function:

```
is_in_profile(profile, [value])
```

For example, let's check whether a specific call belongs to a user, `8590@opensips.org`:

```
is_in_profile("caller","8590@opensips.org")
```

You can count the number of calls belonging to the same profile. Thus, you can count the number of calls per user or domain using the following function:

```
get_profile_size(profile, [value],size)
```

This is very useful if you want to limit calls for a specific user. Take a look at the following example to limit a maximum of five simultaneous calls per user:

```
#This should be included in the module parameters section
#Profiles needs to be declared before usage
modparam("dialog","profiles_with_value","caller")

#This should be included in the routing section.
#Set the new call in the profile
set_dlg_profile("caller","$fU");

# get current calls for from user, current call counts
get_profile_size("caller","$fU","$var(calls)");

# check within limit
if($var(calls) < 5 ) {
  xlog("L_INFO", "User $fU has $var(calls)/5 calls \n");
} else {
  xlog("L_INFO", "User channel limit exceeded $var(calls)/5 \n");
  send_reply("503", "Service unavailable\n");
  exit;
}
```

Counting calls from the MI interface

In some cases, external programs need access related to profiles. You can access the dialog profiles from the MI interface using the following commands:

- `profile_get_size`: You can get the size of a specific profile using `profile_get_size`:

  `opensipsctl fifo profile_get_size caller 8590@opensips.org`

  The following is the output:

  **`profile:: name=caller value=8575@voffice.com.br count=0
    shared=no`**

- `profile_list_dlgs`: You can list all the dialogs belonging to a specific profile:

  `opensipsctl fifo profile_list_dlgs caller 8575@voffice.com.br`

  The following is the output:

  `dialog::  hash=1949:1590881202`

  `state:: 4`

  `...`

  `callee_bind_addr:: udp:10.252.152.221:5060`

Disconnecting calls

Once you have an established dialog, you can disconnect the call at any time by sending a BYE to both sides. There are many ways to disconnect a call using OpenSIPS. Some are initiated by the subscriber and others by the system itself. Fortunately, now there is a PV called $DLG_end_reason that is capable to display the disconnection reason. It returns the reason for the dialog termination. It can be one of the following:

- Upstream BYE: BYE sent by the callee
- Downstream BYE: BYE sent by the caller
- Lifetime Timeout: Lifetime expired
- MI Termination: Ended via the MI interface
- Ping Timeout: Ended by no reply or 481 to in-dialog pings
- RTPProxy Timeout: Timeout signaled by **RTPProxy**

Disconnecting a call using the MI interface

To disconnect a call using the MI interface, you will need to identify the hash number. To identify the hash number of a dialog, you can list the dialogs by call-id using the following command:

```
opensipsctl fifo dlg_list call_id
```

The output of this command will be as follows:

```
dialog::   hash=2354:1623728616
        state:: 4
        user_flags:: 131072
        timestart:: 1422013994
        timeout:: 1422021195
        callid:: 750949327@172.16.200.240
```

After getting the hash number, you can use the MI command, dlg_end_dlg, to terminate a dialog using the hash as a parameter, as follows:

```
opensipsctl fifo dlg_end_dlg 2354 1623728616
```

Topology hiding

There are many cases where you want to hide customer information from your upstream peers. There are three main reasons to use **topology hiding** (TH). The first one is that you do not want to send information that can identify your customer. The second reason is security—the less information a hacker has about your network, the safer you are. The third reason to use TH is when a client is not well-behaved and incapable to work with the Record-Route and Route headers and there are many of them in the field. Using TH tricks the user agent client in seeing the SIP proxy as an endpoint, disregarding these headers.

This is different from the older versions, where topology hiding was a part of the dialog module, but now it is a separate module. It can run on top of the **Transaction Module (TM)** or the dialog module. When using the TM module, OpenSIPS will encode the information in the Contact header. On the other hand, when using the dialog module, you will have shorter messages.

To enable topology hiding is not simple because you have to rewrite some parts of the script. We will explain how to implement it in two parts, initial and sequential requests. For initial requests, you can use the following code:

```
#Load the module in the loading section of the config file
loadmodule "topology_hiding.so"

#The lines below goes in the routing section of the config file
# if it's an INVITE dialog, create the dialog, this will lead to
# cleaner SIP messages
if (is_method("INVITE")) create_dialog();

# we do topology hiding, preserving the Contact Username and also
# hiding the Call-ID
topology_hiding("UC");
t_relay();
exit;
```

After the topology_hiding() command, the system will strip the headers—Via, Record_Route, and Route—and replace the Contact header with the IP address of the interface from where it received the request.

The optional parameters of the topology_hiding() command are as follows:

- U: Propagates the username in the Contact header URI
- C: Encodes the Call-ID header

Initial request before topology hiding

A packet trace for the initial request is displayed here. Pay attention to the Via and Contact headers:

```
U 192.168.255.1:39198 -> 192.168.255.131:5060
INVITE sip:1001@opensips.org SIP/2.0.
Via: SIP/2.0/UDP 192.168.255.1:39198;branch=z9hG4bK-d8754z-
   54408b44c993d315-1---d8754z-;
Max-Forwards: 70.
Contact: <sip:1000@192.168.255.1:39198>.
To: <sip:1001@opensips.org>.
From: "1000"<sip:1000@opensips.org>;tag=129cde14.
Call-ID: ZmNhZDYyNjg1ZTA5MWRkMGI3Y2Y3MmRhMzA5NWJkOTY
```

Initial request after topology hiding

Here is a captured trace of the INVITE request. Again, pay attention to the Via and Contact headers.:

```
U 192.168.255.131:5060 -> 192.168.255.1:5060
INVITE sip:1001@192.168.255.1:5060;
   rinstance=411662bbee9840e7;transport=UDP SIP/2.0.
Via: SIP/2.0/UDP
   192.168.255.131:5060;branch=z9hG4bK3dfc.f7560155.0.
Max-Forwards: 69.
Contact: <sip:192.168.255.131;did=f9f.e10e9697>.
To: <sip:1001@opensips.org>.
From: "1000"<sip:1000@opensips.org>;tag=129cde14.
Call-ID: ZmNhZDYyNjg1ZTA5MWRkMGI3Y2Y3MmRhMzA5NWJkOTY.
```

If you pay attention to the Contact and Via headers, you will see that the IP address changed from the IP address of the client to the IP address of the server hiding the addresses related to the client.

For sequential requests, you have to insert the following code before the existing sequential request section:

```
if (has_totag()) {
  if (topology_hiding_match()) {
    xlog("Succesfully matched this request to a topology hiding
       dialog. \n");
    xlog("Calller side callid is $ci \n");
    xlog("Callee side callid  is $TH_callee_callid \n");
    t_relay();
```

```
      exit;
    } else {
    if ( is_method("ACK") ) {
      if ( t_check_trans() ) {
        t_relay();
        exit;
      } else
        exit;
    }
    sl_send_reply("404","Not here");
    exit;
  }
}
```

Sequential request before topology hiding

Notice the Contact and Via headers. The request coming from the client
(192.168.255.1) contains the original addresses. It is sent straight to the proxy
without the Route headers. Pay attention to the did field as well in the RURI
identifying the dialog:

```
U 192.168.255.1:39198 -> 192.168.255.131:5060
BYE sip:192.168.255.131;did=bd7.88b13634 SIP/2.0.
Via: SIP/2.0/UDP 192.168.255.1:39198;branch=z9hG4bK-d8754z-
  57d1f468a10fc14f-1---d8754z-;rport.
Max-Forwards: 70.
Contact: <sip:1000@192.168.255.1:39198>.
To: "1001"<sip:1001@opensips.org;transport=UDP>;tag=076ad036.
From: <sip:1000@opensips.org;transport=UDP>;tag=19f20a34.
Call-ID: YmFhYTNhODYxZWNkYjE4YmRlYjA1MjNjZjI4NGZlOWI..
CSeq: 2 BYE.
User-Agent: Bria 3 release 3.5.5  stamp 71238.
Content-Length: 0.
```

Sequential request after topology hiding

The process of topology hiding mangles the Contact and Via headers tricking the
User Agent Server (UAS) to think that the proxy is an endpoint completely hiding
the topology and addresses for the internal network:

```
U 192.168.255.131:5060 -> 192.168.255.1:5060
BYE sip:1001@192.168.255.1:5060;transport=UDP SIP/2.0.
Via: SIP/2.0/UDP 192.168.255.131:5060;branch=z9hG4bK0184.d6317a53.0.
Max-Forwards: 69.
```

```
Contact: <sip:192.168.255.131;did=bd7.88b13634>.
To: "1001"<sip:1001@opensips.org;transport=UDP>;tag=076ad036.
From: <sip:1000@opensips.org;transport=UDP>;tag=19f20a34.
Call-ID: YmFhYTNhODYxZWNkYjE4YmRlYjA1MjNjZjI4NGZlOWI..
CSeq: 2 BYE.
User-Agent: Bria 3 release 3.5.5  stamp 71238.
Content-Length: 0.
```

Topology hiding limitations

You cannot easily combine topology hiding with NAT traversal because both the processes mangle the Contact header. Topology hiding will not hide the address and other information contained in other headers such as the display in the From header. To change the From header, you can use the uac_replace_from() function.

Validating a dialog and fixing broken dialogs

One of the most useful features of the dialog module is the dialog validation. There are some cases where this can be very useful. It can prevent malicious BYEs to close dialogs without disconnecting the call causing billing problems and other injected in-dialog requests. The function used to perform dialog validation is validate_dialog() and the result codes are displayed here:

- 1: Dialog exists and is valid
- -1: Invalid cseq
- -2: Invalid remote target
- -3: Invalid route set
- -4: Other errors (parsing, no dlg, and so on)

There are cases where a UAS sends a reply with invalid information in the headers. You can fix these headers based on the dialog information stored in the memory using the fix_route_dialog() function. This function recovers and fixes the RURI and Route headers and the destination URI using the data stored previously in the memory for the current dialog. The typical code for validation is as follows:

```
if (has_totag()) {
  loose_route();
  if($DLG_status!=NULL)
    if(!validate_dialog())
      fix_route_dialog();
}
```

Displaying the dialog statistics

The `dialog` module exports some of the most important statistics of the system.
You can obtain the number of active calls in the system using this module. See the
following example on how to generate the statistics:

```
root@bookosips:~# opensipsctl fifo get_statistics dialog:
dialog:active_dialogs:: 120
dialog:early_dialogs:: 161
dialog:processed_dialogs:: 101002
dialog:expired_dialogs:: 14
dialog:failed_dialogs:: 23434
dialog:create_sent:: 100930
dialog:update_sent:: 12986
dialog:delete_sent:: 100927
dialog:create_recv:: 15
dialog:update_recv:: 23
dialog:delete_recv:: 24
```

Description of the statistics

A detailed description of the statistics is presented here:

- `active_dialogs`: Number of active dialogs (confirmed/ACK or not)
- `early_dialogs`: Number of early dialogs (only provisional responses)
- `processed_dialogs`: Number of processed dialogs since startup
- `expired_dialogs`: Number of expired (timeout) dialogs since startup
- `failed_dialogs`: Number of failed dialogs (never established due to cancels
  and negative replies—internal and external)
- `create_sent`: Number of replicated dialog create requests sent to another
  instance (used when replicating dialogs between servers)
- `update_sent`: Number of replicated dialog update requests sent to another
  instance
- `delete_sent`: Number of replicated dialog delete requests sent to another
  instance
- `create_recv`: Number of dialog create events received from other instances
- `update_recv`: Number of dialog update events received from other instances
- `delete_recv`: Number of dialog delete events received from other instances

SIP session timers

One of the main issues with SIP is to make sure that the call and dialog finishes properly. However, in the SIP protocol, there is no guarantee that either the UAC or UAS will send the BYE request to terminate the call. Network and device issues can lead to unfinished calls. These calls, also called hanged calls, will stay in the dialog table until its default timeout, by default, 43,200 seconds or, in other words, 12 hours. This time is changeable in the `default_timeout` parameter.

The **Internet Engineering Task Force (IETF)** defined a mechanism to detect hanged calls and lack of communication with a specific device. It is now a standard described in RFC 4028. The SIP session timers send periodic messages that continuously update the timeout at the proxy. The **SIP Session Timer (SST)** module in OpenSIPS implements this feature.

How the SIP session timer works

The module receives notifications from the dialog module of any new or updated dialogs. It will look for the value in the Session-Expires header to override the dialog expiry time of the related call. This module is very easy to use and there are no exported functions. All you have to do is mark the initial request with the SST flag defined in the module parameters. The dialog modules disconnect the calls if the timeout expires. To send a BYE to both directions, do not forget to enable BYE on timeout in the dialog module by adding the parameter B in the `create_dialog()` function.

To enable the SIP session timer, you should define the SST flag and set it just before creating the dialog, as shown here:

```
loadmodule "sst.so"

modparam("sst", "sst_flag", "SST_FLAG")
modparam("sst", "min_se", 1800)

route {
  #Initial Requests, track session timers
  if(is_method("INVITE")) {
    setflag(SST_FLAG);
    create_dialog('B');
  }
}
```

It is also possible to define a minimum update time. You can use the `sstCheckMin()` function to verify that the Session-Expires header values are not too small. In this case, it will return `true`, and you should send a reply message, `422 Session Timer Too Small`, as shown in the following code:

```
if (method=="INVITE") {
  if (sstCheckMin("50")) {
    xlog("L_WARN", "422 Session Timer Too Small\n");
    sl_send_reply("422","Session Timer Too Small");
    exit;
  }
}
```

In the following figure, we will explain in detail how SST works in OpenSIPS. For convenience, here we will see part of the text and requests taken from RFC 4028 SIP session timers:

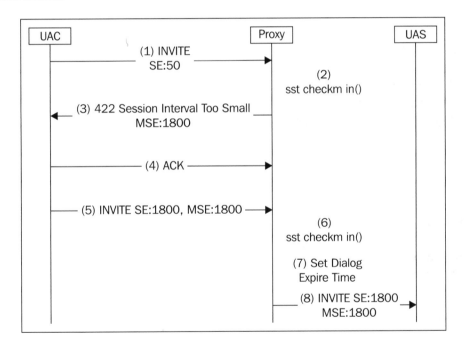

The following steps explain the preceding image in detail:

1. Whenever a **UAC** sends **INVITE**, we will check for the minimum expiration time present in the Session-Expires header:

```
INVITE sips:bob@opensips.org SIP/2.0
Via: SIP/2.0/TLS pc33.opensips.org;branch=z9hG4bKnashds8
Supported: timer
Session-Expires: 50
Max-Forwards: 70
To: Bob <sips:bob@opensips.org>
From: Alice <sips:alice@opensips.org>;tag=1928301774
Call-ID: a84b4c76e66710
CSeq: 314159 INVITE
Contact: <sips:alice@pc33.opensips.org>
Content-Type: application/sdp
Content-Length: 142
```

2. The proxy executes the `sstcheckmin()` function. The minimum expiration time defined is **1800** and the function returns `true`.

3. The proxy now rejects the request with a negative reply using code **422**. In the response, it sends the minimum session expires in the Min-SE header:

```
SIP/2.0 422 Session Interval Too Small
Via: SIP/2.0/TLS pc33.opensips.org;branch=z9hG4bKnashds8
;received=192.0.2.1
Min-SE: 1800
To: Bob <sips:bob@opensips.org>;tag=9a8kz
From: Alice <sips:alice@opensips.org>;tag=1928301774
Call-ID: a84b4c76e66710
CSeq: 314159 INVITE
```

4. The client sends the **ACK** for the negative reply.

5. The UAC sends a new **INVITE** with Min-SE and SE set to **1800** seconds.

6. The minimum SE is checked again.

7. This is the most important part regarding OpenSIPS; it will set the dialog timeout to **1800** seconds. If a sequential request does not arrive in the server in the next **1800** seconds, the session will time out and a BYE request will be sent in both directions if the option BYE on timeout has been set.

8. The server relays the new **INVITE** request to the UAS.

Summary

In this chapter, you learned many new concepts regarding dialogs. To use them is relatively simple: you have to enable the module and create the dialog using the `create_dialog()` function. Make sure that you have understood the concept of dialog matching, which is key to making it work and understanding the possible issues. Dialog variables and flags are useful when you need to persist variables from an initial request to a sequential request. To count calls by the domain, caller, or any other parameter, use the profiling feature. You also learned how to send commands and generate statistics via the MI interface. Overall, this chapter is very important, so do not forget the advanced features such as the SIP session timers, dialog validation, dialog fixing, and topology hiding.

Now, we have covered almost everything including route calls to other subscribers and PSTN. In the next chapter, we will cover accounting, where you will learn how to generate the **call detail record (CDR)**, which is essential if you want to bill your customers.

9
Accounting

In the previous chapter, you learned how to manage dialogs. Now, it is time to focus on one of the most important things for a VoIP provider: **revenue**. The accounting feature will allow you to determine the exact duration of each call. OpenSIPS supports multiple backends such as databases, log files, and RADIUS, simultaneously. There are some scenarios such as call forward that require the accounting of multiple legs. We will cover all of these features in this chapter.

In this chapter, we will cover the following topics:

- Selecting a backend
- Manual and automatic accounting
- Accounting normal, failed, and missed calls
- Integrating the dialog module to obtain the duration
- Adding extra fields to your accounting table
- Configuring OpenSIPS-CP for CDR viewing
- Multi-leg accounting
- Avoiding calls with a missing BYE

Progress check

We are going to work on the billing side of the solution. The proxy server is now working fine, completing calls between users and gateways. Now, we need to account and calculate the duration of the calls. OpenSIPS is capable of giving you a list of completed calls with their duration. The process of putting a price tag on a call is named rating, which is normally done by an external tool. In the following picture you can check your progress towards the complete solution:

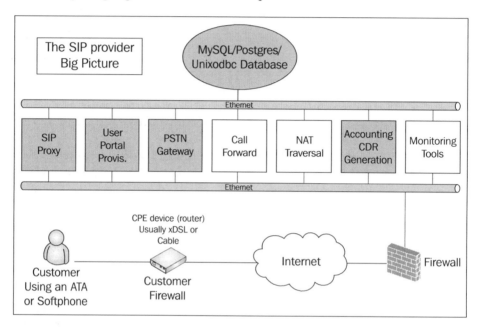

Selecting a backend

The proxy server uses the concept of **Authentication, Authorization, and Accounting (AAA)**. Until now, we have seen how to use a database to only authenticate and authorize users. We can use many different backends such as databases, RADIUS servers, plain text, and log files. Each backend serves a different purpose. The following table compares the most popular choices:

Backend	Pros	Cons
Database	Simple. Fast.	Corruption in a database can lead to billing problems and missing records.

Backend	Pros	Cons
RADIUS	Separation of the billing server. Reusing the existing RADIUS infrastructure in the VoIP provider.	It is more complex. Dictionary additions and server configurations are sometimes tricky and time-consuming. The data will end up in a database.
FlatStore (files)	The fastest backend. No corruption issues.	An external program is required to send CDRs to a central repository.

The accounting configuration

To enable the accounting feature, we will use the ACC module. We will save CDRs in a database server and use OpenSIPS-CP to display them. There are two modes to enable accounting, automatic and manual. In the automatic mode, you will mark the transactions using flags specified in the module's parameters, and the system will account a start or stop event for each completed transaction. In the manual mode, you have to explicitly call a function to generate the event.

Automatic accounting

In the automatic mode, you will mark the transaction that has to be accounted using flags. Usually, it makes sense to account only INVITEs and BYEs. To enable accounting, simply set the corresponding flag in the initial INVITE and the subsequent BYE. To define the flags and backends, check out the following parameters:

```
#### ACCounting module
loadmodule "acc.so"
modparam("acc", "log_flag", "ACC_DO")
modparam("acc", "failed_transaction_flag", "ACC_FAILED")
modparam("acc", "db_flag", "ACC_DO")  # Flag to Account to DB
modparam("acc", "db_url",
  "mysql://opensips:opensipsrw@localhost/acc")
```

In the preceding script, we defined ACC_DO as the flag to activate the automatic accounting for successful requests and ACC_FAILED for failed requests. Now, to enable accounting for a specific transaction, all you have to do is mark the transaction with the flag that has been defined. In the following section, we enabled accounting for any initial INVITE:

```
# account only INVITEs
if (is_method("INVITE")) {
  setflag(ACC_DO); # do accounting
  setflag(ACC_FAILED);
}
```

BYE is a sequential request, so it is handled just after the loose_route() command:

```
if (is_method("BYE")) {
  setflag(ACC_DO);
  setflag(ACC_FAILED); # do accounting ...
```

Whenever you want to account the missed calls, you will need to account the intermediary branches. Let's assume that your subscriber has received an unanswered call and this call was redirected to a voicemail server. The ACC module will account a successful call to your voicemail server, but it does not have any information regarding the unanswered call. To account the intermediary branches, you can enable the missed calls flag:

```
modparam("acc", "log_missed_flag", "ACC_MISSED")
modparam("acc", "db_missed_flag", "ACC_MISSED")
```

If a call is not answered and you have db_missed_flag set, the failed call will be accounted to the missed calls table in the database. This is useful when you redirect calls to a voicemail but still want to log the missed calls. You have to again mark the transaction to account the missed calls. The following code should be inserted before the section handling inbound calls:

```
# when routing via usrloc, log the missed calls also
setflag(ACC_MISSED);
route(relay);
```

It is also possible to account additional data such as 183 replies (early_media), ACK messages (report_ack), and canceled transactions (report_cancels).

Manual accounting

There are special cases where the automatic mode does not handle the accounting properly. One of the practical cases that I had to deal with was the accounting of missed calls to a gateway. To generate the statistics properly, I had to use manual accounting. It is very simple; instead of setting the automatic flags, you simply use the `acc_db_request()` or `acc_log_request()` function. See the following example:

```
acc_db_request("200 BYE without matching dialog", "acc");
acc_log_request("200 BYE without matching dialog");
```

Extra accounting

Automatic accounting only writes the fields, **method, call-id, from_tag, to_tag, sip_code**, and **sip_reason** to a database or log file, as follows:

id	method	from_tag	to_tag	sip_code	sip_reason	time
1	INVITE	5d09d45a	27095f70	200	OK	2008-04-07 09:13:21
2	BYE	5d09d45a	27095f70	200	OK	2008-04-07 09:13:30

Obviously, this is not enough. In most cases, you will have to add extra fields to the accounting table to make it useful, such as the caller and callee identities. To add these fields, you have to extend the database schema to include the new columns and add the additional information with the `db_extra` parameter, as shown here:

```
modparam("acc", "db_extra", "caller_id=$fu; callee_id=$tu")
```

Multi-leg accounting

Operations such as call transfer and call forward can affect accounting. To solve this problem, there is support for multi-leg accounting. Let's suppose that you have a call from A to B and this call is forwarded to C. In normal accounting, the call would be accounted from A to C only, while the right way to do it would be to account two legs, the first one from A to B and the second one from B to C. Multi-leg accounting uses the stack nature of the AVPs (AVPs can have more than one value.) to produce two rows in a database from a single call. To produce multi-leg accounting, perform the following steps:

1. Define the AVPs carrying the multi-leg information. If these fields exist in the parameter, db_extra, you have to move them to the multi_leg_info parameter:

```
modparam("acc", "multi_leg_info",
  "leg_src=$avp(src);leg_dst=$avp(dst)")
```

2. In the initial request, set the AVPs, src and dst, to the username in the From URI and request URI, respectively:

```
$avp(src)=$fU; #Set the first value of the AVP src to A
$avp(dst)=$rU; #Set the first value of the AVP dst to B
```

3. In the call forward section, again set the AVPs:

```
if(avp_db_load("$ru","$avp(callfwd)")) { #Local callfwd
  info from DB
  $avp(src)=$rU; #Set the second value of the AVP src to B
  $ru = $avp(callfwd);
  $avp(dst)=$rU; #Set the second value of the AVP dst to C
  route(1);
  exit;
}
```

4. Check the database and see the multi-leg records in inverse order:

id	method	from_tag	to_tag	sip_code	sip_reason	time	leg_src	leg_dst
1	INVITE	5d09d4	27095	200	OK	2008-04-07 09:13	B	C
2	INVITE	5d09d4	27095	200	OK	2008-04-07 09:13	A	B
3	BYE	5d09d4	27095	200	OK	2008-04-07 09:13		

Lab - accounting using MySQL

In this lab, we will enhance the accounting by adding two extra fields, as shown in the following steps:

1. Add the following fields to the acc table:

```
mysql  -u root
USE OPENSIPS;
ALTER TABLE 'acc' ADD 'caller_id' CHAR( 64 ) NOT NULL ;
ALTER TABLE 'acc' ADD 'callee_id' CHAR( 64 ) NOT NULL ;
```

2. Make the highlighted changes to the script:

```
#### ACCounting module
loadmodule "acc.so"
/* what special events should be accounted ? */
modparam("acc", "early_media", 0)
modparam("acc", "report_cancels", 0)
/* by default we do not adjust the direction of the
   sequential requests.
modparam("acc", "detect_direction", 0)
    if you enable this parameter, be sure to enable
   "append_fromtag"
    in "rr" module */
modparam("acc", "failed_transaction_flag", "ACC_FAILED")
/* account triggers (flags) */
modparam("acc", "log_flag", "ACC_DO")
modparam("acc", "log_missed_flag", "ACC_MISSED")
modparam("acc", "db_flag", "ACC_DO")
modparam("acc", "db_missed_flag", "ACC_MISSED")
modparam("acc",      "db_url",
   "mysql://opensips:opensipsrw@localhost/opensips")
modparam("acc", "db_extra", "caller_id=$fu;
   callee_id=$tu")#Extra Data

# account only INVITEs
if (is_method("INVITE")) {
   setflag(ACC_DO); # Do accounting
   setflag(ACC_FAILED); # Account failed transactions
}

if (is_method("BYE")) {
   setflag(ACC_DO); # do accounting ...
   setflag(ACC_FAILED); # ... even if the transaction fails
}
```

3. Make a call between two available SIP devices.

4. Verify the accounting table using the MySQL command-line interface:

```
#mysql -u root
mysql>use opensips
mysql>select * from acc;
```

Using the dialog module to obtain the duration

You can now combine the accounting module with the `dialog` module in order to produce a CDR that is based on the ACC module with the duration, setup time, and created time. Setup time is the difference between the first INVITE and the final reply received. It is very simple to use; all you have to do is create a dialog in the initial request and mark the transaction with `cdr_flag` defined as a module parameter:

```
modparam("acc", "cdr_flag", "CDR_FLAG")
```

All the transactions will still be accounted to the acc table. A transaction marked with CDR_FLAG will have three new fields populated, as follows:

```
id: 5
method: INVITE
from_tag: a55b2f4cd4744e18b477471f29ca3166
to_tag: d05e7548
callid: 5bbe0471d97f417891ec2843b316cc60
sip_code: 200
sip_reason: OK
time: 2015-02-14 09:31:07
cdr_id: 0
duration: 22
setuptime: 5
created: 2015-02-14 09:31:02
caller_id: sip:1000@opensips.org
callee_id: sip:1001@opensips.org
```

When you get the duration directly in the INVITE record, you can choose not to account BYEs, but for now, I still recommend it, mainly to discover the source of a disconnection. Another risk for dialog accounting is a power failure or computer freeze. You can potentially lose all CDRs for current calls in such events.

Call end reason

The `dialog` module now exports the pseudo-variable, `$DLG_end_reason`, as a reason for disconnection. The reasons are detailed here:

- **Upstream BYE**: Callee has sent a BYE
- **Downstream BYE**: Caller has sent a BYE
- **Lifetime timeout**: Dialog lifetime expired

- **MI termination**: Dialog ended via the MI interface
- **Ping timeout**: Dialog ended because no reply to in-dialog pings
- **RTP proxy timeout**: Media timeout signaled by RTP proxy

You can safely add this variable to extra accounting as shown here, but it appears only after the BYE request:

```
        id: 10
    method: BYE
  from_tag: 34dcc3cbded54f7b93fc0c3ed3369ed4
    to_tag: 87040d36
    callid: ZjU1ZTQ1ODdjODUxOTFiOGMzNmNmZjQ1ZDQwMjg1YmI.
  sip_code: 200
sip_reason: OK
      time: 2015-02-14 09:45:53
    cdr_id: 0
  duration: 0
 setuptime: 0
   created: NULL
 caller_id: sip:1000@opensips.org
 callee_id: sip:1001@opensips.org
end_reason: Upstream BYE
```

Generating CDRs

To generate CDRs, you will have to track INVITE and BYEs. An INVITE and its respective BYE belong to the same dialog. Thus, they share the same call-id, from-tag, and to-tag. We will use a slightly modified MySQL stored procedure to generate CDRs. A MySQL stored procedure is a script that runs directly from the MySQL database. The procedure for the generation of a CDR for MySQL is displayed here:

```
USE opensips;
ALTER TABLE acc ADD COLUMN cdr_id bigint(11) not null default 0
  AFTER time;
DROP PROCEDURE IF EXISTS 'opensips_cdrs';
DELIMITER //
CREATE PROCEDURE opensips_cdrs()
BEGIN
  DECLARE done INT DEFAULT 0;
  DECLARE bye_record INT DEFAULT 0;
  DECLARE v_callid,v_from_tag, v_to_tag VARCHAR(64);
  DECLARE v_inv_time, v_bye_time DATETIME;
  DECLARE inv_cursor CURSOR FOR SELECT time, callid, from_tag,
    to_tag FROM acc where method='INVITE' and cdr_id='0';
```

```
DECLARE CONTINUE HANDLER FOR SQLSTATE '02000' SET done = 1;
OPEN inv_cursor;
REPEAT
  FETCH inv_cursor INTO v_inv_time, v_callid, v_from_tag,
    v_to_tag;
  IF NOT done THEN
    SET bye_record = 0;
    SELECT 1, time INTO bye_record, v_bye_time FROM acc WHERE
      method='BYE' AND callid=v_callid AND ((from_tag=v_from_tag
      AND to_tag=v_to_tag) OR (from_tag=v_to_tag AND
      to_tag=v_from_tag)) ORDER BY time ASC LIMIT 1;
    IF bye_record = 1 THEN
      INSERT INTO cdrs (call_start_time,duration,sip_call_id,
        sip_from_tag,sip_to_tag,created) VALUES
        (v_inv_time,UNIX_TIMESTAMP(v_bye_time)-
        UNIX_TIMESTAMP(v_inv_time),v_callid,v_from_tag,
        v_to_tag,NOW());
      UPDATE acc SET cdr_id=last_insert_id() WHERE
        callid=v_callid AND ( (from_tag=v_from_tag AND
        to_tag=v_to_tag) OR (from_tag=v_to_tag AND
        to_tag=v_from_tag));
    END IF;
    SET done = 0;
  END IF;
UNTIL done END REPEAT;
END
//
DELIMITER ;
```

We have to insert the script into the database and call it, from time to time, from the CRON daemon.

Lab – generating CDRs

The following steps are to generate the CDR from the accounting records:

1. Install the CDR table schema:

   ```
   cd /var/www/opensips-cp/config/tools/system/cdrviewer
   mysql -D opensips -p < cdrs.sql
   mysql -u root -p
   mysql> use opensips
   ```

2. Edit the `cron_job/generate-cdrs.sh` file and change the MySQL connection data (hostname, username, password, and database):

```
cd /var/www/opensips-cp/cron-job
vi generate_cdrs_mysql.sh
```

3. To generate the CDRs regularly, insert the shell script in crontab. Edit the `/etc/crontab` file and add the following line for a three-minute interval:

```
Vi /etc/crontab
*/3 * * * * root /var/www/opensips-cp/cron_job/
   generate_cdrs_mysql.sh
#The line above is a single line
```

4. Execute the CDR generation stored procedure:

```
/var/www/opensips-cp/cron-job/generate-cdrs.sh
```

5. Go to the OpenSIPS control panel and check `cdrviewer`. You should see the following image:

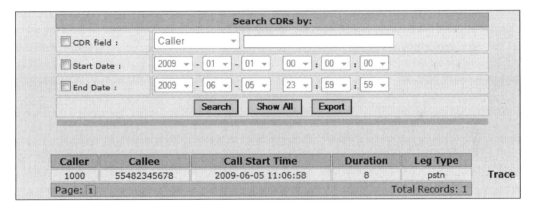

Caller	Callee	Call Start Time	Duration	Leg Type	
1000	55482345678	2009-06-05 11:06:58	8	pstn	Trace

Page: 1 Total Records: 1

CDRviewer and extra accounting

By default, OpenSIPS-CP uses a stored procedure that does not include `caller_id`. You have to follow a few additional steps to have the source and destination in your CDRs:

1. Modify the stored procedure call to include `caller_id` and `callee_id`. This script is provided in the companion files as `opensips_cdrs_btso.sql`:

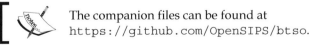

The companion files can be found at `https://github.com/OpenSIPS/btso`.

```
USE opensips ;
ALTER TABLE acc ADD COLUMN cdr_id bigint(11) not null
  default 0 AFTER time;
DROP PROCEDURE IF EXISTS 'opensips_cdrs' ;
DELIMITER //
CREATE PROCEDURE opensips_cdrs()
BEGIN
  DECLARE done INT DEFAULT 0;
  DECLARE bye_record INT DEFAULT 0;
  DECLARE v_callid,v_from_tag, v_to_tag VARCHAR(64);
  DECLARE v_inv_time, v_bye_time DATETIME;
  DECLARE v_callee_id,v_caller_id VARCHAR(128);
  DECLARE inv_cursor CURSOR FOR SELECT time, callid,
    from_tag, to_tag,caller_id,callee_id FROM acc where
    method='INVITE' and cdr_id='0';
  DECLARE CONTINUE HANDLER FOR SQLSTATE '02000' SET done =
    1;
  OPEN inv_cursor;
  REPEAT
    FETCH inv_cursor INTO v_inv_time, v_callid, v_from_tag,
      v_to_tag,v_callee_id,v_caller_id;
    IF NOT done THEN
      SET bye_record = 0;
      SELECT 1, time INTO bye_record, v_bye_time FROM acc
        WHERE method='BYE' AND callid=v_callid AND
        ((from_tag=v_from_tag AND to_tag=v_to_tag) OR
        (from_tag=v_to_tag AND to_tag=v_from_tag)) ORDER BY
        time ASC LIMIT 1;
      IF bye_record = 1 THEN
        INSERT INTO cdrs (call_start_time,duration,
          sip_call_id,sip_from_tag,sip_to_tag,created,
          caller_id,callee_id) VALUES
          (v_inv_time,UNIX_TIMESTAMP(v_bye_time)-
          UNIX_TIMESTAMP(v_inv_time),v_callid,v_from_tag,
          v_to_tag,NOW(),v_caller_id,v_callee_id);
        UPDATE acc SET cdr_id=last_insert_id() WHERE
          callid=v_callid AND ( (from_tag=v_from_tag AND
          to_tag=v_to_tag) OR (from_tag=v_to_tag AND
          to_tag=v_from_tag));
      END IF;
      SET done = 0;
    END IF;
  UNTIL done END REPEAT;
END
//
DELIMITER ;
```

2. Add the `caller_id` and `callee_id` columns to the CDR's database:

```
alter table cdrs add column caller_id varchar(128);
alter table cdrs add column callee_id varchar(128);
```

3. Run the script:

```
/var/www/opensips-cp/cron-job/generate-cdrs.sh
```

4. Add the new columns to the `cdrviewer` module. Edit the file:

```
vi /var/www/opensips-cp/config/tools/
   system/cdrviewer/local.inc.php
```

   Add the new fields to the **fields to show** section:

```
// what fields to show
$show_field[0]['sip_call_id'] = "Sip Call ID" ;
//$show_field[1]['sip_from_tag'] = "Sip From Tag" ;
//$show_field[2]['sip_to_tag'] = "Sip To Tag";
$show_field[1]['call_start_time'] = "Call Start Time";
$show_field[2]['duration'] = "Duration";
$show_field[3]['caller_id'] = "Caller_ID";
$show_field[4]['callee_id'] = "Callee_ID";
```

5. Check `cdrviewer` on the OpenSIPS-CP:

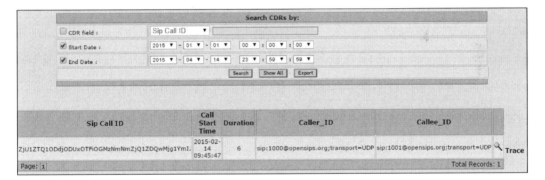

Accounting using RADIUS

Remote Authentication Dial-in User Service (RADIUS) is a kind of an AAA service. Providers often use it for AAA. You can implement a RADIUS server using the open source package called FreeRADIUS. There are other RADIUS packages licensed open-source and commercial.

RADIUS was defined primarily in two RFCs:

- **RFC 2865**: Authentication
- **RFC 2866**: Accounting

In this chapter, we will use RADIUS only for the accounting. MySQL will be used for authentication.

Lab – accounting using a FreeRADIUS server

The installation of the FreeRADIUS server is unquestionably a challenge. Several steps have to be strictly followed in order to have a working configuration. To do this, we will divide the installation into the following steps:

- Installing packages and dependencies
- Installing FreeRADIUS and radius Client
- Configuring OpenSIPS

Package and dependencies

To install the RADIUS components, we need to install some libraries and software packages:

1. For FreeRADIUS, install the following packages:

   ```
   apt-get install freeradius libradiusclient-ng2
     libradiusclient-ng-dev
   ```

2. Compile OpenSIPS to use RADIUS.

3. Go to the source code and run the configuration command, `make menuconfig` in `/usr/src/opensips_21`:

   Select **Configure Compile Options | Configure Excluded Modules | aaa_radius**:

4. Compile and install using the menu.

FreeRADIUS client and server configuration

Now, let's configure the RADIUS client and server:

1. Configure both the client and server to share the same secret.

    In the RADIUS protocol architecture, you have to define the devices that will send the authentication and accounting packets to the RADIUS server. Usually, these devices are remote access gateways, 802.1X switches, and access points. In our case, the RADIUS client is the SIP proxy server that will be sending the account requests.

2. Edit the `clients.conf` file in the FreeRADIUS configuration directory:

    ```
    vi /etc/freeradius/clients.conf
    ```

    Add the following:

    ```
    client 127.0.0.1 {
            secret=opensips
            shortname=OpenSIPS
            nastype=other
    }
    ```

3. Edit the servers in the RADIUS client:

    ```
    vi /etc/radiusclient-ng/servers
    ```

    Add the following:

    ```
    #Server Name or Client/Server pair          Key
    127.0.0.1                                    opensips
    ```

4. Copy the dictionary to the FreeRADIUS shared files and configure it for both the client and server:

    ```
    cd /etc/opensips
    cp dictionary.opensips
      /usr/share/freeradius/dictionary.opensips
    chmod -R 664 /usr/local/etc/opensips/
    cd /usr/share/freeradius/dictionary

    vi dictionary

    $INCLUDE        /usr/share/freeradius/dictionary.openser
    $INCLUDE        /etc/opensips/dictionary.opensips
    ```

Be sure to add the include lines to the end of the file.

```
cd /etc/opensips
cp dictionary.opensips /etc/radiusclient-ng/
   dictionary.opensips


vi /etc/radiusclient-ng/dictionary
$INCLUDE          /usr/share/freeradius/dictionary.openser
$INCLUDE          /etc/opensips/dictionary.opensips
```

 Be sure to add the include lines to the end of the file.

5. Adjust the file permissions. FreeRADIUS needs access to the `dictionary.opensips` file. Use the following command to allow access:

```
chmod 655 /etc/opensips/dictionary.opensips
   chmod 655 /etc/radiusclient-ng -R
   touch /var/run/radius.seq
   chmod 777 /var/run/radius.seq
```

6. Restart the FreeRADIUS server:

```
/etc/init.d/freeradius restart
```

 Warning: Sometimes, it is tricky to edit the FreeRADIUS configuration files. For your convenience, I have copied all the edited files (`radiusd.conf` and `clients.conf`) and servers for this section to the files companion. The opensips configuration file for the tests were copied with the name, `opensips_radius.cfg`.

Configuring the OpenSIPS server

Now, let's configure the OpenSIPS server to send the accounting to the FreeRADIUS database:

1. Add the following lines to the system in the proper places:

```
#--- Modules Loading
loadmodule "aaa_radius.so" # Load the Radius Base API

# --- Modules Parameters
modparam("acc", "aaa_url",
   "radius:/etc/radiusclient-ng/radiusclient.conf")
   # Point the configuration file
modparam("acc", "aaa_extra",
   "Calling-Station-Id=$fU;Called-Station-Id=$rU")
   # Add extra data
modparam("acc", "aaa_flag", "ACC_DO")
   #Use the same flag for Radius
modparam("acc", "service_type", 15)
   # Set the service_type to 15

# ----- radius params ----
modparam("aaa_radius", "radius_config",
   "/etc/radiusclient-ng/radiusclient.conf")
```

2. Restart OpenSIPS and FreeRADIUS.

3. Make some calls.

4. Check for the RADIUS accounting in the `/var/log/freeradius/ radacct/127.0.0.1` directory.

You should see the following image:

```
root@bookosips:/var/log/freeradius/radacct/127.0.0.1# cat detail-20151012
Mon Oct 12 18:23:00 2015
        Acct-Status-Type = Start
        Service-Type = Sip-Session
        Sip-Response-Code = 200
        Sip-Method = INVITE
        Event-Timestamp = "Oct 12 2015 18:23:00 EDT"
        Sip-From-Tag = "d163ec0e"
        Sip-To-Tag = "ff98650a"
        Acct-Session-Id = "JTKhsQ-P_DfPvMv1bftMFA.."
        Calling-Station-Id = "1001"
        Called-Station-Id = "1000"
        NAS-Port = 5060
        Acct-Delay-Time = 0
        NAS-IP-Address = 127.0.0.1
        Acct-Unique-Session-Id = "18c95fffdb171470"
        Timestamp = 1444688580

Mon Oct 12 18:23:04 2015
        Acct-Status-Type = Stop
        Service-Type = Sip-Session
        Sip-Response-Code = 200
        Sip-Method = BYE
        Event-Timestamp = "Oct 12 2015 18:23:04 EDT"
        Sip-From-Tag = "ff98650a"
        Sip-To-Tag = "d163ec0e"
        Acct-Session-Id = "JTKhsQ-P_DfPvMv1bftMFA.."
        Calling-Station-Id = "1000"
        Called-Station-Id = "1001"
        NAS-Port = 5060
        Acct-Delay-Time = 0
        NAS-IP-Address = 127.0.0.1
        Acct-Unique-Session-Id = "18c95fffdb171470"
        Timestamp = 1444688584
```

Missing BYEs and CDRs

One of the biggest issues with SIP accounting is the occurrence of missing BYEs. If one leg of a call is abruptly disconnected from the network, the BYE request is not generated. In this case, it is not possible to receive the BYE message and determine the duration of the call correctly. There are some approaches to solve this issue:

- **The SIP session timers**

  The SIP session timers, described in RFC 4028, enhance the SIP protocol by adding the capability to refresh the SIP sessions by resending periodic re-INVITEs or UPDATEs. To implement SIP session timers, it is necessary to have support on at least one of the SIP endpoints, the client, or the gateway. The advantage of this method is that it uses only signaling without any control of the media. In the *Chapter 8, Managing Dialogs*, we have already discussed the setup of the **SIP Session Timers (SST)**.

- **The RTP proxy timeout**

  Recently, a timeout socket was included in the RTP proxy. You can use an external program connected to this socket to catch the timeout events and fix the accounting. You will also need to force the media for billable calls through the RTP proxy. The main disadvantage is the overhead caused by forcing all the connections through the RTP proxy. The main advantage is the complete control over the solution. To activate the RTP proxy timeout notification, you have to enable it on OpenSIPS and the RTP proxy daemon as follows:

  1. Enable the `rtpproxy` notification on OpenSIPS:

     ```
     modparam("rtpproxy", "rtpp_notify_socket",
       "tcp:127.0.0.1:7891")
     ```

  2. Add the following line to the options for the `rtpproxy` daemon (/`etc/default/rtpproxy`, usually):

     ```
     -n tcp 127.0.0.1:7891
     ```

> OpenSIPS only accepts notifications from the `rtpproxy` servers listed in the `rtpproxy_sock` module parameter or the `rtpproxy_sockets` table.

- **In-dialog pinging**

  In-dialog pinging is one of the simplest methods. It is activated when you create a dialog with the parameter p or P to ping the gateway or client, respectively. An in-dialog ping depends on the answer of the UAC or UAS. Most IP phones and ATAs answer the in-dialog OPTIONS correctly. However, there are some platforms that either do not respond at all or respond to everything with 200 OK without checking the state of the dialog. So, if you are going to use this method, check whether the UAC or UAS responds correctly to the in-dialog OPTIONS request.

Summary

In this chapter, you learned how to implement one of the most sensitive components of a VoIP provider: the accounting. The first step is to choose a backend. Databases are the primary choice, but if you want to have redundancy and encryption, RADIUS can be an option. Remember that it can be tricky to add all the extra attributes to RADIUS. In the end, the records will finish in a database. Make sure that you use at least one method to handle missing BYEs. For residential implementations, an in-dialog ping makes sense. For wholesale, the SIP session timers and a media timeout are more appropriate. You can use OpenSIPS-CP to view CDRs, but in this case, only MySQL and PostgreSQL are supported.

10
SIP NAT Traversal

NAT, also known as **Network Address Translation**, was the solution found to solve the shortage of IP version 4 addresses. It uses a small range of IP addresses (in most cases, a single IP address) on the external port of a firewall and a range of private addresses (see RFC 1918) on the internal port of the firewall.

Unfortunately, NAT affects SIP communication because SIP uses IP addresses inside its headers. In this chapter, we will look at some ways to solve the NAT traversal challenge.

In this chapter, we will cover the following topics:

- Explaining why and where NAT breaks SIP communications
- Describing the different types of NAT devices and their implications
- Describing the most common solutions available for NAT traversal
- Implementing a universal solution for OpenSIPS combining STUN and TURN

Port address translation

Routers and firewalls implement NAT by mapping the internal addresses to external addresses using an address-mapping table. Sometimes, people refer to NAT as **PAT (Port Address Translation)**. PAT maintains a mapping table of the `ip:port` pairs. This allows users to navigate the Internet using different UDP or TCP ports and a single address at the same time. You can search for more information in RFC 1631.

RFC 1918 defines the address allocation for private networks. It defines the following blocks as private networks:

- **10.0.0.0**: 10.255.255.255 (10/8 prefix)
- **172.16.0.0**: 172.31.255.255 (172.16/12 prefix)
- **192.168.0.0**: 192.168.255.255 (192.168/16 prefix)

Where does NAT break SIP?

NAT affects SIP because SIP is a session protocol. The translation of the address occurs in the network headers leaving the SIP headers in the session layer untouched. Thus, the server is unable to contact the user using the addresses provided in the SIP headers. The following headers, Contact, Via, Route, and Record-Route are not automatically translated by the NAT device. **Session Description Protocol (SDP)** is also affected. See the points where some layer-3 addresses appear in a SIP request in the following highlighted code:

```
U 189.101.207.211:11266 -> 208.109.122.193:5060
INVITE sip:8580@opensips.org SIP/2.0.
Via: SIP/2.0/UDP 192.168.1.160:11266;
  branch=z9hG4bK-d8754z-1f2cd509;rport.
Max-Fowards: 70.
Contact: <sip:flavio@192.168.1.160:11266>.
To: "8580"<sip:8580@opensips.org>.
From: "flavio"<sip:flavio@opensips.org>;tag=99494a4b.
Call-ID: NmYwNjAzMDE3MTE0YWM5MWIxNjNiMWNjZDY3NjI0MWQ..
CSeq: 1 INVITE.
Allow: INVITE, ACK, CANCEL, OPTIONS, BYE, REFER, NOTIFY, MESSAGE,
  SUBSCRIBE
Content-Type: application/sdp.
User-Agent: MyPhone.
Content-Length: 188.
.
v=0.
o=- 4 2 IN IP4 192.168.1.160.
s=MyPhone.
c=IN IP4 192.168.1.160.
t=0 0.
m=audio 8616 RTP/AVP 0 8 3 101.
a=fmtp:101 0-15.
a=rtpmap:101 telephone-event/8000.
a=sendrecv
```

The routers and firewalls are able to change the address of IP packets. However, they usually don't understand the SIP layer to translate IP addresses described in the SIP headers. Some routers now have a feature called **Application Layer Gateway (ALG)**, which is capable of performing such translations.

How to solve one-way audio problems when ALG is present?

If you are having audio-related issues such as one-way audio, and there is an ALG router/firewall in the path, try to disable the ALG feature (sometimes referred to as a VoIP feature or fixup). The solution presented in this chapter does not require ALG. A good reference on how to disable ALG is available at http://www.voip-info.org/wiki/view/Routers+SIP+ALG.

Before we can discuss mechanisms to traverse NAT, we need to explain the existing types of NAT. Some mechanisms will work only for specific types of NAT.

Types of NAT

The way in which various NAT devices work is different and varies based on the vendor and models. It is not easy to predict the type of NAT before buying. There are four kinds of NAT devices and they are different in the way they map the internal addresses to external addresses:

- Full cone
- Restricted cone
- Port-restricted cone
- Symmetric

We will cover each of these devices in the following sections.

Full cone

Full cone devices use a **static mapping** from the external `ip:port` pair to the internal `ip:port` pair. Any external computer can connect to it using the external `ip:port` pair. This is the case in non-stateful firewalls implemented with the use of filters. The external address is predictable after the first interaction.

A full cone device does not allow incoming packets from a destination that has not received any traffic yet, as shown in the following image:

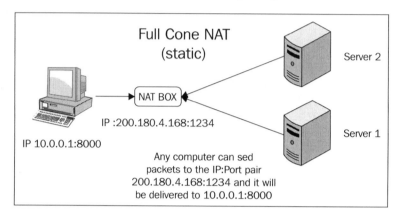

Restricted cone

A restricted cone device is similar to the full cone in the way it maps the addresses. However, it is dynamic and opens the `ip:port` pair when the internal computer sends data outside. It blocks any packets coming from a different address.
A restricted cone device does not allow incoming packets from a destination that has not received any traffic yet, as shown in the following image:

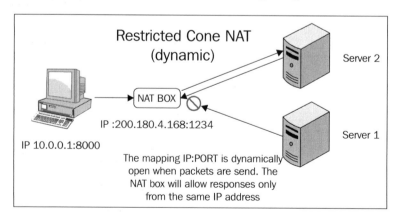

Port-restricted cone

The port-restricted cone firewall is almost identical to the restricted cone. The only difference is that the incoming packet should come from exactly the same `ip:port` pair of the sent packet. The port-restricted cone restricts not only the IP, but also port, as shown in the following image:

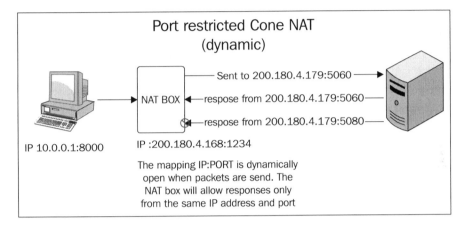

Symmetric

The last type of NAT is the most difficult to traverse and is called symmetric. It creates a new map entry using a different external port for each interaction, while the cone types of NAT always use the same external port for the mappings. It is not possible now to predict the external `ip:port` pair used by the NAT device after the first interaction.

In the following diagram, pay attention to the different public address for each destination. This is the opposite of the previous device types that used the same public address for all destinations:

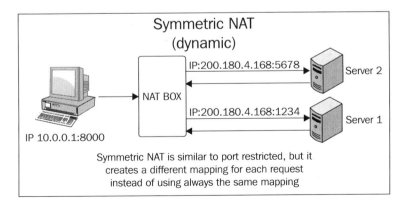

With the other three types of NAT, it was possible to use an external server to discover the external IP address used.

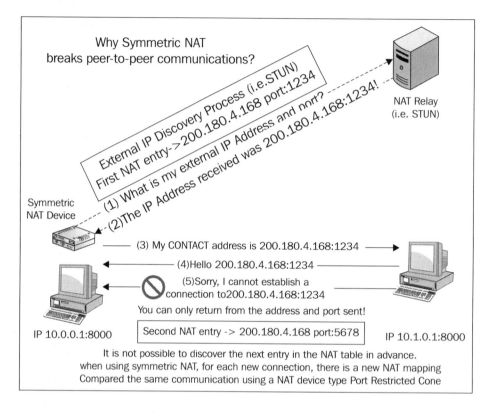

When using symmetric NAT, you can discover the external IP address using a mechanism such as STUN. However, in this case, this discovered address is useless because the NAT device will open a different one in the next interaction.

The NAT firewall table

Here is a summary table of all the NAT types. This table is very useful to understand the differences between the various types of NAT:

NAT types	Need to send data before receiving	It is possible to determine the next IP:port that is open	It restricts packets to the destination IP:port
Full cone	No	Yes	No
Restricted cone	Yes	Yes	Only IP

NAT types	Need to send data before receiving	It is possible to determine the next IP:port that is open	It restricts packets to the destination IP:port
Port-restricted cone	Yes	Yes	Yes
Symmetric	Yes	No	Yes

Solving the SIP NAT traversal challenge

There are many ways to solve the NAT puzzle with many different types of NAT. So, for a beginner, the problem becomes very confusing We will see a table with the following valid methods of solving SIP for the NAT issue:

- **STUN**: Simple traversal of UDP over NAT
- **TURN**: Traversal of UDP over Relay NAT
- **ALG**: Application Layer Gateways
- **MANUAL**: Manual configuration (port forwarding)
- **UPNP**: Universal Plug and Play

Method	STUN	TURN	ALG	MANUAL	UPNP
Symmetric NAT	No	Yes	Yes	Yes	Yes
It requires phone support?	Yes	No	No	No	No
Scalability	Good	Poor	Good	Good	Good
User effort	Small	Small	Small	High	Small
Reliability	Good	Good	Poor	Good	?
Industry support	Good	Good	Average	Good	Poor

Most customers use the NAT device (cable, DSL, or optical fiber) provided by its Internet Service Provider. Thus, for the residential market, we have to deal with whatever the customer has and support all kinds of NAT. For the commercial SIP trunk market, you will be able to choose the device in many cases.

The simplest and most scalable solution for NAT is STUN. However, STUN does not work over symmetric NAT. In this case, we can use the universal solution called TURN. A combination of STUN and TURN can solve 99% of the NAT cases affordably and with good scalability.

A solution proposed for the NAT issue

The solution proposed in this book is as follows:

- Let as many phones as possible use STUN for scalability
- Detect the cases where NAT can't be solved autonomously
- When a hard NAT is detected, use a media relay server

Thus, we can have the best of both worlds: scalability of STUN and support for any kind of device.

For the SIP trunk market, we strongly encourage you to disable ALG when possible. There are many corporate firewalls with some kind of VoIP support (ALG). It is tricky to find the configuration sometimes referred to as fixup, VoIP, and other names. Check the documentation of your firewall to disable these features.

The solution's topology

There are two ways to build the NAT solution. You can build it on the proxy routing script or in an external proxy via a specialized **Session Border Controller (SBC)**.

The following are the features of the main proxy:

- **Pros(+)**: Compact solution
- **Pros(+)**: Efficient and scalable in terms of load
- **Cons(-)**: Increases the complexity of the script

The following are the features of the SBC:

- Detaches the NAT logic and simplifies the proxy script
- Suitable for geographic distribution
- Introduces some overhead as extra hops and headers
- Not so efficient as data becomes redundant between the SBC and proxy

Building the solution

The solution for NAT is a little complex and requires several steps. We will split the solution into three pieces and a few steps for each segment in order to simplify the understanding:

1. Installing STUN
2. Solving the SIP signaling
3. Using a media relay server
4. Engaging a media relay server

Installing STUN

Simple traversal of UDP over NAT, or simply STUN, is the most common method for near-end NAT traversal. The IETF standardized STUN in three RFCs: 3489, 5389, and 7350. STUN is a near-end NAT traversal solution. STUN's biggest advantage is to fix addresses in the client side. Clients using STUN appear to the proxy as a client using a valid IP address. You do not require any extra configuration on the server. On the other hand, STUN does not work with symmetric NAT. The STUN protocol enables IP endpoints behind NAT to discover their external IP addresses, ports, and NAT type. Use STUN to discover if the client is in any of the following situations:

- In an open Internet
- Behind a firewall that blocks UDP
- Behind a NAT device
- What kind of device it is (symmetric, cone, open Internet, or blocked)

STUN handles all the cases in the green boxes in the following image. STUN cannot solve the ones in the red boxes. For symmetric NAT devices, you can use a media relay server:

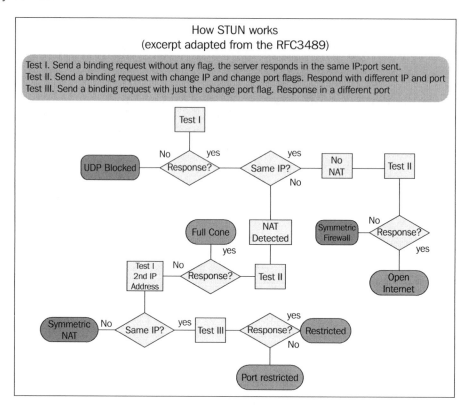

You can implement STUN using OpenSIPS in the same port as the proxy server. You will need two public IP addresses. All you have to do is load the STUN module and set some specific parameters. See the following example:

```
listen=udp:IP1:5060
listen=udp:IP2:5060
loadmodule "stun.so"
# ---- Stun ----
modparam("stun","primary_ip","IP1")
modparam("stun","primary_port","5060")
modparam("stun","alternate_ip","IP2")
modparam("stun","alternate_port","5060")
```

It is possible to test STUN without configuring a server. Simply use a public STUN server. Usually, IP phone vendors keep a public STUN server; you can check with your vendor.

If you use STUN in the client side, you do not need to make any changes in the `opensips.cfg` script. It will work as it is directly connected to the Internet.

Why STUN does not work with symmetric NAT devices

The main characteristic of a symmetric NAT device is to create a new mapping for each external device that is contacted. So, if you contact the STUN device, it will inform you about the `ip:port` pair from whom it has been contacted. Unfortunately, this `ip:port` pair informed won't be the next mapping created for any other device, so this information is useless. In the first three kinds of NAT devices (full cone, restricted cone, and port-restricted), the mapping created for one device is exactly the same as the others as it reuses the same external `ip:port` for all the mappings.

Solving SIP signaling

The first part of the puzzle is to solve SIP signaling. The solution requires the following steps:

1. Implementing NAT detection.
2. Solving the Via header using rport.
3. Fixing the Contact header for initial requests and replies
4. Handling REGISTER requests for devices behind NAT
5. Pinging the client to keep the NAT mapping open
6. Handling sequential requests

Implementing NAT detection

We will use the `nat_uac_test()` function from the `nathelper` module to detect if the client is behind NAT. This function has some flags described here. You can combine flags adding the values:

- `1` - Search the Contact header for the RFC 1918 addresses.
- `2` - Test received parameter in Via whether it is different from the source address.
- `4` - Top most Via is searched for occurrence of RFC1918 / RFC6598 addresses
- `8` - Search for occurrence of RFC1918 / RFC6598 addresses in the SDP header
- `16` - Test whether the source port is different from the port in Via

- 32 - Compare the address in Contact against the source IP address of signaling
- 64 - Compare the Port in Contact against source port of signaling

All flags can be combined bit per bit, the test returns true if any of the tests succeed.

Consider the following example for clarity:

If you select 18 as the parameter, it is the combination of the tests 16+2. The function will return true if any individual test returns true (The OR logic).

Solving the Via header using rport

The process to solve the Via header is described in RFC 3581 and is implemented transparently in the SIP proxy itself. The only thing that you need to do is eventually force rport in the initial request to fix clients without rport support. The proxy verifies the existence of the field and includes the received= and rport= fields using the address from the interface where it received the request. Now it is easy to forward responses to SIP devices.

Fixing the Contact header for requests and replies

It is very easy to confuse the Via headers with the Contact headers. The difference is simple: SIP uses the Via headers to handle replies such as 183 and 200 and Contact headers for sequential requests such as BYEs and UPDATEs. If you do not fix the Contact headers properly, you will have problems with calls not disconnecting. The fix_nated_contact() function fixes the address of the Contact header with the request's address. It is very simple and important. We will also need to fix the Contact header for all the temporary and final replies (183 and 200)

Handling the REGISTER requests and pings

The NAT detection process is good when the caller is behind NAT. Let's assume that the source of a call is not behind NAT and the destination is. How do we detect NAT for the destination? Actually, the best way to do it is detect when the client is registering itself. We will mark this specific registration with a transaction flag. When the user receives a call, we recover this flag in the process of the lookup. We will also include the ping process for each client registered in order to keep the dynamic NAT mappings open in the UAC. For the pings, you can use the dummy UDP ping or SIP ping using OPTIONS. Personally, I always use the SIP ping because it is more reliable. We will describe the SIP ping process here. The following is a sample code on how to implement and set the inter-communication parameters for modules registrar and nathelper:

```
#### USeR LOCation module
loadmodule "usrloc.so"
```

```
modparam("usrloc", "nat_bflag", "NAT_FLAG")

#### REGISTRAR module
loadmodule "registrar.so"
modparam("registrar", "tcp_persistent_flag", "TCP_PERSISTENT")
modparam("registrar", "received_avp", "$avp(received_nh)")

####   NAT modules
loadmodule "nathelper.so"
modparam("nathelper", "natping_interval", 10)
modparam("nathelper", "ping_nated_only", 1)
modparam("nathelper", "received_avp", "$avp(received_nh)")
modparam("nathelper", "sipping_from", "sip:pinger@opensips.org")
modparam("nathelper", "natping_interval", 30)
modparam("nathelper", "sipping_bflag", "SIP_PING_FLAG") #OPTIONS
   ping
```

Detect the clients behind NAT and fix the Contact header on REGISTER and the other requests:

```
## NAT Detection
#
force_rport();
if (nat_uac_test("19")) {
  if (method=="REGISTER")is_method() {
    fix_nated_register();
    setbflag(NAT_FLAG);
    setbflag(SIP_PING_FLAG);
  } else {
    fix_nated_contact();
    setflag(NAT_FLAG);
  };
};
```

In the preceding code, we force `rport` for all the requests. After testing the request using the `nat_uac_test()` function, we fix the Contact using `fix_nated_register()` for the REGISTER requests and save the correct address in the location table. The `fix_nated_register()` function will create a new URI with the source IP + port + protocol in an AVP (in our case, `received_avp`, `avp(nat)`). The system appends the URI with the `received` parameter in the Contact header field and stores it in the user location table. To check whether it is working properly, verify that you have the external address of your client stored in the user location table. The `fix_nated_contact()` function simply rewrites the Contact header field to contain the request's source `ip:port`.

Mark contacts behind NAT using the flag defined in the `nat_bflag` parameter of the `usrloc` module. Set the defined flag before saving the location of the UAC. The `NAT_FLAG` flag will be saved to the user location table and recovered when you use the `lookup("location")` function. In the future, this will help you discover if the destination called is behind NAT. Here, we will use a `branch` flag to support multiple registrations from a subscriber with Contacts behind NAT. We will also set `SIP_PING_FLAG` to mark the clients for the SIP ping process.

Handling the responses

The 183 Session Progress and 200 OK reply messages returned from the UAC will also require manipulation. Thus, a NAT handling code must be included in the `onreply_route[]` section:

```
onreply_route[RELAY] {
   if ((isflagset(NAT_FLAG) || isbflagset(NAT_FLAG)) &&
      status=~"(183)|(2[0-9][0-9])"){
      ENGAGE_MEDIA_RELAY (Check the documentation of your MRS)
   }

#---- If the CALLEE is behind NAT, fix the CONTACT HF ----#
   if (isbflagset(NAT_FLAG)) {
      #--    Insert nat=yes at the end of the Contact header   --#
      #--                This helps with REINVITEs,            --#
      #- nat=yes will be included in the R-URI for seq.requests-#
      search_append('Contact:.*sip:[^>[:cntrl:]]*', ';nat=yes');
      fix_nated_contact();
   }
   exit;
}
```

If the NAT flag or the branch flag NAT are set, in other words, if the caller or callee are behind NAT and the status of the request is 183 or 200, we have to force the usage of a media relay server and fix the Contact header.

Handling sequential requests

During a call, the proxy may receive sequential requests such as re-INVITEs, UPDATEs, and BYEs.

For sequential requests, we have to again fix the Contact header. For sequential requests, we follow the Route headers instead of relying on registrations. In other words, there is no way to know if the destination is behind NAT.

To solve this problem, there are a few approaches. The first one is to insert a parameter in the Contact header. Any URI parameter in the Contact header should be included in sequential requests. See the following example, where this string will be added to the Contact header of the initial request:

```
#--- Insert nat=yes at the end of the Contact header      ----#
#----               This helps with REINVITEs,            ----#
#- nat=yes will be included in the R-URI for sequential requests -
   #
search_append('Contact:.*sip:[^>[:cntrl:]]*', ';nat=yes');
```

The sequential request URI should include any parameter sent previously in the Contact header. In the preceding line, we are appending the nat=yes parameter to the Contact header. Now, in sequential requests, we have this parameter in the Request-URI. In the following example, we will check the presence of the nat=yes string in the Request-URI. If found, it indicates the presence of NAT and should be handled properly:

```
#----          This is used to Process REINVITES          ----#
if (subst_uri('/(sip:.*);nat=yes/\1/')){
   setbflag(NAT_FLAG);
};
```

Unfortunately, not all gateways behave properly in including the parameters in the Request-URI. We got a few cases in the field where the re-INVITEs were not handled properly because the gateway or SBC were not including the parameter inserted in the Contact header. There are two alternatives: the first one is to include the parameter in Record-Route or set a dialog flag for NAT requests and not depend whatsoever on the external components. The following is an example on how to insert the Record_Route parameter:

```
if (isflagset(NAT_FLAG) || isbflagset(NAT_FLAG)) {
   add_rr_param(";nat=yes");
}
```

To check the parameter in sequential requests after the loose_route() command, you can use the following command:

```
if (check_route_param("nat=yes")) setflag(NAT_FLAG);
```

The last method is the one that I am currently using. If you have created a dialog before processing the call, set a dialog flag as follows:

```
if (isflagset(NAT_FLAG) || isbflagset(NAT_FLAG)) {
   set_dlg_flag(NAT_FLAG);
}
```

In the sequential request, after the `loose_route()` command, you can check the setting with the following command:

```
if (is_dlg_flag_set("5")) setflag(NAT_FLAG);
```

The advantage of the last method is not depending on any other component to send back the mark. The disadvantage is requiring the `dialog` module and the small extra overhead associated.

Using a media relay server

Now that we have solved the SIP signaling, it is time to solve the RTP issue. A prerequisite for this solution is to have symmetric UACs. Do not get confused, here we are not talking about the NAT device but the UAC phone or softphone. Symmetric for a UAC means to send and receive in the same UDP port for both SIP (5060) and RTP (usually, in the range of 10000 to 20000). Most UACs, as of today, are symmetric, so do not worry about this. One notorious exception is the Cisco gateway based on the iOS.

There are three popular media relay servers in use with OpenSIPS:

- **RTPProxy**: From Sippy software (http://www.rtpproxy.org/)
- **MediaProxy**: From AG-projects (http://www.ag-projects.com/MediaProxy.html)
- **RTPEngine**: From SipWise (https://github.com/sipwise/rtpengine)

As a SIP proxy project, we should not take sides. You should evaluate which media relay server fits best for your purposes. Check the documentation of your media relay server on how to install the daemon and integrate it with OpenSIPS. From now on, we will refer to this service as simply **media relay server** (**MRS**).

Solving the traversal of the RTP packets

For those cases where the UAC is behind a symmetric NAT device, we need to employ an MRS to bridge the RTP traffic. RTP uses dynamic UDP ports described in the SDP. A symmetric NAT device creates a new mapping for each destination. Thus, it is not possible for a UAC to inform a UAS about the correct UDP port from whom it received the RTP packet in order to send the response. The solution for this problem is to send both RTP sessions directly to a device called MRS with a known IP address and port, and bridge the RTP flow in this box, as shown in the following image:

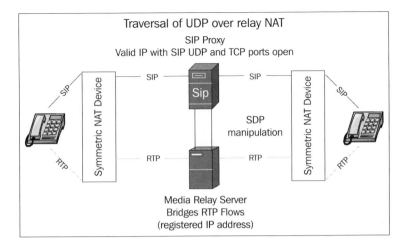

The MRS bridges the media flows coming from the UAC to the UAS. It is one of the few solutions for a symmetric NAT. For the OpenSIPS script, you will have to call an procedure to activate the MRS in the initial and sequential requests. Check the documentation of your MRS.

Understanding the solution flow

Here, we will describe the solution request by request and instruction by instruction. Pay attention to the request number and the corresponding process on the script.

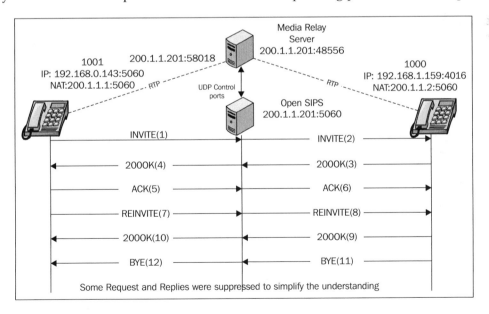

Note the following request and reply numbers. We will show the relevant requests only. Pay special attention to the IP present on the headers, Via, Contact, and the `c=` line of the SDP header. These are the fields modified by the NAT algorithms. Check the Contact header of the INVITE relayed (2) for the presence of `nat=yes` in the Contact header as well. In the ACK, pay close attention to the `nat=yes` parameter, now in the Request-URI. ACK is a sequential request and includes the parameter. We will fix the Contact header based on this information.

(1) First INVITE

This is the first INVITE of the preceding figure:

```
U 200.1.1.1:63493 ->200.1.1.201:5060
INVITE sip:1000@200.1.1.201 SIP/2.0.
Date: Tue, 15 Sep 2009 16:44:08 GMT.
CSeq: 1 INVITE.
Via: SIP/2.0/UDP 192.168.0.143:5060;
   branch=z9hG4bKb224e5a7-8a33-;rport.
User-Agent: UAC
From: "Flavio" <sip:1001@200.1.1.201>;
   tag=8a9ae2a7-8a33-000c29254d97.
Call-ID: 1894e2a7-84a0-de11-8a33-000c29254d97@debian.
To: <sip:1000@200.1.1.201>.
Contact: <sip:1001@192.168.0.143:5060;transport=udp>.
Allow: INVITE,ACK,OPTIONS,BYE,CANCEL,NOTIFY,REFER,MESSAGE.
Content-Type: application/sdp.
Content-Length: 389.
Max-Forwards: 70.
v=0.
o=- 1253033048 1253033048 IN IP4 192.168.0.143.
c=IN IP4 192.168.0.143.
t=0 0.
m=audio 5016 RTP/AVP 96 3 107 110 0 8 101.
a=rtpmap:96 SPEEX/16000.
a=rtpmap:101 telephone-event/8000.
a=fmtp:101 0-15.
```

Once the first INVITE arrives, we will detect if it is behind NAT. It does not have the To tag, so it is an initial request using the following code:

```
force_rport();
if (nat_uac_test("19")) {
  if (method=="REGISTER") {
    fix_nated_register();
  } else {
    fix_nated_contact();
  };
  setflag(NAT_FLAG);
};
```

Additionally, for the first INVITE, note the following:

```
route[RELAY] {
  ##If the request has the parameter nat=yes, insert previously
    set ## the UAC as behind NAT. This is for REINVITES or UPDATES
  if (subst_uri('/(sip:.*);nat=yes/\1/')){
    setbflag(NAT_FLAG);
  };
  ##If the UAC or UAC is behind NAT route to the media relay
  if (isflagset(NAT_FLAG)||isbflagset(NAT_FLAG)) {
    route(MEDIARELAY);
  };

  ## Use to Contact header to insert a mark in the request
  ## Later we are going to use this mark on REINVITEs and UPDATEs
  if (isflagset(NAT_FLAG)){
    search_append('Contact:.*sip:[^>[:cntrl:]]*', ';nat=yes');
  }..

route[MEDIARELAY] {
  if (is_method("BYE|CANCEL")) {
    #UNENGAGE_MEDIA_RELAY; #(Please check the documentation of your
      MRS for the exact command and syntax)
  } else if (is_method("INVITE")){
    #ENGAGE_MEDIA_RELAY; #(Please check the documentation of your
      #MRS for the exact command and syntax)
    t_on_failure("1");
  };
}
```

(2) INVITE relayed by the server

The following is the request after it is relayed by the SIP proxy:

```
U 200.1.1.201:5060 -> 200.1.1.2:5060
INVITE sip:1000@200.1.1.2 SIP/2.0.
Date: Tue, 15 Sep 2009 16:44:08 GMT.
CSeq: 2 INVITE.
Via: SIP/2.0/UDP 200.1.1.1:5060;branch=z9hG4bK64d3e8a7-8a33;rport.
User-Agent: UAC.
From: "flavio" <sip:1001@200.1.1.201>;
  tag=8a9ae2a7-8a33-000c29254d97.
Call-ID: 1894e2a7-84a0-de11-8a33-000c29254d97@debian.
To: <sip:1000@200.1.1.201>.
Contact: <sip:1001@200.1.1.1:5060;transport=udp>
Allow: INVITE,ACK,OPTIONS,BYE,CANCEL,NOTIFY,REFER,MESSAGE.
Content-Type: application/sdp.
Content-Length: 389.
Max-Forwards: 70.
.
v=0.
o=- 1253033048 1253033048 IN IP4 192.168.0.143.
c=IN IP4 200.1.1.201.-> (IP address of the Media Realy Server)
t=0 0.
m=audio 48556 RTP/AVP 96 3 107 110 0 8 101.
a=rtpmap:96 SPEEX/16000.
a=rtpmap:101 telephone-event/8000.
a=fmtp:101 0-15.

a=fmtp:101 0-15.
m=video 38902 RTP/AVP 31.
a=rtpmap:31 H261/90000.
```

(3) Reply 200 OK with SDP

The following code produces the results in the reply (number 4 in the preceding image). Pay attention to the IP addresses in the Contact header, the c= line of the SDP header, and the nat=yes parameter included in the Contact header.

```
onreply_route[RELAY] {
  if ((isflagset(NAT_FLAG) || isbflagset(NAT_FLAG)) &&
    status=~"(183)|(2[0-9][0-9])"){
```

```
        ENGAGE_MEDIA_RELAY (Check the documentation of your MRS)
    }

    #---- If the CALLEE is behind NAT, fix the CONTACT HF ----#
    if (isbflagset(NAT_FLAG)) {
        #--    Insert nat=yes at the end of the Contact header    --#
        #--             This helps with REINVITEs,                --#
        #- nat=yes will be included in the R-URI for seq.requests-#
        search_append('Contact:.*sip:[^>[:cntrl:]]*', ';nat=yes');
        fix_nated_contact();
    }
    exit;
}
```

```
U 200.1.1.2:4106 -> 200.1.1.201:5060
SIP/2.0 200 OK.
Via: SIP/2.0/UDP 192.168.1.159:4106;branch=z9hG4bKcf89.06472571.1.
Via: SIP/2.0/UDP 192.168.0.143:5067;
  received=200.1.1.1;branch=z9hG4bK64d3e8a7-8a33;rport=63493.
Record-Route: <sip:200.1.1.201;lr>.
Contact: <sip:1000@192.168.1.159:4106;rinstance=d22dcb0534217188>.
To: <sip:1000@200.1.1.201>;tag=96694179.
From: "Flavio"<sip:1001@200.1.1.201>;
  tag=8a9ae2a7-8a33-000c29254d97.
Call-ID: 1894e2a7-84a0-de11-8a33-000c29254d97@debian.
CSeq: 2 INVITE.
Allow: INVITE, ACK, CANCEL, OPTIONS, BYE, REFER, NOTIFY, INFO.
Content-Type: application/sdp.
Content-Length: 237.
.
v=0.
o=- 3 2 IN IP4 192.168.1.159
c=IN IP4 192.168.1.159.
t=0 0.
m=audio 51752 RTP/AVP 96 0 8 101.
a=fmtp:101 0-15.
a=rtpmap:96 SPEEX/16000.
a=rtpmap:101 telephone-event/8000.
a=sendrecv.

U 200.1.1.201:5060 -> 200.1.1.1:63493
SIP/2.0 200 OK.
```

```
Via: SIP/2.0/UDP 192.168.0.143:5067;received=200.1.1.1;
   branch=z9hG4bK64d3e8a7-84a0-de11-8a33-000c29254d97;rport=63493.
Record-Route: <sip:200.1.1.201;lr>.
Contact: <sip:1000@200.1.1.2:4106;
   rinstance=d22dcb0534217188;nat=yes>.
To: <sip:1000@200.1.1.201>;tag=96694179.
From: "Flavio"<sip:1001@200.1.1.201>;
   tag=8a9ae2a7-84a0-de11-8a33-000c29254d97.
Call-ID: 1894e2a7-84a0-de11-8a33-000c29254d97@debian.
CSeq: 2 INVITE.
Allow: INVITE, ACK, CANCEL, OPTIONS, BYE, REFER, SUBSCRIBE, INFO.
Content-Type: application/sdp.
Content-Length: 255.
   .
v=0.
o=- 3 2 IN IP4 200.1.1.1.
s=CounterPath X-Lite 3.0.
c=IN IP4 200.1.1.201. -> (IP address of the Media Realy Server)
t=0 0.
m=audio 58018 RTP/AVP 96 0 8 101.
a=fmtp:101 0-15.
a=rtpmap:96 SPEEX/16000.
a=rtpmap:101 telephone-event/8000.
a=sendrecv.
```

Acknowledgements (ACK packets)

For the sequential requests, the following code is triggered. The nat=yes parameter indicates that the callee is behind NAT, so the branch flag NAT is activated again. As the ACK does not have an SDP, it does not need to reactivate the media relay server.

```
#----          This is used to Process REINVITES        ----#
if (subst_uri('/(sip:.*);nat=yes/\1/')){
  setbflag(NAT_FLAG);
};


U 200.1.1.1:63493 -> 200.1.1.201:5060
ACK sip:1000@200.1.1.1:4106;nat=yes;
   rinstance=d22dcb0534217188 SIP/2.0.
Route: <sip:200.1.1.201;lr>.
Via: SIP/2.0/UDP 192.168.0.143:5067;
   branch=z9hG4bK94ce60aa-;rport=63493.
From: "Flavio" <sip:1001@200.1.1.201>;
   tag=8a9ae2a7-84a0-de11-8a33-000c29254d97.
```

Call-ID: 1894e2a7-84a0-de11-8a33-000c29254d97@debian.
To: <sip:1000@200.1.1.201>;tag=96694179.
Contact: <sip:1001@**192.168.0.143**:63493;transport=udp>.
Allow: INVITE,ACK,OPTIONS,BYE,CANCEL,NOTIFY,REFER,MESSAGE.
Content-Length: 0.
Max-Forwards: 69.

...

U 200.1.1.201:5060 -> 200.1.1.1:4106
ACK sip:1000@200.1.1.1:4106;rinstance=d22dcb0534217188 SIP/2.0.
CSeq: 2 ACK.
Via: SIP/2.0/UDP 200.1.1.201;branch=z9hG4bKcf89.06472571.3.
Via: SIP/2.0/UDP 192.168.0.143:5067;received=200.1.1.1;
  branch=z9hG4bK94ce60aa-84a0-de11-8a33-000c29254d97;rport=63493.
From: "Flavio" <sip:1001@200.1.1.201>;
  tag=8a9ae2a7-84a0-de11-8a33-000c29254d97.
Call-ID: 1894e2a7-84a0-de11-8a33-000c29254d97@debian.
To: <sip:1000@200.1.1.201>;tag=96694179.
Contact: <sip:1001@**200.1.1.1**:63493;transport=udp>.
Allow: INVITE,ACK,OPTIONS,BYE,CANCEL,NOTIFY,REFER,MESSAGE.
Content-Length: 0.
Max-Forwards: 69.

U 200.1.1.1:4106 -> 200.1.1.201:5060
BYE sip:1001@200.1.1.1:63493;transport=udp SIP/2.0.
Via: SIP/2.0/UDP 200.1.1.1:4106;branch=z9hG4bK-d87543-
...

U 200.1.1.201:5060 -> 200.1.1.1:63493
BYE sip:1001@200.1.1.1:63493;transport=udp SIP/2.0.
Via: SIP/2.0/UDP 200.1.1.201;branch=z9hG4bKcf89.26472571.0.

U 200.1.1.1:63493 -> 200.1.1.201:5060
SIP/2.0 200 OK.
CSeq: 2 BYE.
...
U 200.1.1.201:5060 -> 200.1.1.1:4106
SIP/2.0 200 OK.
CSeq: 2 BYE.
...

...

Summary

In this chapter, we explained the different NAT types and devices. Then, you learned about the available methods to traverse NAT. After discovering the pros and cons of the different methods, we suggested the use of STUN and detected cases where STUN does not work properly and so switched to the traversal of UDP over Relay NAT. We also saw what algorithms are in use to traverse NAT and its corresponding code. Finally, we published the entire call flow for a call behind a NAT device. In the next chapter, we are going to cover phone features implemented as SIP services.

11
Implementing SIP Services

The usual role of OpenSIPS is a SIP proxy. In this role, a SIP server—in most cases—can only route requests and replies between user agents. In this chapter, we will explain how to implement SIP services such as call forward and call transfer in this type of an environment. This chapter uses the best practices document *RFC 5359*, *Session Initiation Protocol Service Examples*, and assumes that endpoints and gateways support the required RFCs.

One important aspect regarding OpenSIPS is that it does not handle media or RTP. Thus, even simple services such as playing an announcement require an external media server. The most common media servers in use with OpenSIPS are Asterisk™, FreeSWITCH™, and SEMS. In this chapter, you will learn how to implement a series of SIP services integrating OpenSIPS with a media server. We have chosen Asterisk because of its popularity and simplicity.

In this chapter, we will cover the following topics:

- Distinguishing where you should implement SIP services
- Describing the purpose of RFC 5359
- Playing announcements from a media server
- Implementing call forward immediately on busy and no answer
- Integrating a voicemail service
- Implementing call transfer

In this chapter, we are working with the media server, Asterisk. The call forwarding feature will help us understand important concepts such as serial forking and failure routing. You can check your progress in the following figure:

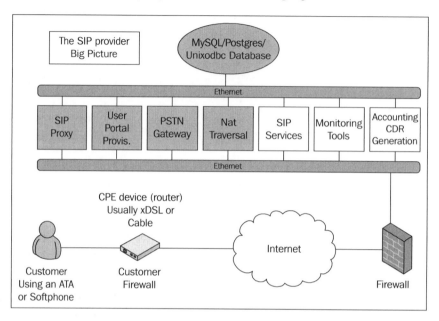

Where to implement SIP services

A SIP proxy is just a component of a voice platform. IP telephony has many services such as call transfer, call pickup, paging, call completion services, and distinctive ringing. A legacy PBX implements all these services in its own firmware and old analog phones were simply dumb terminals. Now, IP phones are intelligent and the SIP server, in most cases, simply relays the requests and replies from endpoints. In other words, to implement the same PBX services that we had in the old analog PBXs, we need full cooperation between phones, proxies, and gateways. As you can see in the following table, there is a straight cooperation between the components to implement a service. It is not possible to implement some services in SIP without support from all the components.

Service	Proxy	IP Phone/ATA	Gateway/SBC	Media server
Call forward	Yes	Some IP phones implement call forward using 3XX redirect messages without any role of the server.	No role.	No role
Call transfer	Yes, processes requests and replies	Yes, requires RFC 3515, RFC 3891, and RFC 3892 (processes the method, REFER, and the headers, Referred-By and Replaces).	Yes, requires RFC 3515, RFC 3891, and RFC 3892 (processes the method, REFER, and the headers, Referred-By and Replaces).	No role
Call pickup	Yes, processes requests and replies	Yes, the system uses SUBSCRIBE and NOTIFY to share the dialog information. The Replaces header in RFC 3892 is required.	Yes, the system uses SUBSCRIBE and NOTIFY to share the dialog information. The Replaces header in RFC 3892 is required.	No role
Three-way conferencing	Yes, processes requests and replies	Yes, the conference bridge is implemented in the phone itself.	No role.	No role
Room conferencing	Sends requests to the destination	No role.	No role.	Yes, implements a URI with the conference room
Voicemail	Sends requests to the destination	Displays the message waiting indicator. Some phones automate the process of recovering the voicemail.	No role.	Yes, it implements the voicemail service
IVR	Relays requests and replies	No role.	No role.	Yes, it implements the IVR service

Explaining RFC 5359 with SIP service examples

There are many ways to implement a PBX feature using SIP. Fortunately, RFC 5359 details the best practices on how to implement them. It will be our guide while implementing PBX services in a SIP ecosystem. It describes call flows and the role of user agent clients, user agent servers, and proxies in the process in detail. Following the examples in RFC 5359 will simplify your work as many IP phone manufacturers also use the same standard to implement the services in their own phones. In the next section, we will demonstrate in detail how to implement some of the services in the RFC.

Playing announcements

To send calls to a media server is not *rocket science*. All you have to do is rewrite the host and port of the R-URI to the IP address of the media server.

Playing demo-thanks

The demo-thanks.gsm file is a recording present in each Asterisk server that is installed. Let's create a number such as *100 to send a call to the Asterisk server. From now on, each number prefixed by the character, *, will be sent to the media server. In the route section of the file, insert the following just after the alias processing:

```
if($rU=~"^\*") {
  rewritehostport("ip_address_of_the_media_server");
  route(1);
}
```

It is very simple; any number starting with * will be sent to the media server. Now, in the Asterisk server, we have to receive the call. To do this, we will edit the sip. conf and extensions.conf files in the /etc/asterisk directory. Usually, for the purposes of testing and education, we install both Asterisk and OpenSIPS in the same server, OpenSIPS in the port 5060, and Asterisk in the port 5062.

Edit the `sip.conf` file as follows:

```
[general]
context=from-sip
bindaddr=0.0.0.0
bindport=5062
allowguest=no

[opensips]
type=peer
host=192.168.1.201
context=from-sip
insecure=invite
allow=ulaw;alaw;gsm
deny=0.0.0.0/0.0.0.0
permit=192.168.1.201/255.255.255.255
```

Although we are allowing calls without authentication (`insecure=invite`), we are preventing other users with an exception made for the SIP proxy itself to send calls using `iptables`.

> **Do not allow unauthenticated calls to your Asterisk server from any IP address, allow only from the SIP server**. Unauthorized calls are very dangerous. The average spending for victims of toll fraud is beyond tens of thousands of dollars. You can further improve your security by configuring `iptables` in your Asterisk server to receive calls only from the OpenSIPS server where users are being authenticated. The `iptables` configuration is beyond the scope of this book.

Edit the `extensions.conf` file as follows:

```
[from-sip]
exten=*100,1,answer()
exten=*100,n,playback(demo-thanks)
exten=*100,n,hangup()
```

The `extensions.conf` file includes just the basics, redirecting calls starting with *100 to a playback message.

Call forwarding

Now, we will work with call forwarding on OpenSIPS. There are usually three kinds of call forwards:

- **Call forward unconditional**: The system redirects all the INVITE requests sent to this phone number to the phone stored in the usr_preferences table. The SIP server will simply replace the request URI before sending the request ahead.

- **Forward on busy**: In this case, we will use the failure_route feature to intercept the 486 Busy Here message and create a new leg sending the INVITE request to the final destination.

- **Forward on no answer**: If a phone replies to an INVITE request with a 480 Temporarily Unavailable or the SIP proxy generates a timeout with a 408 request Timeout, then OpenSIPS will again use failure_route to intercept the message and create a new leg sending the INVITE to the final destination.

To implement any of these services, we need to store data related to the called number. During the authentication process, it is possible to load data from the caller but not from the called number. We will use the usr_preferences table and avp_db_load() function. Use opensipsctl to insert data into the usr_preferences table. The username will be the key, so pay attention to the attribute name and value for each username. For a multidomain system, you can use the username and domain as a key.

```
opensipsctl avp add 1001 callfwd 0 sip:1004@yourdomain
opensipsctl avp add 1002 fwdbusy 0 sip:1000@yourdomain
opensipsctl avp add 1002 callfwd 0 sip:1000@yourdomain
```

After adding all these attributes, you can check the table using the following command:

```
opensipsctl db show usr_preferences
```

The output should look as follows:

Username	Type	Attribute	Value
1001	0	callfwd	sip:1004@yourdomain
1002	0	fwdnoansw	sip:1000@yourdomain
1002	0	fwdbusy	sip:1000@yourdomain

In the preceding table, the username is the key, `callfwd` is an attribute, and the value is the URI containing the destination for the call forward. The field type is the AVP type and 0 means a string attribute with a string value. Check the AVPops module documentation for further details.

Implementing blind call forwarding

For blind call forwarding, we will use an AVP named `callfwd` to store the URI of the call forward destination. In the `avp_db_load()` function, the first parameter is the source and the second is `avp_name`. This function will load the value of the `callfwd` attribute for the user matching the requested URI ($rU) in the username and domain columns.

```
avp_db_load("$rU","$avp(callfwd)")
```

The preceding command is explained as follows:

- $rU is the username of the request URI
- $avp(callfwd) is the name of the AVP storing the call forward destination URI

Later on, we will push this AVP to the SIP request changing the original $ru URI to the new one:

```
$ru = $avp(callfwd);
```

In other words, if the call forward number exists for this user, we will call the URI stored in the `callfwd` AVP rather than calling the original user. The magic in the call forward is inserting the call forward numbers in the `usr_preference` table.

Loading the AVPops module and its parameters

When loading the module, we will specify the database location, access parameters, and AVP table as follows:

```
loadmodule "/usr/lib/openser/modules/avpops.so"
modparam("avpops", "db_url",
   "mysql://opensips:opensipsrw@localhost/opensips")
modparam("avpops", "avp_table", "usr_preferences")
```

In the initial request, load the AVP named `callfwd` from the `usr_preferences` table in the database. If the `callfwd` preference is set to this specific user, it will push it to the R-URI before forwarding the request:

```
if(avp_db_load("$rU","$avp(callfwd)")) {
$ru = $avp(callfwd);
  sl_send_reply("181","Call is being forwarded");
  route(relay);
  exit;
}
```

Lab – implementing blind call forwarding

To implement blind call forwarding, follow these steps:

1. Insert the AVP pairs using `opensipsctl`:

    opensipsctl avp add 1001 callfwd 0 sip:1004@yourdomain

2. Edit the `opensips.cfg` file to include the following instructions. The file should stay as shown here. Include the following lines in the `opensips.cfg` file.

    In the module loading section, include the following:

    ```
    loadmodule "avpops.so"
    loadmodule "xlog.so"
    ```

    In the module parameters section, include the following:

    ```
    modparam("avpops", "db_url",
      "mysql://openser:openserrw@localhost/openser")
    modparam("avpops", "avp_table", "usr_preferences")
    ```

    Just after the `alias_db_lookup` section, insert the following excerpt:

    ```
    if(avp_db_load("$rU","$avp(callfwd)")) {
      $ru = $avp(s:callfwd);
      xlog("forwarded to: $avp(callfwd)");
      route(relay);
      exit;
    }
    ```

3. Register the phones, 1000 and 1004. From the phone 1000, call 1001. The call is forwarded to the device registered as 1004 as instructed in the usr_ preferences table.

Implementing call forward on busy or unanswered

Now, we will review an important concept called `failure_route`. We will handle the following failure situations:

- 408: Request Timeout (phone not registered or disconnected)
- 480: Temporarily Unavailable (no answer)
- 486: Busy Here

To implement call forward on busy and call forward when unanswered, we will use the concept of the failure route. In this logic, we will call the `t_on_failure("missed_call")` function just before sending the INVITE to the destination. This allows the handling of SIP negative replies (codes higher than 299).

We will use a logic similar to blind call forwarding; load an AVP to redirect the call to a specific URI as follows:

```
if(avp_db_load("$rU","$avp(fwdbusy)")) {
  $ru = $avp(fwdbusy);
  xlog("forwarded to: $avp(fwdbusy)");
}
```

Here is an excerpt of the route section with the changes highlighted:

```
####### Routing Logic ########
# main request routing logic

route{

  # apply DB based aliases (uncomment to enable)
  alias_db_lookup("dbaliases");

  # Just after the command alias_db_lookup, add the blind
  # forward

  # Blind call forward
  if(avp_db_load("$rU","$avp(callfwd)")) {
    $ru = $avp(callfwd);
    xlog("Call forward to $avp(callfwd)");
    route(relay);
    exit;
```

```
      }
  }

  failure_route[missed_call] {
    if (t_was_cancelled()) {
      exit;
    }

    # Call forward on busy
    if (t_check_status("486")) {
      #If there is an AVP called fwdbusy send to it
      if(avp_db_load("$rU","$avp(fwdbusy)")) {
        $ru = $avp(fwdbusy);
        xlog("Call forward on busy to: $avp(fwdbusy)");
        t_relay();
      }
    }

    # Redirect unanswered calls to the media server
    if (t_check_status("480|408") and t_local_replied("all")) {
      #If there is an AVP called fwdbusy send to it
      if(avp_db_load("$rU","$avp(fwdnoansw)")) {
        $ru = $avp(fwdbusy);
        xlog("Call forward on busy to $avp(fwdnoansw)");
      }
    t_relay();
    }
  }
```

Debugging the routing script

To better test and debug the routing script, we will use the xlog() function as a way
to insert debugging and informational messages in our script:

```
loadmodule "xlog.so"
xlog("L_ERR","Marker 480 ruri=<$ru>");
```

You can check the latest XLOG messages with the following command:

```
tail /var/log/syslog
```

The t_on_failure() function tells OpenSIPS to handle the SIP failure (negative/unsuccessful replies) conditions. Failure conditions in this context are error messages of codes, 4XX and 5XX. When you call t_on_failure() just before calling the t_relay() function, you will tell OpenSIPS to transfer the control to failure_route[missed_call] when a failure message is detected:

> IMPORTANT: OpenSIPS does not execute the failure route when you perform t_on_failure() but executes it in the future when (if any) a SIP failure is detected:
>
>   t_on_failure("missed_call");

The first part of the failure_route section handles cancelled messages (487). The script simply terminates the processing for this kind of message. In the following section, we will process busy messages. The reply is still relayed to the destination.

```
failure_route[missed_call] {
  ##--
  ##-- If cancelled, exit.
  ##--
  if (t_was_cancelled()) {
    exit;
  }
}
```

If the status is equal to 486 (Busy Here), the action is to load a call forward on busy for the called number, if it exists:

```
# Call forward on busy
if (t_check_status("486")) {
  #If there is an AVP called fwdbusy send to it
  if(avp_db_load("$rU","$avp(fwdbusy)")) {
    $ru = $avp(fwdbusy);
    xlog("L_INFO","Call forward on busy to: $avp(fwdbusy)");
    t_relay();
  }
}
```

Now, if the status is 480 Temporarily Unavailable or 408 Timeout, use the `fwdnoansw` attribute. OpenSIPS provides you with two timeouts defined by the `transaction` module. These parameters are `fr_timeout` and `fr_inv_timeout`. The first is the time between a request and first provisional reply (usually, a 100 Trying stating that the destination is alive). The second timer, `fr_inv_timeout`, is the time between a request and final reply (positive 2XX or negative [3-6]XX). It's possible to get an internally generated 408 Timeout message before the SIP client sends a response such as 480 Temporarily Unavailable. This can happen more often if `fr_inv_timeout` is not long enough for the client to respond but you intend to forward the call in a shorter time period. In this case, the call will be cancelled (OpenSIPS will actually send a CANCEL to the endpoint.) and will generate an internal 408 Timeout. This is why we check both 480 and 408 in this section as follows:

```
# Redirect unanswered calls to the media server
if ((t_check_status("408") && t_local_replied("all")) || t_check_
status("480")) {
   #If there is an AVP called fwdbusy send to it
   if(avp_db_load("$rU","$avp(fwdnoansw)")) {
     $ru = $avp(fwdbusy);
     xlog("Call forward on busy to $avp(fwdnoansw)");
   }
   t_relay();
}
```

Lab – testing the call forwarding feature

To create this lab, some experience with Asterisk is required for the voicemail integration. This lab is relatively hard to implement. Some IP phones hardly send the busy message because they have more than a single line. It is important to use all the lines before to get the 486 Busy Here message. I like to do this test with two softphones, Xlite and Zoiper, in the same computer. When you reject a call in Zoiper, it sends a 486 Busy Here message to the SIP server. We will reduce the INVITE timeout in order to make the tests easier and less cumbersome. We can change the SIP timers using the following parameters:

```
modparam("tm", "fr_timeout", 5)
modparam("tm", "fr_inv_timeout", 10)
```

The test for call forward is done on two occasions:

- **Test the call forward for unanswered calls**: From the extension 1001, call the extension 1002. Do not answer the call at the user 1002. The system will forward the unanswered call to the user 1000.

- **Test the call forward on busy**: Call the extension 1002 from the extension 1001 and reject the call. The system will forward the call to the user 1000.

Implementing an integrated voicemail

We will now see how to integrate the voicemail system present on Asterisk servers with OpenSIPS. This example will show you how to integrate services provided by media servers.

User integration

If you have only five or ten users, you can go straight to the `/etc/asterisk/voicemail.conf` file and create the users there manually. However, in VoIP providers, you possibly have tens of thousands of users, and changing the configuration files manually would not be cost effective. Using real-time tables and MySQL views, it is possible to make Asterisk see OpenSIPS as a native database source for voicemail users.

Another important issue is where to store the voicemail messages. Let's assume that you want to use more than one voicemail server for scalability purposes. In this case, you will need to use centralized storage. Fortunately, Asterisk allows the use of centralized storage using **Open Database Connectivity (ODBC)**.

Integrating Asterisk Realtime with OpenSIPS

To integrate Asterisk with OpenSIPS, follow these steps. I have created this example using Asterisk 1.8.

1. First, install the ODBC driver for MySQL. You can configure Asterisk Realtime with native MySQL, but the voicemail storage is always made using ODBC. Install the `unixodbc` driver if not already installed:

   ```
   apt-get install unixodbc libmyodbc
   ```

2. Configure the ODBC driver for MySQL:

```
vi odbcinst.ini
[MySQL]
Description                  = MySQL driver for Linux & Win32
Driver           = /usr/lib/odbc/libmyodbc.so
Setup            = /usr/lib/odbc/libodbcmyS.so
FileUsage          = 1
UsageCount         = 2


cd /etc
odbcinst -i -d -f odbcinst.ini
vi odbc.ini
[asterisk]
Description = MySQL Asterisk
Driver      = MySQL
SERVER      = localhost
USER        = opensips
PASSWORD    = opensipsrw
PORT        = 3306
DATABASE    = opensips
Option      = 3
```

3. Test your connectivity using `isql`:

```
isql asterisk
```

4. Create the views and tables in OpenSIPS for Asterisk. Add the `vmail_password` column to the subscriber's table:

```
mysql -u root -p
use opensips;


##Add the column vmail_password ##
ALTER TABLE subscriber add column vmail_password varchar(16);
ALTER TABLE subscriber add column datetime_created datetime;


## Create the Asterisk View from OpenSIPS subscriber table ##
CREATE VIEW vmusers AS
SELECT id as uniqueid,
```

```
username as customer_id,
'default' as context,
username as mailbox,
vmail_password as password,
username as fullname,
email_address as email,
NULL as pager,
datetime_created as stamp
FROM opensips.subscriber;


## Create the voicemessages table
CREATE TABLE 'voicemessages' (
  'id' int(11) NOT NULL auto_increment,
  'msgnum' int(11) NOT NULL default '0',
  'dir' varchar(80) default '',
  'context' varchar(80) default '',
  'macrocontext' varchar(80) default '',
  'callerid' varchar(40) default '',
  'origtime' varchar(40) default '',
  'duration' varchar(20) default '',
  'mailboxuser' varchar(80) default '',
  'mailboxcontext' varchar(80) default '',
  'recording' longblob,
  PRIMARY KEY  ('id'),
  KEY 'dir' ('dir')
) ENGINE=InnoDB;
```

5. Configure Asterisk to use the OpenSIPS database:

```
cd /etc/asterisk
vi res_odbc.conf
[asterisk]
enabled => yes
dsn => asterisk
username => opensips
password => opensipsrw
pre-connect => yes
```

6. Reload the Asterisk server:

```
asterisk -rx "core restart now"
```

7. Check if the ODBC driver is connected using the following:

    ```
    asterisk -r
    CLI> odbc show
    Name: asterisk
    DSN: asterisk
    Pooled: no
    Connected: yes
    ```

8. Configure the Asterisk Realtime configuration file:

    ```
    vi extconfig.conf
    ; Static and realtime external configuration
    ; engine configuration
    ;
    ; Please read doc/extconfig.txt for basic table
    ; formatting information.
    ;
    [settings]
    voicemail => odbc, asterisk, vmusers
    ```

9. Configure the `voicemail.conf` file and uncomment the lines related to the ODBC storage:

    ```
    ; Voicemail can be stored in a database using the ODBC
      driver.
    ; The value of odbcstorage is the database connection
      configured
    ; in res_odbc.conf.
    odbcstorage=asterisk
    ; The default table for ODBC voicemail storage is
      voicemessages.
    odbctable=voicemessages
    ```

Troubleshooting: Use the `modules show` command to check whether the `res_config_odbc.so` module has been loaded on the Asterisk server. If it has not been loaded, look at the `/etc/asterisk/modules.conf` file to check whether you have any line preventing the load. Additionally, check the Asterisk compilation options using `make menuselect`; check whether this module was compiled during the Asterisk installation. Check specifically the option, `voicemail build options`, for ODBC support.

10. Configure the Asterisk dialplan in the `extensions.conf` file.

    In the VIEW definition, use `from-sip` as the context for the calls incoming from OpenSIPS:

```
vi extensions.conf
[from-sip]
exten=_u.,1,voicemail(${EXTEN:1},u)
exten=_u.,n,hangup()
exten=_b.,1,voicemail(${EXTEN:1},b)
exten=_b.,n,hangup()
exten=*99,1,voicemailmain(${CALLERID(num)},s)
exten=*99,2,hangup()
```

11. Test the access to the voicemail menu using `*99`.

Call transfer

To transfer a call between two user agents on SIP requires a lot of coordination. All the devices should support the REFER message and, for attended transfers, the Replaces and Referred-By headers. To explain how a transfer occurs, we will see a scenario where a PSTN user sends a call to the PSTN gateway, and this extension transfers the call to another extension—a typical scenario for an operator. We will see these scenarios for unattended (blind) and attended transfers.

An unattended transfer

Looking at the following call flow, you will notice that the function of the SIP proxy in a call transfer process is simply to relay messages between the gateway and endpoints. You do not need to change anything in the routing script to support transfers. However, you have to make sure that your gateway supports a REFER message and has a route to the extensions. A common mistake in this scenario is forgetting to insert a route in the PSTN gateway or **Session Border Controller (SBC)** pointing the extensions back to the SIP proxy:

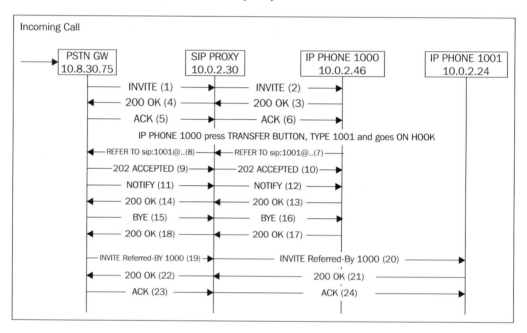

As you can see, for an incoming call, the gateway needs to support the REFER message as described in RFC 3515. The Referred-By header carries the identity of the referrer. Gateways handle REFERs in the same way as INVITEs, so you need to have a route to the extensions with the 1XXX pattern pointing back to the SIP proxy to complete the transfer. You can see the full trace here:

```
(1) U 10.8.30.75:5060 -> 10.0.2.30:5060
INVITE sip:1000@10.0.2.30 SIP/2.0.
Via: SIP/2.0/UDP 10.8.30.75:5060;branch=z9hG4bK00411d5c;rport.
From: "4733990000" <sip:4733990000@10.8.30.75>;tag=as54e9679e.
To: <sip:1000@10.0.2.30>.
Contact: <sip:4733990000@10.8.30.75:5060>.
```

Call-ID: 745b8b6b21aa0e535258c83c31b5e08c@10.8.30.75:5060.
User-Agent: Test Gateway 1.0.

...

(2) U 10.0.2.30:5060 -> 10.0.2.46:50217
INVITE sip:1000@10.0.2.46:50217;ob SIP/2.0.
Record-Route: <sip:10.0.2.30;lr;did=641.5571dba1>.
Via: SIP/2.0/UDP 10.0.2.30:5060;branch=z9hG4bK7103.3c2dff36.0.
Via: SIP/2.0/UDP 10.8.30.75:5060;
   received=10.8.30.75;branch=z9hG4bK00411d5c;rport=5060.
From: "4733990000" <sip:4733990000@10.8.30.75>;tag=as54e9679e.
To: <sip:1000@10.0.2.30>.
Contact: <sip:4733990000@10.8.30.75:5060>.
Call-ID: 745b8b6b21aa0e535258c83c31b5e08c@10.8.30.75:5060.
User-Agent: Test Gateway 1.0.

(3) U 10.0.2.46:50217 -> 10.0.2.30:5060
SIP/2.0 200 OK.
Via: SIP/2.0/UDP 10.0.2.30:5060;received=10.0.2.30;branch=z9hG4bK7103
.3c2dff36.0.
Via: SIP/2.0/UDP 10.8.30.75:5060;
   rport=5060;received=10.8.30.75;branch=z9hG4bK00411d5c.
Record-Route: <sip:10.0.2.30;lr;did=641.5571dba1>.
Call-ID: 745b8b6b21aa0e535258c83c31b5e08c@10.8.30.75:5060.
From: "4733990000" <sip:4733990000@10.8.30.75>;tag=as54e9679e.
To: <sip:1000@10.0.2.30>;tag=mSbllSh4jlY-SG9IPiFdemNa7Scd37Ql.
CSeq: 102 INVITE.
Contact: "1000" <sip:1000@10.0.2.46:50217;ob>.

(4) U 10.0.2.30:5060 -> 10.8.30.75:5060
SIP/2.0 200 OK.
Via: SIP/2.0/UDP 10.8.30.75:5060;
   rport=5060;received=10.8.30.75;branch=z9hG4bK00411d5c.
Record-Route: <sip:10.0.2.30;lr;did=641.5571dba1>.
Call-ID: 745b8b6b21aa0e535258c83c31b5e08c@10.8.30.75:5060.
From: "4733990000" <sip:4733990000@10.8.30.75>;tag=as54e9679e.
To: <sip:1000@10.0.2.30>;tag=mSbllSh4jlY-SG9IPiFdemNa7Scd37Ql.
CSeq: 102 INVITE.
Contact: "1000" <sip:1000@10.0.2.46:50217;ob>.

(5) U 10.8.30.75:5060 -> 10.0.2.30:5060
ACK sip:1000@10.0.2.46:50217;ob SIP/2.0.

```
Via: SIP/2.0/UDP 10.8.30.75:5060;branch=z9hG4bK486a63e9;rport.
Route: <sip:10.0.2.30;lr;did=641.5571dba1>.
From: "4733990000" <sip:4733990000@10.8.30.75>;tag=as54e9679e.
To: <sip:1000@10.0.2.30>;tag=mSbllSh4jlY-SG9IPiFdemNa7Scd37Ql.
Contact: <sip:4733990000@10.8.30.75:5060>.
Call-ID: 745b8b6b21aa0e535258c83c31b5e08c@10.8.30.75:5060.
CSeq: 102 ACK.
User-Agent: Test Gateway 1.0.


(6) U 10.0.2.30:5060 -> 10.0.2.46:50217
ACK sip:1000@10.0.2.46:50217;ob SIP/2.0.
Via: SIP/2.0/UDP 10.0.2.30:5060;branch=z9hG4bK7103.3c2dff36.2.
Via: SIP/2.0/UDP 10.8.30.75:5060;
   received=10.8.30.75;branch=z9hG4bK486a63e9;rport=5060.
From: "4733990000" <sip:4733990000@10.8.30.75>;tag=as54e9679e.
To: <sip:1000@10.0.2.30>;tag=mSbllSh4jlY-SG9IPiFdemNa7Scd37Ql.
Contact: <sip:4733990000@10.8.30.75:5060>.
Call-ID: 745b8b6b21aa0e535258c83c31b5e08c@10.8.30.75:5060.
User-Agent: Test Gateway 1.0.


(7) U 10.0.2.46:50217 -> 10.0.2.30:5060
REFER sip:4733990000@10.8.30.75:5060 SIP/2.0.
Via: SIP/2.0/UDP 10.0.2.46:50217;
   rport;branch=z9hG4bKPjcz0hNYTTUTZYOZ9sCMANZAYObdHMpwr2.
From: <sip:1000@10.0.2.30>;tag=mSbllSh4jlY-SG9IPiFdemNa7Scd37Ql.
To: "4733990000" <sip:4733990000@10.8.30.75>;tag=as54e9679e.
Contact: "1000" <sip:1000@10.0.2.46:50217;ob>.
Call-ID: 745b8b6b21aa0e535258c83c31b5e08c@10.8.30.75:5060.
CSeq: 25623 REFER.
Route: <sip:10.0.2.30;lr;did=641.5571dba1>.
Event: refer.
Expires: 600.
Supported: Replaces, 100rel, timer, norefersub.
Accept: message/sipfrag;version=2.0.
Refer-To: "" <sip:1001@opensips.org>.
Referred-By: <sip:1000@10.0.2.30>.
User-Agent: Bria iOS 3.0.5.
Content-Length:  0.
.


(8) U 10.0.2.30:5060 -> 10.8.30.75:5060
REFER sip:4733990000@10.8.30.75:5060 SIP/2.0.
```

Via: SIP/2.0/UDP 10.0.2.30:5060;branch=z9hG4bK6e4d.92131fc2.0.
Via: SIP/2.0/UDP 10.0.2.46:50217;
  received=10.0.2.46;rport=50217;
  branch=z9hG4bKPjcz0hNYTTUTZYOZ9sCMANZAYObdHMpwr2.
Max-Forwards: 69.
From: <sip:1000@10.0.2.30>;tag=mSbllSh4jlY-SG9IPiFdemNa7Scd37Ql.
To: "4733990000" <sip:4733990000@10.8.30.75>;tag=as54e9679e.
Contact: "1000" <sip:1000@10.0.2.46:50217;ob>.
Call-ID: 745b8b6b21aa0e535258c83c31b5e08c@10.8.30.75:5060.
CSeq: 25623 REFER.
Event: refer.
Expires: 600.
Refer-To: "" <sip:1001@opensips.org>.
Referred-By: <sip:1000@10.0.2.30>.
User-Agent: Bria iOS 3.0.5.
Content-Length: 0.
  .

(9) U 10.8.30.75:5060 -> 10.0.2.30:5060
SIP/2.0 202 Accepted.
Via: SIP/2.0/UDP 10.0.2.30:5060;
  branch=z9hG4bK6e4d.92131fc2.0;received=10.0.2.30;rport=5060.
Via: SIP/2.0/UDP 10.0.2.46:50217;
  received=10.0.2.46;rport=50217;
  branch=z9hG4bKPjcz0hNYTTUTZYOZ9sCMANZAYObdHMpwr2.
From: <sip:1000@10.0.2.30>;tag=mSbllSh4jlY-SG9IPiFdemNa7Scd37Ql.
To: "4733990000" <sip:4733990000@10.8.30.75>;tag=as54e9679e.
Call-ID: 745b8b6b21aa0e535258c83c31b5e08c@10.8.30.75:5060.
CSeq: 25623 REFER.
Server: Test Gateway 1.0.
Contact: <sip:4733990000@10.8.30.75:5060>.
Content-Length: 0.

(10) U 10.0.2.30:5060 -> 10.0.2.46:50217
SIP/2.0 202 Accepted.
Via: SIP/2.0/UDP 10.0.2.46:50217;
  received=10.0.2.46;rport=50217;
  branch=z9hG4bKPjcz0hNYTTUTZYOZ9sCMANZAYObdHMpwr2.
From: <sip:1000@10.0.2.30>;tag=mSbllSh4jlY-SG9IPiFdemNa7Scd37Ql.
To: "4733990000" <sip:4733990000@10.8.30.75>;tag=as54e9679e.
Call-ID: 745b8b6b21aa0e535258c83c31b5e08c@10.8.30.75:5060.
CSeq: 25623 REFER.
Server: Test Gateway 1.0.

```
Allow: INVITE, ACK, CANCEL, OPTIONS, BYE, REFER, SUBSCRIBE,
  NOTIFY, INFO, PUBLISH.
Supported: Replaces, timer.
Contact: <sip:4733990000@10.8.30.75:5060>.
Content-Length: 0.
.


(11) U 10.8.30.75:5060 -> 10.0.2.30:5060
NOTIFY sip:1000@10.0.2.46:50217;ob SIP/2.0.
Via: SIP/2.0/UDP 10.8.30.75:5060;branch=z9hG4bK768e6ef0;rport.
Route: <sip:10.0.2.30;lr;did=641.5571dba1>.
From: "4733990000" <sip:4733990000@10.8.30.75>;tag=as54e9679e.
To: <sip:1000@10.0.2.30>;tag=mSbllSh4jlY-SG9IPiFdemNa7Scd37Ql.
Contact: <sip:4733990000@10.8.30.75:5060>.
Call-ID: 745b8b6b21aa0e535258c83c31b5e08c@10.8.30.75:5060.
User-Agent: Test Gateway 1.0.
Event: refer;id=25623.
Subscription-state: terminated;reason=noresource.
Content-Type: message/sipfrag;version=2.0.


(12) U 10.0.2.30:5060 -> 10.0.2.46:50217
NOTIFY sip:1000@10.0.2.46:50217;ob SIP/2.0.
Via: SIP/2.0/UDP 10.0.2.30:5060;branch=z9hG4bK5103.f1dcd8d4.0.
Via: SIP/2.0/UDP
  10.8.30.75:5060;received=10.8.30.75;
  branch=z9hG4bK768e6ef0;rport=5060.
From: "4733990000" <sip:4733990000@10.8.30.75>;tag=as54e9679e.
To: <sip:1000@10.0.2.30>;tag=mSbllSh4jlY-SG9IPiFdemNa7Scd37Ql.
Contact: <sip:4733990000@10.8.30.75:5060>.
Call-ID: 745b8b6b21aa0e535258c83c31b5e08c@10.8.30.75:5060.
User-Agent: Test Gateway 1.0.
Event: refer;id=25623.
Subscription-state: terminated;reason=noresource.
Content-Type: message/sipfrag;version=2.0.


(13) U 10.0.2.46:50217 -> 10.0.2.30:5060
SIP/2.0 200 OK.
Via: SIP/2.0/UDP 10.0.2.30:5060;received=10.0.2.30;branch=z9hG4
bK8103.74472343.0.
Via: SIP/2.0/UDP
  10.8.30.75:5060;rport=5060;received=10.8.30.75;
  branch=z9hG4bK005abb57.
Call-ID: 745b8b6b21aa0e535258c83c31b5e08c@10.8.30.75:5060.
```

From: "4733990000" <sip:4733990000@10.8.30.75>;tag=as54e9679e.
To: <sip:1000@10.0.2.30>;tag=mSbllSh4jlY-SG9IPiFdemNa7Scd37Ql.
CSeq: 103 NOTIFY.
Contact: "1000" <sip:1000@10.0.2.46:50217;ob>.

(14) U 10.0.2.30:5060 -> 10.8.30.75:5060
SIP/2.0 200 OK.
Via: SIP/2.0/UDP 10.8.30.75:5060;
  rport=5060;received=10.8.30.75;branch=z9hG4bK005abb57.
Call-ID: 745b8b6b21aa0e535258c83c31b5e08c@10.8.30.75:5060.
From: "4733990000" <sip:4733990000@10.8.30.75>;tag=as54e9679e.
To: <sip:1000@10.0.2.30>;tag=mSbllSh4jlY-SG9IPiFdemNa7Scd37Ql.
CSeq: 103 NOTIFY.
Contact: "1000" <sip:1000@10.0.2.46:50217;ob>.
Content-Length: 0.
.

(15) U 10.0.2.46:50217 -> 10.0.2.30:5060
BYE sip:4733990000@10.8.30.75:5060 SIP/2.0.
Via: SIP/2.0/UDP 10.0.2.46:50217;rport;
  branch=z9hG4bKPjjPYiHxbr98avTAX9urTl31tih4wdxAiQ.
From: <sip:1000@10.0.2.30>;tag=mSbllSh4jlY-SG9IPiFdemNa7Scd37Ql.
To: "4733990000" <sip:4733990000@10.8.30.75>;tag=as54e9679e.
Call-ID: 745b8b6b21aa0e535258c83c31b5e08c@10.8.30.75:5060.
Route: <sip:10.0.2.30;lr;did=641.5571dba1>.
User-Agent: Bria iOS 3.0.5.
Content-Length: 0.
.

(16) U 10.0.2.30:5060 -> 10.8.30.75:5060
BYE sip:4733990000@10.8.30.75:5060 SIP/2.0.
Via: SIP/2.0/UDP 10.0.2.30:5060;branch=z9hG4bK3e4d.b605e994.0.
Via: SIP/2.0/UDP 10.0.2.46:50217;received=10.0.2.46;
  rport=50217;branch=z9hG4bKPjjPYiHxbr98avTAX9urTl31tih4wdxAiQ.
From: <sip:1000@10.0.2.30>;tag=mSbllSh4jlY-SG9IPiFdemNa7Scd37Ql.
To: "4733990000" <sip:4733990000@10.8.30.75>;tag=as54e9679e.
Call-ID: 745b8b6b21aa0e535258c83c31b5e08c@10.8.30.75:5060.
CSeq: 25624 BYE.
User-Agent: Bria iOS 3.0.5.
Content-Length: 0.
.

(17) U 10.8.30.75:5060 -> 10.0.2.30:5060
SIP/2.0 200 OK.

```
Via: SIP/2.0/UDP 10.0.2.30:5060;
  branch=z9hG4bK3e4d.b605e994.0;received=10.0.2.30;rport=5060.
Via: SIP/2.0/UDP 10.0.2.46:50217;
  received=10.0.2.46;rport=50217;
  branch=z9hG4bKPjjPYiHxbr98avTAX9urTl31tih4wdxAiQ.
From: <sip:1000@10.0.2.30>;tag=mSbllSh4jlY-SG9IPiFdemNa7Scd37Ql.
To: "4733990000" <sip:4733990000@10.8.30.75>;tag=as54e9679e.
Call-ID: 745b8b6b21aa0e535258c83c31b5e08c@10.8.30.75:5060.
CSeq: 25624 BYE.
Server: Test Gateway 1.0.



(18) U 10.0.2.30:5060 -> 10.0.2.46:50217
SIP/2.0 200 OK.
Via: SIP/2.0/UDP 10.0.2.46:50217;received=10.0.2.46;
  rport=50217;branch=z9hG4bKPjjPYiHxbr98avTAX9urTl31tih4wdxAiQ.
From: <sip:1000@10.0.2.30>;tag=mSbllSh4jlY-SG9IPiFdemNa7Scd37Ql.
To: "4733990000" <sip:4733990000@10.8.30.75>;tag=as54e9679e.
Call-ID: 745b8b6b21aa0e535258c83c31b5e08c@10.8.30.75:5060.
CSeq: 25624 BYE.


(19) U 10.8.30.75:5060 -> 10.0.2.30:5060
INVITE sip:1001@10.0.2.30 SIP/2.0.
Via: SIP/2.0/UDP 10.8.30.75:5060;branch=z9hG4bK7aad50bf;rport.
Max-Forwards: 70.
From: "4733990000" <sip:4733990000@10.8.30.75>;tag=as7980b69b.
To: <sip:1001@10.0.2.30>.
Contact: <sip:4733990000@10.8.30.75:5060>.
Call-ID: 0338e22c47ea867f7f85b7657e5f8b66@10.8.30.75:5060.
CSeq: 102 INVITE.
User-Agent: Test Gateway 1.0.


(20) U 10.0.2.30:5060 -> 10.0.2.24:26724
INVITE sip:1001@10.0.2.24:26724;
  rinstance=0f9522053bd37f41;transport=udp SIP/2.0.
Record-Route: <sip:10.0.2.30;lr;did=2d7.ed05f5e5>.
Via: SIP/2.0/UDP 10.0.2.30:5060;branch=z9hG4bK2a6c.d0a1bbd1.0.
Via: SIP/2.0/UDP 10.8.30.75:5060;received=10.8.30.75;
  branch=z9hG4bK7aad50bf;rport=5060.
Max-Forwards: 69.
```

```
From: "4733990000" <sip:4733990000@10.8.30.75>;tag=as7980b69b.
To: <sip:1001@10.0.2.30>.
Contact: <sip:4733990000@10.8.30.75:5060>.
Call-ID: 0338e22c47ea867f7f85b7657e5f8b66@10.8.30.75:5060.
CSeq: 102 INVITE.
User-Agent: Test Gateway 1.0.


(21) U 10.0.2.24:26724 -> 10.0.2.30:5060
SIP/2.0 200 OK.
Via: SIP/2.0/UDP 10.0.2.30:5060;branch=z9hG4bK2a6c.d0a1bbd1.0.
Via: SIP/2.0/UDP 10.8.30.75:5060;
   received=10.8.30.75;branch=z9hG4bK7aad50bf;rport=5060.
Record-Route: <sip:10.0.2.30;lr;did=2d7.ed05f5e5>.
Contact: <sip:1001@10.0.2.24:26724>.
To: <sip:1001@10.0.2.30>;tag=d8eeb72d.
From: "4733990000"<sip:4733990000@10.8.30.75>;tag=as7980b69b.
Call-ID: 0338e22c47ea867f7f85b7657e5f8b66@10.8.30.75:5060.
CSeq: 102 INVITE.


(22) U 10.0.2.30:5060 -> 10.8.30.75:5060
SIP/2.0 200 OK.
Via: SIP/2.0/UDP 10.8.30.75:5060;received=10.8.30.75;branch=z9hG4bK7a
ad50bf;
   rport=5060.
Record-Route: <sip:10.0.2.30;lr;did=2d7.ed05f5e5>.
Contact: <sip:1001@10.0.2.24:26724>.
To: <sip:1001@10.0.2.30>;tag=d8eeb72d.
From: "4733990000"<sip:4733990000@10.8.30.75>;tag=as7980b69b.
Call-ID: 0338e22c47ea867f7f85b7657e5f8b66@10.8.30.75:5060.
CSeq: 102 INVITE.
Allow: INVITE, ACK, CANCEL, OPTIONS, BYE, REFER, NOTIFY, MESSAGE,
   SUBSCRIBE, INFO.
Content-Type: application/sdp.
Supported: Replaces, eventlist.
User-Agent: Bria 3 release 3.5.5  stamp 71238.
```

The last packets are suppressed as they are irrelevant.

The following image shows the full call flow of an attended call transfer using OpenSIPS and Asterisk as the PSTN gateway. Now, beyond the support for REFERs, the IP phones and gateways need support for the Replaces header as defined in RFC 3892. The Replaces header is an in-dialog request; it carries the Call-ID, From-Tag, and To-Tag from the original call. Thus, the destination phone (1001) will actually replace the original dialog with this new one, completing the transfer. Call transfers work on SIP only if all the available components support these advanced features. Most IP phones and paid softphones support call transfers; however, gateways and SIP VoIP providers rarely do so. Sometimes, it is wiser to insert B2BUA between the SIP network and PSTN to honor all REFERs and Replaces. The OpenSIPS B2BUA module, at the time of writing this, supports blind, but not attended, transfers:

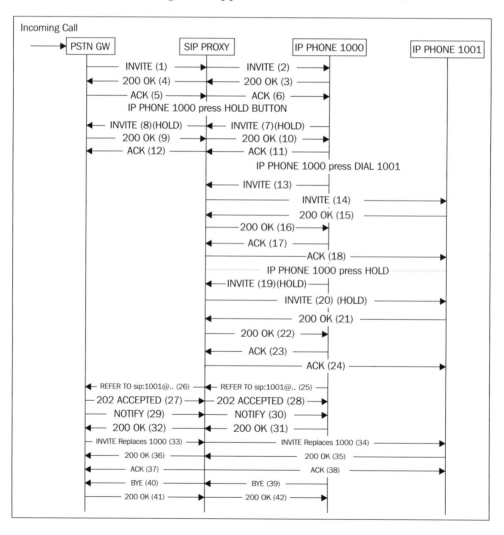

In the following trace, we have removed the provisional replies, ACKs, and SDP content to reduce the size of the trace:

```
(1) U 10.8.30.75:5060 -> 10.0.2.30:5060
INVITE sip:1000@10.0.2.30 SIP/2.0.
Via: SIP/2.0/UDP 10.8.30.75:5060;branch=z9hG4bK65410ec4;rport.
From: "4733990000" <sip:4733990000@10.8.30.75>;tag=as6fa7d95c.
To: <sip:1000@10.0.2.30>.
Contact: <sip:4733990000@10.8.30.75:5060>.
Call-ID: 0c4ac8a67f1c69311d5a9dbc4ae59678@10.8.30.75:5060.
User-Agent: Test Gateway 1.0.


(2) U 10.0.2.30:5060 -> 10.0.2.46:61814
INVITE sip:1000@10.0.2.46:61814;ob SIP/2.0.
Record-Route: <sip:10.0.2.30;lr;did=cb4.691d7dd2>.
Via: SIP/2.0/UDP 10.0.2.30:5060;branch=z9hG4bKd834.f583db61.0.
Via: SIP/2.0/UDP 10.8.30.75:5060;received=10.8.30.75;
  branch=z9hG4bK65410ec4;rport=5060.
From: "4733990000" <sip:4733990000@10.8.30.75>;tag=as6fa7d95c.
To: <sip:1000@10.0.2.30>.
Contact: <sip:4733990000@10.8.30.75:5060>.
Call-ID: 0c4ac8a67f1c69311d5a9dbc4ae59678@10.8.30.75:5060.
CSeq: 102 INVITE.
User-Agent: Test Gateway 1.0.


(3) U 10.0.2.46:61814 -> 10.0.2.30:5060
SIP/2.0 200 OK.
Via: SIP/2.0/UDP 10.0.2.30:5060;received=10.0.2.30;
  branch=z9hG4bKd834.f583db61.0.
Via: SIP/2.0/UDP 10.8.30.75:5060;rport=5060;
  received=10.8.30.75;branch=z9hG4bK65410ec4.
Record-Route: <sip:10.0.2.30;lr;did=cb4.691d7dd2>.
Call-ID: 0c4ac8a67f1c69311d5a9dbc4ae59678@10.8.30.75:5060.
From: "4733990000" <sip:4733990000@10.8.30.75>;tag=as6fa7d95c.
To: <sip:1000@10.0.2.30>;tag=toQEoljqGplWjxgNJZuwxqQSSNTxYlaU.
CSeq: 102 INVITE.


(4) U 10.0.2.30:5060 -> 10.8.30.75:5060
SIP/2.0 200 OK.
Via: SIP/2.0/UDP 10.8.30.75:5060;rport=5060;
  received=10.8.30.75;branch=z9hG4bK65410ec4.
Record-Route: <sip:10.0.2.30;lr;did=cb4.691d7dd2>.
Call-ID: 0c4ac8a67f1c69311d5a9dbc4ae59678@10.8.30.75:5060.
From: "4733990000" <sip:4733990000@10.8.30.75>;tag=as6fa7d95c.
```

```
To: <sip:1000@10.0.2.30>;tag=toQEoljqGplWjxgNJZuwxqQSSNTxYlaU.
CSeq: 102 INVITE.


(5) U 10.8.30.75:5060 -> 10.0.2.30:5060
ACK sip:1000@10.0.2.46:61814;ob SIP/2.0.
Via: SIP/2.0/UDP 10.8.30.75:5060;branch=z9hG4bK7f3317d2;rport.
Route: <sip:10.0.2.30;lr;did=cb4.691d7dd2>.
Max-Forwards: 70.
From: "4733990000" <sip:4733990000@10.8.30.75>;tag=as6fa7d95c.
To: <sip:1000@10.0.2.30>;tag=toQEoljqGplWjxgNJZuwxqQSSNTxYlaU.
Contact: <sip:4733990000@10.8.30.75:5060>.
Call-ID: 0c4ac8a67f1c69311d5a9dbc4ae59678@10.8.30.75:5060.
CSeq: 102 ACK.
User-Agent: Test Gateway 1.0.
Content-Length: 0.
.


(7) U 10.0.2.46:61814 -> 10.0.2.30:5060
INVITE sip:4733990000@10.8.30.75:5060 SIP/2.0.
Via: SIP/2.0/UDP 10.0.2.46:61814;rport;
  branch=z9hG4bKPj4D7PYdj0rNAByE9A.vJ0afnIokfpXmxq.
From: <sip:1000@10.0.2.30>;tag=toQEoljqGplWjxgNJZuwxqQSSNTxYlaU.
To: "4733990000" <sip:4733990000@10.8.30.75>;tag=as6fa7d95c.
Contact: "1000" <sip:1000@10.0.2.46:61814;ob>.
Call-ID: 0c4ac8a67f1c69311d5a9dbc4ae59678@10.8.30.75:5060.
CSeq: 6379 INVITE.
Route: <sip:10.0.2.30;lr;did=cb4.691d7dd2>.
Supported: Replaces, 100rel, timer, norefersub.
User-Agent: Bria iOS 3.0.5.


(8) U 10.0.2.30:5060 -> 10.8.30.75:5060
INVITE sip:4733990000@10.8.30.75:5060 SIP/2.0.
Record-Route: <sip:10.0.2.30;lr>.
Via: SIP/2.0/UDP 10.0.2.30:5060;branch=z9hG4bK15b1.6fc061c2.0.
Via: SIP/2.0/UDP 10.0.2.46:61814;received=10.0.2.46;
  rport=61814;branch=z9hG4bKPj4D7PYdj0rNAByE9A.vJ0afnIokfpXmxq.
From: <sip:1000@10.0.2.30>;tag=toQEoljqGplWjxgNJZuwxqQSSNTxYlaU.
To: "4733990000" <sip:4733990000@10.8.30.75>;tag=as6fa7d95c.
Contact: "1000" <sip:1000@10.0.2.46:61814;ob>.
Call-ID: 0c4ac8a67f1c69311d5a9dbc4ae59678@10.8.30.75:5060.
CSeq: 6379 INVITE.
User-Agent: Bria iOS 3.0.5.
```

```
(9) U 10.8.30.75:5060 -> 10.0.2.30:5060
SIP/2.0 200 OK.
Via: SIP/2.0/UDP 10.0.2.30:5060;
  branch=z9hG4bK15b1.6fc061c2.0;received=10.0.2.30;rport=5060.
Via: SIP/2.0/UDP 10.0.2.46:61814;received=10.0.2.46;
  rport=61814;branch=z9hG4bKPj4D7PYdj0rNAByE9A.vJ0afnIokfpXmxq.
Record-Route: <sip:10.0.2.30;lr>.
From: <sip:1000@10.0.2.30>;tag=toQEoljqGplWjxgNJZuwxqQSSNTxYlaU.
To: "4733990000" <sip:4733990000@10.8.30.75>;tag=as6fa7d95c.
Call-ID: 0c4ac8a67f1c69311d5a9dbc4ae59678@10.8.30.75:5060.
CSeq: 6379 INVITE.
Server: Test Gateway 1.0.
Contact: <sip:4733990000@10.8.30.75:5060>.


(10) U 10.0.2.30:5060 -> 10.0.2.46:61814
SIP/2.0 200 OK.
Via: SIP/2.0/UDP 10.0.2.46:61814;received=10.0.2.46;
  rport=61814;branch=z9hG4bKPj4D7PYdj0rNAByE9A.vJ0afnIokfpXmxq.
Record-Route: <sip:10.0.2.30;lr>.
From: <sip:1000@10.0.2.30>;tag=toQEoljqGplWjxgNJZuwxqQSSNTxYlaU.
To: "4733990000" <sip:4733990000@10.8.30.75>;tag=as6fa7d95c.
Call-ID: 0c4ac8a67f1c69311d5a9dbc4ae59678@10.8.30.75:5060.
CSeq: 6379 INVITE.
Server: Test Gateway 1.0.
Allow: INVITE, ACK, CANCEL, OPTIONS, BYE, REFER, SUBSCRIBE,
  NOTIFY, INFO, PUBLISH.
Supported: Replaces, timer.
Contact: <sip:4733990000@10.8.30.75:5060>.


(11) U 10.0.2.46:61814 -> 10.0.2.30:5060
ACK sip:4733990000@10.8.30.75:5060 SIP/2.0.
Via: SIP/2.0/UDP 10.0.2.46:61814;rport;
  branch=z9hG4bKPj0x3oECScRRVxd2PfPjgBar1QPxB-o9Zo.
Max-Forwards: 70.
From: <sip:1000@10.0.2.30>;tag=toQEoljqGplWjxgNJZuwxqQSSNTxYlaU.
To: "4733990000" <sip:4733990000@10.8.30.75>;tag=as6fa7d95c.
Call-ID: 0c4ac8a67f1c69311d5a9dbc4ae59678@10.8.30.75:5060.
CSeq: 6379 ACK.
Route: <sip:10.0.2.30;lr;did=cb4.691d7dd2>.


(13) U 10.0.2.46:61814 -> 10.0.2.30:5060
INVITE sip:1001@opensips.org SIP/2.0.
```

```
Via: SIP/2.0/UDP 10.0.2.46:61814;rport;branch=z9hG4bKPj9lproHRHfiWHT2
.K-
  hweQQNYxoEa69B..
From: "1000" <sip:1000@opensips.org>;tag=eIrd.nxJQfDFjk3OzVRyJ-
  CjnDaL1sCz.
To: <sip:1001@opensips.org>.
Contact: "1000" <sip:1000@10.0.2.46:61814;ob>.
Call-ID: wiUEvg2atKMRa0pZNHfTM3RC0lbubWWF.
CSeq: 17323 INVITE.
User-Agent: Bria iOS 3.0.5.


(14) U 10.0.2.30:5060 -> 10.0.2.24:26724
INVITE sip:1001@10.0.2.24:26724;
  rinstance=0f9522053bd37f41;transport=udp SIP/2.0.
Record-Route: <sip:10.0.2.30;lr;did=cee.20906ae2>.
Via: SIP/2.0/UDP 10.0.2.30:5060;branch=z9hG4bKcaf5.e9b376a2.0.
Via: SIP/2.0/UDP 10.0.2.46:61814;received=10.0.2.46;
  rport=61814;branch=z9hG4bKPj9lproHRHfiWHT2.K-hweQQNYxoEa69B..
From: "1000" <sip:1000@opensips.org>;tag=eIrd.nxJQfDFjk3OzVRyJ-
  CjnDaL1sCz.
To: <sip:1001@opensips.org>.
Contact: "1000" <sip:1000@10.0.2.46:61814;ob>.
Call-ID: wiUEvg2atKMRa0pZNHfTM3RC0lbubWWF.
CSeq: 17323 INVITE.
User-Agent: Bria iOS 3.0.5.


(15) U 10.0.2.24:26724 -> 10.0.2.30:5060
SIP/2.0 200 OK.
Via: SIP/2.0/UDP 10.0.2.30:5060;branch=z9hG4bKcaf5.e9b376a2.0.
Via: SIP/2.0/UDP 10.0.2.46:61814;received=10.0.2.46;
  rport=61814;branch=z9hG4bKPj9lproHRHfiWHT2.K-hweQQNYxoEa69B..
Record-Route: <sip:10.0.2.30;lr;did=cee.20906ae2>.
Contact: <sip:1001@10.0.2.24:26724>.
To: <sip:1001@opensips.org>;tag=d022987a.
From: "1000"<sip:1000@opensips.org>;tag=eIrd.nxJQfDFjk3OzVRyJ-
  CjnDaL1sCz.
Call-ID: wiUEvg2atKMRa0pZNHfTM3RC0lbubWWF.
CSeq: 17323 INVITE.
Allow: INVITE, ACK, CANCEL, OPTIONS, BYE, REFER, NOTIFY, MESSAGE,
  SUBSCRIBE, INFO.
Content-Type: application/sdp.
Supported: Replaces, eventlist.
User-Agent: Bria 3 release 3.5.5  stamp 71238.
```

```
(16) U 10.0.2.30:5060 -> 10.0.2.46:61814
SIP/2.0 200 OK.
Via: SIP/2.0/UDP 10.0.2.46:61814;received=10.0.2.46;
   rport=61814;branch=z9hG4bKPj9lproHRHfiWHT2.K-hweQQNYxoEa69B..
Record-Route: <sip:10.0.2.30;lr;did=cee.20906ae2>.
Contact: <sip:1001@10.0.2.24:26724>.
To: <sip:1001@opensips.org>;tag=d022987a.
From: "1000"<sip:1000@opensips.org>;tag=eIrd.nxJQfDFjk3OzVRyJ-
   CjnDaL1sCz.
Call-ID: wiUEvg2atKMRa0pZNHfTM3RC0lbubWWF.
CSeq: 17323 INVITE.


(19) U 10.0.2.46:61814 -> 10.0.2.30:5060
INVITE sip:1001@10.0.2.24:26724 SIP/2.0.
Via: SIP/2.0/UDP 10.0.2.46:61814;rport;
   branch=z9hG4bKPjDu0EGRnwIYDVg5.D7Dyvt8h4Q91H16VJ.
From: "1000" <sip:1000@opensips.org>;tag=eIrd.nxJQfDFjk3OzVRyJ-
   CjnDaL1sCz.
To: <sip:1001@opensips.org>;tag=d022987a.
Contact: "1000" <sip:1000@10.0.2.46:61814;ob>.
Call-ID: wiUEvg2atKMRa0pZNHfTM3RC0lbubWWF.
CSeq: 17325 INVITE.
Route: <sip:10.0.2.30;lr;did=cee.20906ae2>.
User-Agent: Bria iOS 3.0.5.


(20) U 10.0.2.30:5060 -> 10.0.2.24:26724
INVITE sip:1001@10.0.2.24:26724 SIP/2.0.
Record-Route: <sip:10.0.2.30;lr>.
Via: SIP/2.0/UDP 10.0.2.30:5060;branch=z9hG4bKaaf5.274569b.0.
Via: SIP/2.0/UDP 10.0.2.46:61814;received=10.0.2.46;
   rport=61814;branch=z9hG4bKPjDu0EGRnwIYDVg5.D7Dyvt8h4Q91H16VJ.
From: "1000" <sip:1000@opensips.org>;tag=eIrd.nxJQfDFjk3OzVRyJ-
   CjnDaL1sCz.
To: <sip:1001@opensips.org>;tag=d022987a.
Contact: "1000" <sip:1000@10.0.2.46:61814;ob>.
Call-ID: wiUEvg2atKMRa0pZNHfTM3RC0lbubWWF.
CSeq: 17325 INVITE.
User-Agent: Bria iOS 3.0.5.


(21) U 10.0.2.24:26724 -> 10.0.2.30:5060
SIP/2.0 200 OK.
Via: SIP/2.0/UDP 10.0.2.30:5060;branch=z9hG4bKaaf5.274569b.0.
Via: SIP/2.0/UDP 10.0.2.46:61814;received=10.0.2.46;
   rport=61814;branch=z9hG4bKPjDu0EGRnwIYDVg5.D7Dyvt8h4Q91H16VJ.
```

Record-Route: <sip:10.0.2.30;lr>.
Contact: <sip:1001@10.0.2.24:26724>.
To: <sip:1001@opensips.org>;tag=d022987a.
From: "1000"<sip:1000@opensips.org>;tag=eIrd.nxJQfDFjk3OzVRyJ-
    CjnDaL1sCz.
Call-ID: wiUEvg2atKMRa0pZNHfTM3RC01bubWWF.
CSeq: 17325 INVITE.
Allow: INVITE, ACK, CANCEL, OPTIONS, BYE, REFER, NOTIFY, MESSAGE,
    SUBSCRIBE, INFO.
Content-Type: application/sdp.
User-Agent: Bria 3 release 3.5.5 stamp 71238.

(22) U 10.0.2.30:5060 -> 10.0.2.46:61814
SIP/2.0 200 OK.
Via: SIP/2.0/UDP 10.0.2.46:61814;received=10.0.2.46;
    rport=61814;branch=z9hG4bKPjDu0EGRnwIYDVg5.D7Dyvt8h4Q91H16VJ.
Record-Route: <sip:10.0.2.30;lr>.
Contact: <sip:1001@10.0.2.24:26724>.
To: <sip:1001@opensips.org>;tag=d022987a.
From: "1000"<sip:1000@opensips.org>;tag=eIrd.nxJQfDFjk3OzVRyJ-
    CjnDaL1sCz.
Call-ID: wiUEvg2atKMRa0pZNHfTM3RC01bubWWF.
CSeq: 17325 INVITE.
User-Agent: Bria 3 release 3.5.5 stamp 71238.

(25) U 10.0.2.46:61814 -> 10.0.2.30:5060
REFER sip:4733990000@10.8.30.75:5060 SIP/2.0.
Via: SIP/2.0/UDP 10.0.2.46:61814;rport;
    branch=z9hG4bKPjHXE6B5RmGvasu7o0fW0S8RqTd-Wejvzz.
Max-Forwards: 70.
From: <sip:1000@10.0.2.30>;tag=toQEoljqGplWjxgNJZuwxqQSSNTxYlaU.
To: "4733990000" <sip:4733990000@10.8.30.75>;tag=as6fa7d95c.
Contact: "1000" <sip:1000@10.0.2.46:61814;ob>.
Call-ID: 0c4ac8a67f1c69311d5a9dbc4ae59678@10.8.30.75:5060.
CSeq: 6380 REFER.
Route: <sip:10.0.2.30;lr;did=cb4.691d7dd2>.
Event: refer.
Expires: 600.
Supported: Replaces, 100rel, timer, norefersub.
Accept: message/sipfrag;version=2.0.
Allow-Events: presence, message-summary, refer.
Refer-To: <sip:1001@opensips.org?Replaces=wiUEvg2atKMRa0pZNHfTM3RC01b
ubWWF%3
    Bto-tag%3Dd022987a%3Bfrom-tag%3DeIrd.nxJQfDFjk3OzVRyJ-
    CjnDaL1sCz>.

```
Referred-By: <sip:1000@10.0.2.30>.
User-Agent: Bria iOS 3.0.5.
Content-Length:  0.

.


(26) U 10.0.2.30:5060 -> 10.8.30.75:5060
REFER sip:4733990000@10.8.30.75:5060 SIP/2.0.
Via: SIP/2.0/UDP 10.0.2.30:5060;branch=z9hG4bKba82.251e69b1.0.
Via: SIP/2.0/UDP 10.0.2.46:61814;received=10.0.2.46;
   rport=61814;branch=z9hG4bKPjHXE6B5RmGvasu7o0fW0S8RqTd-Wejvzz.
Max-Forwards: 69.
From: <sip:1000@10.0.2.30>;tag=toQEoljqGplWjxgNJZuwxqQSSNTxYlaU.
To: "4733990000" <sip:4733990000@10.8.30.75>;tag=as6fa7d95c.
Contact: "1000" <sip:1000@10.0.2.46:61814;ob>.
Call-ID: 0c4ac8a67f1c69311d5a9dbc4ae59678@10.8.30.75:5060.
CSeq: 6380 REFER.
Event: refer.
Expires: 600.
Supported: Replaces, 100rel, timer, norefersub.
Accept: message/sipfrag;version=2.0.
Allow-Events: presence, message-summary, refer.
Refer-To: <sip:1001@opensips.org?
   Replaces=wiUEvg2atKMRa0pZNHfTM3RC0lbubWWF%3Bto-
   tag%3Dd022987a%3Bfrom-tag%3DeIrd.nxJQfDFjk3OzVRyJ-CjnDaL1sCz>.
Referred-By: <sip:1000@10.0.2.30>.
User-Agent: Bria iOS 3.0.5.
Content-Length:  0.

.


(27) U 10.8.30.75:5060 -> 10.0.2.30:5060
SIP/2.0 202 Accepted.
Via: SIP/2.0/UDP 10.0.2.30:5060;branch=z9hG4bKba82.251e69b1.0;
   received=10.0.2.30;rport=5060.
Via: SIP/2.0/UDP 10.0.2.46:61814;received=10.0.2.46;
   rport=61814;branch=z9hG4bKPjHXE6B5RmGvasu7o0fW0S8RqTd-Wejvzz.
From: <sip:1000@10.0.2.30>;tag=toQEoljqGplWjxgNJZuwxqQSSNTxYlaU.
To: "4733990000" <sip:4733990000@10.8.30.75>;tag=as6fa7d95c.
Call-ID: 0c4ac8a67f1c69311d5a9dbc4ae59678@10.8.30.75:5060.
CSeq: 6380 REFER.
Server: Test Gateway 1.0.
Allow: INVITE, ACK, CANCEL, OPTIONS, BYE, REFER, SUBSCRIBE,
   NOTIFY, INFO, PUBLISH.
Supported: Replaces, timer.
Contact: <sip:4733990000@10.8.30.75:5060>.
Content-Length: 0.
```

```
 .
 (28) U 10.0.2.30:5060 -> 10.0.2.46:61814
SIP/2.0 202 Accepted.
Via: SIP/2.0/UDP 10.0.2.46:61814;received=10.0.2.46;
  rport=61814;branch=z9hG4bKPjHXE6B5RmGvasu7o0fW0S8RqTd-Wejvzz.
From: <sip:1000@10.0.2.30>;tag=toQEoljqGplWjxgNJZuwxqQSSNTxYlaU.
To: "4733990000" <sip:4733990000@10.8.30.75>;tag=as6fa7d95c.
Call-ID: 0c4ac8a67f1c69311d5a9dbc4ae59678@10.8.30.75:5060.
CSeq: 6380 REFER.
Server: Test Gateway 1.0.
Allow: INVITE, ACK, CANCEL, OPTIONS, BYE, REFER, SUBSCRIBE,
  NOTIFY, INFO, PUBLISH.
Supported: Replaces, timer.
Contact: <sip:4733990000@10.8.30.75:5060>.
Content-Length: 0.
 .


 (29) U 10.8.30.75:5060 -> 10.0.2.30:5060
NOTIFY sip:1000@10.0.2.46:61814;ob SIP/2.0.
Via: SIP/2.0/UDP 10.8.30.75:5060;branch=z9hG4bK51c68eba;rport.
Route: <sip:10.0.2.30;lr;did=cb4.691d7dd2>.
Max-Forwards: 70.
From: "4733990000" <sip:4733990000@10.8.30.75>;tag=as6fa7d95c.
To: <sip:1000@10.0.2.30>;tag=toQEoljqGplWjxgNJZuwxqQSSNTxYlaU.
Contact: <sip:4733990000@10.8.30.75:5060>.
Call-ID: 0c4ac8a67f1c69311d5a9dbc4ae59678@10.8.30.75:5060.
CSeq: 103 NOTIFY.
User-Agent: Test Gateway 1.0.
Event: refer;id=6380.
Subscription-state: terminated;reason=noresource.
Content-Type: message/sipfrag;version=2.0.
Allow: INVITE, ACK, CANCEL, OPTIONS, BYE, REFER, SUBSCRIBE,
  NOTIFY, INFO, PUBLISH.
Supported: Replaces, timer.
Content-Length: 16.
 .
SIP/2.0 200 Ok.

 (33) U 10.8.30.75:5060 -> 10.0.2.30:5060
INVITE sip:1001@10.0.2.30 SIP/2.0.
Via: SIP/2.0/UDP 10.8.30.75:5060;branch=z9hG4bK3f3b7eeb;rport.
Max-Forwards: 70.
From: "4733990000" <sip:4733990000@10.8.30.75>;tag=as559d93a0.
To: <sip:1001@10.0.2.30>.
```

Contact: <sip:4733990000@10.8.30.75:5060>.
Call-ID: 058f177724cc3a991bf8c24661120764@10.8.30.75:5060.
CSeq: 102 INVITE.
User-Agent: Test Gateway 1.0.
Date: Fri, 01 May 2015 00:42:35 GMT.
Replaces: wiUEvg2atKMRa0pZNHfTM3RC0lbubWWF;to-tag=d022987a;
   from-tag=eIrd.nxJQfDFjk3OzVRyJ-CjnDaL1sCz.
Require: Replaces.

(34) U 10.0.2.30:5060 -> 10.0.2.24:26724
INVITE sip:1001@10.0.2.24:26724;rinstance=0f9522053bd37f41;
   transport=udp SIP/2.0.
Record-Route: <sip:10.0.2.30;lr;did=921.e88cdfa6>.
Via: SIP/2.0/UDP 10.0.2.30:5060;branch=z9hG4bKafff.9f571202.0.
Via: SIP/2.0/UDP 10.8.30.75:5060;received=10.8.30.75;
   branch=z9hG4bK3f3b7eeb;rport=5060.
Max-Forwards: 69.
From: "4733990000" <sip:4733990000@10.8.30.75>;tag=as559d93a0.
To: <sip:1001@10.0.2.30>.
Contact: <sip:4733990000@10.8.30.75:5060>.
Call-ID: 058f177724cc3a991bf8c24661120764@10.8.30.75:5060.
CSeq: 102 INVITE.
User-Agent: Test Gateway 1.0.
Replaces: wiUEvg2atKMRa0pZNHfTM3RC0lbubWWF;to-tag=d022987a;
   from-tag=eIrd.nxJQfDFjk3OzVRyJ-CjnDaL1sCz.

(35) U 10.0.2.24:26724 -> 10.0.2.30:5060
SIP/2.0 200 OK.
Via: SIP/2.0/UDP 10.0.2.30:5060;branch=z9hG4bKafff.9f571202.0.
Via: SIP/2.0/UDP 10.8.30.75:5060;received=10.8.30.75;branch=z9hG4bK3f
3b7eeb;
   rport=5060.
Record-Route: <sip:10.0.2.30;lr;did=921.e88cdfa6>.
Contact: <sip:1001@10.0.2.24:26724>.
To: <sip:1001@10.0.2.30>;tag=1e2ae359.
From: "4733990000"<sip:4733990000@10.8.30.75>;tag=as559d93a0.
Call-ID: 058f177724cc3a991bf8c24661120764@10.8.30.75:5060.
CSeq: 102 INVITE.
Allow: INVITE, ACK, CANCEL, OPTIONS, BYE, REFER, NOTIFY, MESSAGE,
   SUBSCRIBE, INFO.
User-Agent: Bria 3 release 3.5.5   stamp 71238.

(36) U 10.0.2.24:26724 -> 10.0.2.30:5060
BYE sip:1000@10.0.2.46:61814;ob SIP/2.0.

```
User-Agent: Bria 3 release 3.5.5  stamp 71238.
.


(37) U 10.0.2.30:5060 -> 10.8.30.75:5060
SIP/2.0 200 OK.
Via: SIP/2.0/UDP 10.8.30.75:5060;
  received=10.8.30.75;branch=z9hG4bK3f3b7eeb;
  rport=5060.
Record-Route: <sip:10.0.2.30;lr;did=921.e88cdfa6>.
Contact: <sip:1001@10.0.2.24:26724>.
To: <sip:1001@10.0.2.30>;tag=1e2ae359.
From: "4733990000"<sip:4733990000@10.8.30.75>;tag=as559d93a0.
Call-ID: 058f177724cc3a991bf8c24661120764@10.8.30.75:5060.
CSeq: 102 INVITE.
Allow: INVITE, ACK, CANCEL, OPTIONS, BYE, REFER, NOTIFY, MESSAGE,
  SUBSCRIBE, INFO.
Content-Type: application/sdp.
Supported: Replaces, eventlist.
User-Agent: Bria 3 release 3.5.5  stamp 71238.
.

Last packets suppressed
```

Tips for call transfer

Before you attempt a call transfer, make sure that you can make a simple call between all the components. I did this by registering a phone on Asterisk and simulating an inbound external call. Then, I called the extensions 1000 and 1001 from this phone, successfully. Later, I tested calling from 1000 and 1001 to 4733990000, our PSTN number. Once everything was okay, I proceeded with the transfer tests. The things to pay attention to are that all the components need to have support for the REFERs and Replaces header. The REFER requests are handled exactly in the same way as an INVITE. Make sure that you have the REFER destination in your dialplan.

There is no change required in opensips.cfg to make a call transfer work. The script from *Chapter 7, Dialplan and Routing* is sufficient; just make sure that you can complete all the calls described previously.

In the Asterisk server, you need to have the `allowtransfers=yes` line in the general section in the `sip.conf` file. You should also have a peer created for OpenSIPS as follows:

```
[opensips]
type=peer
host=10.0.2.30
disallow=all
allow=ulaw
context=from-internal
dtmf=rfc2833
insecure=invite,port
```

In the Asterisk server, you need to have the options `tT` in the `extensions.conf` file on the dialplan in order to allow the transfer:

```
[from-internal]
exten=_1XXX,1,dial(SIP/opensips/${EXTEN},tT)
exten=4733990000,1,dial(SIP/4733990000,20,tT)
```

Summary

In this chapter, you learned how to implement SIP services in order to implement telephony features found in legacy PBXs. You learned that RFC 5359 is our guide when implementing such services. Then, we explained how to implement simple services such as announcements, call forward, integration with voicemail, and call transfer. New services are being created every year; these services are usually proposed in drafts. A few good examples are RFC 6910 describing Call Completion Services and RFC 6341 for SIP-based Media Recording. After implementing all these features, we now have to understand how to troubleshoot them.

In the next chapter, we will cover troubleshooting tools.

12
Monitoring Tools

In the previous chapters, we finished the installation of the VoIP provider. Now, it is time to start production and operation. On a daily basis, you will need some tools to deal with customers complaining about connectivity and voice quality issues. In this chapter, we will see some of the best tools that will help you with this task. You may check your progress in the following figure:

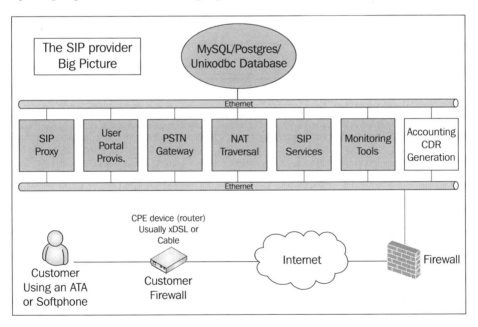

After installing the whole system, there comes a new phase: testing, operation, and maintenance. In this chapter, we will cover some tools and utilities that will help you with this task. We will start with built-in monitoring tools such as **OpenSIPS statistics** and **SIPTRACE**, followed by testing tools such as **SIPp** and **sipsak**.

By the end of this chapter, you will be able to perform the following operations:

- Understanding how to use built-in tools such as opensipsctl
- Understanding the control panel's statistics monitor
- Troubleshooting customer signaling using SIPTRACE
- Troubleshooting the script using Script trace
- Troubleshooting syntax errors and scripts that won't start
- What to do when the system crashes, handling core dumps
- Understanding the benchmark sections of the script using benchmark
- Stress testing OpenSIPS using SIPp and sipsak
- Using **Wireshark** and **ngrep** to troubleshoot

Built-in tools

The OpenSIPS version 2.x provides you with a bunch of new management tools. The shell script, opensipsctl, has some options to generate statistics. Let's go through some of these commands:

Command	Result
opensipsctl fifo which	Displays all the available commands
opensipsctl fifo ps	Displays all the processes
opensipsctl fifo get_statistics core:	Displays statistics about the core
opensipsctl fifo get_statistics net:	Displays Net sockets
opensipsctl fifo get_statistics pkmem:	Displays private memory of each process
opensipsctl fifo get_statistics tm:	Displays TM module statistics
opensipsctl fifo get_statistics sl:	Displays SL module statistics
opensipsctl fifo get statistics shmem:	Displays shared memory statistics
opensipsctl fifo get statistics usrloc:	Displays user location statistics
opensipsctl fifo get statistics registrar:	Displays Registrar statistics
opensipsctl fifo get statistics uri:	Displays URI statistics
opensipsctl fifo get statistics load:	Displays load statistics

The first question that my students ask me after presenting these options is: which ones are the most significant? If I had to monitor an OpenSIPS server, I would examine the following parameters:

- The memory available. Graph shmem and pkgmem and check for memory leaks.
- The number of simultaneous calls from the `dialog` module.
- The number of users registered on the `registrar` module.
- The number of simultaneous transactions from the TM module.
- The load. A load of one hundred means that all the children processes are busy. It means that your server is dropping requests. It is usually counterproductive to add more children processes. Normally, this happens because of slow DNS queries, SQL queries, or HTTP queries. Check anything in your system taking more than a few milliseconds to process. The `benchmark` module can help you, with an exception for the DNS queries.

Statistics may be graphed using the OpenSIPS control panel, as shown in the following image:

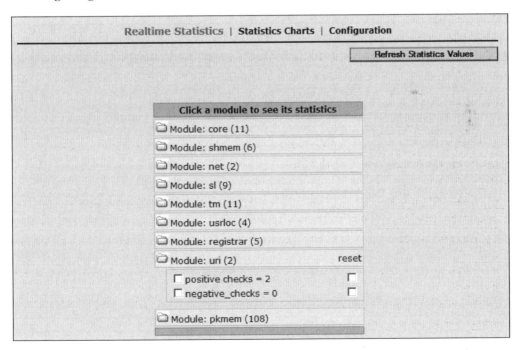

Trace tools

OpenSIPS has an exceptional tool called **SIPTRACE**. With this tool, you can trace calls from a specific user in real time. SIPTRACE can severely affect the performance of your system when enabled. The SIPTRACE module logs the SIP signaling to a database for the inbound and outbound traffic. Remember that a good magnetic hard disk is usually able to write up to 200 **IO operations per second (IOPS)**. With SIPTRACE turned on, it will insert at least eight records for a simple authenticated call along with indexes. If you are running a system with 100 calls per second, it can significantly affect the performance and ultimately block your system to the point of dropping requests. Use with care; enable it only to troubleshoot and for a specific traffic target. If you need to have a history of traces, you should try a separate disk. Solid-state disks are becoming mainstream and can improve the write performance dramatically.

SIPTRACE

The SIPTRACE module is simple to use; you need to load the module and mark the transactions that you want to record using a specific flag. Define this flag using the module parameter, trace_flag. You probably don't want to record all the messages to the database because of the overhead. It is possible to start the trace for a single user.

Set the module parameter, traced_user_avp, to trace a specific user. The traced_user column of the siptrace table shows the target user. You can store multiple values in the AVP if you want to trace more than a single user. The SIPTRACE module can be enabled and disabled using the fifo command, sip_trace on/off. It is possible to visualize the results of the traced call using the OpenSIPS control panel.

Configuring SIPTRACE

The following are the steps to configure SIPTRACE:

1. To enable the SIPTRACE, add the following instructions to your script:

```
loadmodule "siptrace.so"

modparam("siptrace", "db_url", "mysql://opensips:opensipsrw@
localhost/opensips")
modparam("siptrace", "trace_flag", TRACE_FLAG)
modparam("siptrace", "traced_user_avp", "$avp(traceuser)")
modparam("siptrace", "trace_local_ip", "ip_address_of_your_
server")
```

```
if(avp_db_load("$fu","$avp(trace)")) {
    $avp(s:traceuser)=$fu;
    setflag(TRACE_FLAG);
    xlog("L_INFO","User $fu being traced");
}
```

2. After restarting the script, add the user to the trace as follows:

    ```
    opensipsctl avp add -T usr_preferences 1000@youripaddress trace 0
    1
    ```

3. Now, start SIPTRACE using the following command:

    ```
    opensipsctl fifo sip_trace on
    ```

If everything has been configured correctly, try making a call from the user 1000 to user 1001. See the results in the `sip_trace` table or in the OpenSIPS control panel, as shown in the following image:

Date Time	Method	Status	Path	Details
2009-10-20 23:24:32	BYE	200	👤 ← 🖥	🔍
2009-10-20 23:24:32	BYE	200	🖥 ← 👤	🔍
2009-10-20 23:24:32	BYE		🖥 → 👤	🔍
2009-10-20 23:24:30	INVITE	200	👤 ← 🖥	🔍
2009-10-20 23:24:30	INVITE	200	🖥 ← 👤	🔍
2009-10-20 23:24:27	INVITE	180	👤 ← 🖥	🔍
2009-10-20 23:24:27	INVITE	180	🖥 ← 👤	🔍
2009-10-20 23:24:27	INVITE		🖥 → 👤	🔍

👤 Caller 🖥 Proxy 👤 Callee

Script trace

This tool helps you understand the execution flow. It shows what line it is in and what function it is executing. It is also able to trace AVPs and pseudo-variables. Define the code segment that you want to script. The format of the command is as follows:

```
script_trace( log_level, pv_format_string[, info_string])
```

The parameters of `script_trace()` are described as follows:

- `log_level`: This is the level where the messages are shown
- `pv_format_string`: This is a string with pseudo-variables to show
- `info_string`: This identifies the block of the script trace

An example of their usage is as follows:

```
script_trace( 1, "$rm/$si/f=$fu/r=$ru/$ci/$si", "me");
```

The preceding example will produce the following output:

```
Oct 14 22:39:54 [Script Trace][opensips.cfg:301][me][core if] ->
(REGISTER/10.8.30.53/f=sip:1000@10.8.30.45/r=sip:10.8.30.45/20915a8a365347a99eb1e8734faa6a69/10.8.30.53)
Oct 14 22:39:54 [Script Trace][opensips.cfg:294][me][module www_authorize] ->
(REGISTER/10.8.30.53/f=sip:1000@10.8.30.45/r=sip:10.8.30.45/20915a8a365347a99eb1e8734faa6a69/10.8.30.53)
Oct 14 22:39:54 [Script Trace][opensips.cfg:296][me][module www_challenge] ->
(REGISTER/10.8.30.53/f=sip:1000@10.8.30.45/r=sip:10.8.30.45/20915a8a365347a99eb1e8734faa6a69/10.8.30.53)
Oct 14 22:39:54 [Script Trace][opensips.cfg:301][me][core if] ->
(REGISTER/10.8.30.53/f=sip:1000@10.8.30.45/r=sip:10.8.30.45/20915a8a365347a99eb1e8734faa6a69/10.8.30.53)
Oct 14 22:39:54 [Script Trace][opensips.cfg:294][me][module www_authorize] ->
(REGISTER/10.8.30.53/f=sip:1000@10.8.30.45/r=sip:10.8.30.45/20915a8a365347a99eb1e8734faa6a69/10.8.30.53)
Oct 14 22:39:54 [Script Trace][opensips.cfg:303][me][core if] ->
(REGISTER/10.8.30.53/f=sip:1000@10.8.30.45/r=sip:10.8.30.45/20915a8a365347a99eb1e8734faa6a69/10.8.30.53)
Oct 14 22:39:54 [Script Trace][opensips.cfg:305][me][core if] ->
(REGISTER/10.8.30.53/f=sip:1000@10.8.30.45/r=sip:10.8.30.45/20915a8a365347a99eb1e8734faa6a69/10.8.30.53)
Oct 14 22:39:54 [Script Trace][opensips.cfg:303][me][module save] ->
(REGISTER/10.8.30.53/f=sip:1000@10.8.30.45/r=sip:10.8.30.45/20915a8a365347a99eb1e8734faa6a69/10.8.30.53)
Oct 14 22:39:54 [Script Trace][opensips/opensips.cfg:305][me][core script_trace] ->
(REGISTER/10.8.30.53/f=sip:1000@10.8.30.45/r=sip:10.8.30.45/20915a8a365347a99eb1e8734faa6a69/10.8.30.53)
```

 Don't forget to use `script_trace()` without parameters after the end of the segment of code that is of interest.

Troubleshooting routing scripts

Sometimes, it is hard to debug an existing script. We strongly encourage you to use a versioning system such as subversion or Git for your scripts. Always create a backup before editing a production script. Try to avoid changing the routing script (`opensips.cfg`) as much as possible. Use the database for the daily configuration changes to subscribers, dialplans, and routes. It is usual to run the same script for years.

You can test the syntax of a script without running it using the following command:

```
opensips -c
```

It will show you the syntax errors and related lines. Some common syntax errors are as follows:

- A missing semi-column at the end of the line
- Missing brackets ([]) and curly brackets ({ })
- Command not available because the module was not loaded
- A global parameter pointing to the wrong library path (mpath)

Missing parentheses, curly braces, and brackets are hard to spot because the system will point to the line where it detected the mistake, but the error is usually before this point. Indentation is key for the troubleshooting of syntax errors.

After getting rid of all the syntax errors, try to start OpenSIPS using the following command:

```
opensipsctl start
```

You can also use the following command to do so:

```
/etc/init.d/opensips start
```

Once started, check the status as follows:

```
/etc/init.d/opensips status
```

> If your script does not start, check for errors in the log file. The log file is usually at /var/log/syslog in Debian/Ubuntu systems and /var/log/messages for Red Hat/CentOS/Fedora. You can redirect the log files to a specific file configuring your server's syslog (usually at /etc/rsyslog.conf).

As a last resource, in a few cases, you will have to start OpenSIPS in the foreground using a maximum debug level. You can do it using the following command:

```
opensips -D -E -dddddddddddd
```

A system crash

In some very specific cases, OpenSIPS can crash just as any other system. Crashed systems are not easy to troubleshoot. However, you can get some clues regarding the crash using core dumps. To enable core dumps, you have to edit the initialization file at /etc/init.d/opensips. Edit the core dump section and remove the comments from the highlighted lines:

```
if test "$DUMP_CORE" = "yes" ; then
    # set proper ulimit
    ulimit -c unlimited

    # directory for the core dump files
    COREDIR=/home/corefiles -d $COREDIR ] || mkdir $COREDIR
    chmod 777 $COREDIR
    echo "$COREDIR/core.%e.sig%s.%p" >
      /proc/sys/kernel/core_pattern
fi
```

After a crash, a core dump file is created in the /home/corefiles directory. You can use gdb (the GNU debugger) to do a backtrace of the core dump. It can give you some clues regarding the crash such as what command the system was running at the moment of the crash. Send the full backtrace to the developers of OpenSIPS for further analysis.

To generate a backtrace, use the following:

gdb opensips core.126327051987.sig11

Here, core.126327051987.sig11 is the core dump file found at /home/corefiles.

Type bt full in the debugger prompt (gdb).

An example of the output is as follows:

```
Program terminated with signal 11, Segmentation fault.
#0  0x00007fe93ab05491 in unlink_unsafe_dlg (dlg=0x7fe915eccd30,
  cnt=1) at
dlg_hash.c:706
706 dlg->next->prev = dlg->prev;

(gdb) bt full
#0  0x00007fe93ab05491 in unlink_unsafe_dlg (dlg=0x7fe915eccd30,
  cnt=1) at
```

```
dlg_h
ash.c:706
No locals.
#1  unref_dlg (dlg=0x7fe915eccd30, cnt=1) at dlg_hash.c:740
        d_entry = 0x7fe915c3f990
        __FUNCTION__ = "unref_dlg"
#2  0x00007fe93ab0e7f5 in dlg_ping_routine (ticks=<value optimized
  out>,
attr=<v
alue optimized out>) at dlg_timer.c:529
        expired = <value optimized out>
        it = 0x0
        curr = 0x0
        dlg = 0x7fe915eccd30
        __FUNCTION__ = "dlg_ping_routine"
#3  0x000000000047d4ca in timer_ticker () at timer.c:355
        t = 0x7fe93c19c810
#4  run_timer_process () at timer.c:425
        multiple = 10
      cnt = <value optimized out>
        tv = {tv_sec = 0, tv_usec = 0}
#5  start_timer_processes () at timer.c:522
        tpl = 0x7fe93c20aa60
        pid = <value optimized out>
        __FUNCTION__ = "start_timer_processes"
#6  0x000000000042a814 in main_loop (argc=<value optimized out>,
argv=<value optimized out>) at main.c:933
        i = <value optimized out>
        pid = <value optimized out>
        si = 0x0
        startup_done = 0x0
        chd_rank = 0
        rc = <value optimized out>
        load_p = 0x0
#7  main (argc=<value optimized out>, argv=<value optimized out>)
  at
main.c:1520
        cfg_log_stderr = <value optimized out>
        cfg_stream = <value optimized out>
        c = <value optimized out>
        r = <value optimized out>
```

```
tmp = 0x1 <Address 0x1 out of bounds>
tmp_len = <value optimized out>
port = <value optimized out>
proto = <value optimized out>
options = 0x4eb5a8
    "f:cCm:M:b:l:n:N:rRvdDETSVhw:t:u:g:P:G:W:o:"
ret = -1
seed = 1183817865
rfd = <value optimized out>
__FUNCTION__ = "main"
```

Benchmarking segments of code

The benchmark module is capable of timing specific segments of the script. We use it often to detect slow queries and avoid blocking. The standard timeout before a client or peer sends a retransmission is usually 500 ms. Depending on the number of calls per second, segments of code lasting more than 500 ms are like an eternity. DB queries should be as fast as possible to avoid blocking the processes that are waiting for a query answer. To use the benchmark module, follow these steps:

1. Set the module parameters:

```
loadmodule "benchmark.so"
modparam("benchmark", "enable", 1)
modparam("benchmark", "granularity", 500)
modparam("benchmark", "loglevel", 3)
```

The preceding lines enable the module and set the granularity to 500, where granularity is the number of request samples to consider; in our example, one call on each 500. The log level is 3 (L_INFO), so if the debug level is set to 3, the benchmark statistics will appear.

2. Find the segment of interest and insert the start and stop of the benchmark:

```
bm_start_timer("register");
#Segment Start
...

...
#Segment end
bm_log_timer("register");
```

Here, register is an arbitrary name for the segment.

3. Look for the statistics in **syslog**:

```
Oct 14 23:26:43 benchmark (timer register [0]): 1483 [ msgs/total/min/max/avg - LR:
10/15925/1378/2096/1592.500000 | GB: 20/57338/1378/17060/2866.900000]
Oct 14 23:27:14 benchmark (timer register [0]): 1711 [ msgs/total/min/max/avg - LR:
10/16634/1420/2105/1663.400000 | GB: 30/73972/1378/17060/2465.733333]
```

In the preceding figure, note the number of messages in the first line (**20**) and the minimum, average, and maximum time to execute the segment of code. Durations are given in microseconds.

Stress testing tools

Now, we will present some tools to stress test your server before going live. The first tool is sipsak (http://sourceforge.net/projects/sipsak.berlios/) and the second is SIPp (http://sipp.sourceforge.net/).

The sipsak tool

The sipsak is a command-line tool used by SIP administrators. It is able to run simple tests against the SIP server. It is a good tool to check the security of the server because you can create the SIP request exactly in the way you want. Further information on this can be found at http://sourceforge.net/projects/sipsak.berlios/. Let's show an example on how to use it. Install it using the following:

```
apt-get install sipsak
```

An example of its use is as follows:

- You can ping a UAC using the OPTIONS method by issuing the following command:

  ```
  sipsak -vv -s sip:1000@opensips.org
  ```

- To register a user and return a completion code, you can use the following:

  ```
  sipsak -U -s sip:1000@192.168.1.185 -a 1000 -W 1 -vvvvv
  ```

- Place a call as follows:

  ```
  sipsak -T -s sip:1000@opensips.org
  ```

- Send a message using the MESSAGE method:

  ```
  sipsak -M -s sip:1000@opensips.org -c flavio@opensips.org -B
     "time for a coffee break"
  ```

You can also use the stress (-F) and torture (-R) modes. You can find the complete documentation in the sipsak website, `http://sourceforge.net/projects/sipsak.berlios/`. The best results are obtained by combining sipsak with Nagios (`http://www.nagios.org/`) or even a simple shell script.

SIPp

To explain each detail of SIPp is beyond the scope of this book. The idea here is to give you an overview of SIPp and teach you how to start it. Allocate enough time to test your platform and build a test lab.

SIPp is a traffic generation tool to stress test the server. It is a good tool to submit traffic to your SIP server and test it before going to the production phase. It establishes and releases multiple calls with methods such as INVITE and BYE. The call rate is adjusted dynamically by pressing the keys (+) plus and (-) minus. More information is available at `http://sipp.sourceforge.net/doc/reference.html`.

Let's see some examples with real-world scenarios of what we can do with this tool.

Installing SIPp

We begin by installing the dependencies:

```
apt-get install g++ libncurses5-dev libssl-dev libnet1-dev libpcap0.8-dev
```

Then, we Download and decompress the `sipp` source file:

 File names on the Internet change often, please download the latest version available.

```
wget http://downloads.sourceforge.net/sipp/sipp-3.3.990.tar.gz
tar -xzvf sipp-3.3.990.tar.gz
```

Compile and include the `ssl` libraries to allow authentication:

```
./configure -with-openssl
make
./sipp
```

Stress testing

We will not get in the details of SIPp's scenario customizations. For this, you
can check the SIPp documentation (refer to http://sipp.sourceforge.net/
doc/) if you intend to test with authentication and record routing. We will test the
registration process for the SIP server. Follow these steps:

1. After installing SIPp, create the register scenario file or simply copy the reg.
   xml file available in the book-related downloads:

```xml
<?xml version="1.0" encoding="ISO-8859-1" ?>
<scenario name="register">
  <send retrans="500">
    <![CDATA[

        REGISTER sip:[remote_ip] SIP/2.0
        Via: SIP/2.0/[transport] [local_ip]:
          [local_port];branch=[branch]
        From: <sip:[field0]@[field1]>;tag=[call_number]
        To: <sip:[field0]@[field1]>
        Call-ID: [call_id]
        CSeq: 1 REGISTER
        Contact: sip:[field0]@[local_ip]:[local_port]
        Max-Forwards: 5
        Expires: 1800
        User-Agent: SIPP
        Content-Length: 0

    ]]>
  </send>
  <optional="true" recv response="100">
  </recv>

  <recv response="401" auth="true">
  </recv>

  <send retrans="500">
    <![CDATA[

        REGISTER sip:[remote_ip] SIP/2.0
        Via: SIP/2.0/[transport] [local_ip]:
          [local_port];branch=[branch]
        From: <sip:[field0]@[field1]>;tag=[call_number]
        To: <sip:[field0]@[field1]>
```

```
        Call-ID: [call_id]
        CSeq: 2 REGISTER
        Contact: sip:[field0]@[local_ip]:[local_port]
        [field2]
        Max-Forwards: 5
        Expires: 1800
        User-Agent: SIPP
        Content-Length: 0


     ]]>
    </send>

    <recv response="200">
    </recv>
</scenario>
```

2. Add the following users to the `client.csv` file for authentication and name them `users.csv`:

   SEQUENTIAL

   1000;opensips.org;[authentication username=1000 password=1000]

   1001;opensips.org;[authentication username=1001 password=1001]

3. Add the current IP address of your server pointing to `opensips.org`:

   vi /etc/hosts

127.0.0.1	**localhost**
127.0.1.1	**bookosips.opensips.org bookosips**
10.8.30.77	**opensips.org**

4. Use the sample script with authentication generated by **make menuconfig** or any other script that you have with registration and authentication.

5. To start the registration test, use the following command:

   sipp -sf reg.xml -inf users.csv -i 10.8.30.77 -p 5080 -r 10 opensips.org

   The previous command is described as follows:

   - `-sf reg.xml` is the scenario file
   - `-inf users.csv` specifies the authentication information
   - `-i` is the IP local SIPp address
   - `-p` is the local SIPp port
   - `-r 10` sets the message rate of 10 cps
   - `opensips.org` is the domain of the server

It will show you a screen similar to the following screenshot:

```
------------------------------- Scenario Screen --------- [1-9]: Change Screen ---
  Call-rate(length)    Port    Total-time  Total-calls  Remote-host
  10.0(0 ms)/1.000s    5080       8.00 s           79   10.8.30.77:5060(UDP)


  9 new calls during 0.952 s period      11 ms scheduler resolution
  0 calls (limit 30)                     Peak was 1 calls, after 0 s
  0 Running, 82 Paused, 20 Woken up
  0 dead call msg (discarded)            0 out-of-call msg (discarded)
  3 open sockets

                                  Messages  Retrans   Timeout   Unexpected-Msg
     REGISTER ---------->            79        0         0
          100 <----------             0        0         0          0
          401 <----------  E-RTD1    79        0         0          0
     REGISTER ---------->            79        0         0
          100 <----------             0        0         0          0
          200 <----------            79        0         0          0
       Pause [      0ms]            79                             0
--------------------------------- Test Terminated ------------------------------
```

Packet capturing tools

In many situations, you will have to capture SIP packets to analyze the signaling. There are many tools available on the web for this purpose. In this book, we will cover three: ngrep, sipgrep, and Wireshark, the most popular. If you have to keep a large number of captured packets and traces, I strongly recommend Homer (http://www.sipcapture.org/).

Ngrep

Ngrep is one of the simplest tools for packet capture and is readily available in any OS. To install it on Debian/Ubuntu, use the following:

```
apt-get install ngrep
```

After the installation, you can capture packets as follows:

```
ngrep -d any -q -t -W byline port 5060
```

The previous command is described as follows:

- -d any means capture from all interfaces
- -q means quiet
- -t means include a timestamp
- -W byline means an output line by line
- port 5060 is the filter

Sipgrep

This tool is specialized on SIP and very helpful. The project page for this tool is `https://github.com/sipcapture/sipgrep`. To install it, use the following commands:

```
apt-get install libpcap-dev libpcre3-dev
cd /usr/src
git clone https://github.com/sipcapture/sipgrep.git
cd sipgrep
./build.sh
./configure
make && make install
```

After installing, you can start using it by calling from the command line:

```
sipgrep -d any
```

The output is shown as follows:

```
U 2015/04/20 14:41:45.999446 10.8.30.77:5080 -> 10.8.30.77:5060

REGISTER sip:opensips.org SIP/2.0.
Via: SIP/2.0/UDP 10.8.30.77:5080;branch=z9hG4bK-16897-31-0.
From: <sip:1000@opensips.org>;tag=31.
To: <sip:1000@opensips.org>.
Call-ID: 31-16897@10.8.30.77.
CSeq: 1 REGISTER.
Contact: sip:1000@10.8.30.77:5080.
Max-Forwards: 5.
Expires: 1800.
User-Agent: SIPP.
Content-Length: 0.
```

Wireshark

Wireshark (formerly, Ethereal) is the most popular open source protocol analyzer. To teach you exactly how to use a protocol analyzer is beyond the scope of this book. However, we will give you some tips on analyzing SIP and RTP packets. Wireshark has some special statistics for SIP and RTP. After loading the captured packets, you can start analyzing the statistics of the SIP protocol. In the Wireshark menu, select the following:

Telephony | SIP

It will ask you for **Filter**; use `sip`:

Press the **Create Stat** button:

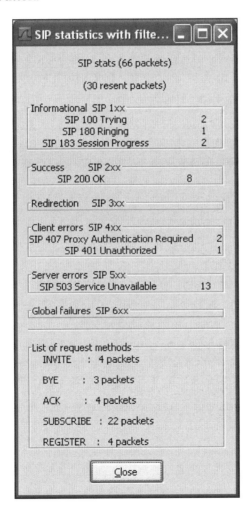

It is a nice trick. You can now check the general statistics about your SIP messages. Well, this is not our best trick, but it can help to spot abnormal behavior.

Let's go to the second trick; graphing the SIP dialog. In the Wireshark menu, select the following:

Statistics | VoIP Calls

You will see the following screen:

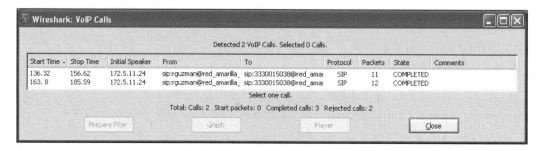

In this screen, you can select the call that you want to graph. After selecting the call, press the **Graph** button:

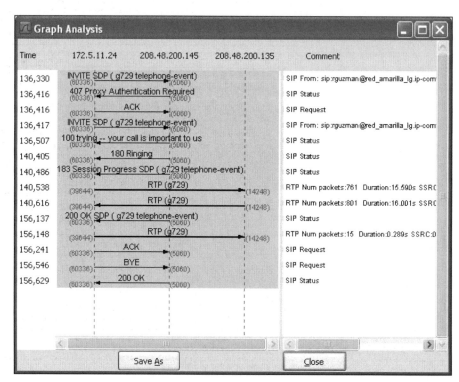

You will receive this amazing graph with the SIP dialog. Now you can spot specific problems in a single dialog. You can even play a call in the previous menu if it is coded using g.711 alaw or ulaw.

Well, now let's check the RTP packets. After all, the RTP packets will determine the voice quality. There is no single recommendation; we consider having a good voice quality when the latency is below 150 ms (the one-way equivalent to a round-trip time of 300 ms), jitter below 20 ms, and packet loss below 3%. You can have a good voice quality with higher latencies. However, the interactivity of the conversation is deteriorated after 150 ms. You can experiment this when using satellite links, where the latency is typically 500 ms. Check to see what works for you, and use Wireshark to measure voice quality in in your own standards. To help you in this task, let's use the following statistics. In the Wireshark menu, select **Telephony | RTP | Show All Streams** as shown here:

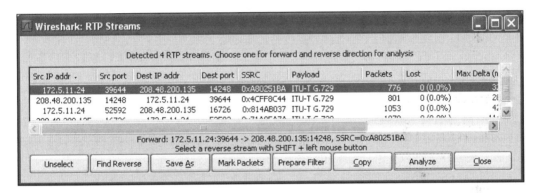

Select a stream to analyze. Use *Shift* + left mouse button to select a reverse stream:

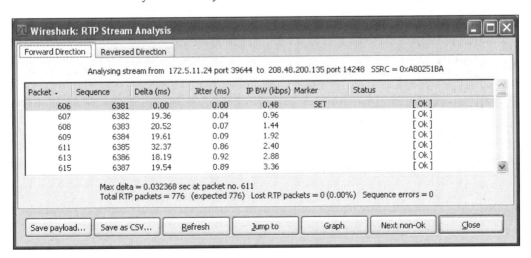

Now, you can analyze the jitter, latency (delta), IP bandwidth, and packet loss of your RTP streams packet by packet. You can even graph the RTP stream as follows:

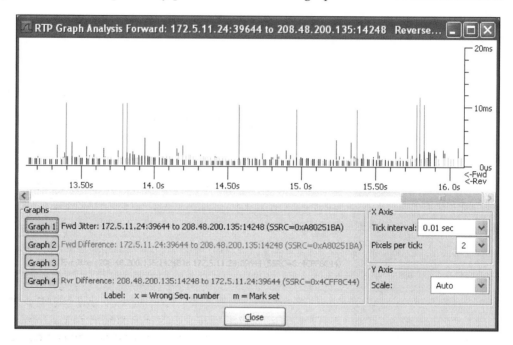

In our case, we can see that our jitter is below 5 ms in both directions in the graph. The difference is the inter-arrival time between packets.

To monitor OpenSIPS you can use a set of utilities along with network monitoring tools. You can use Nagios along with sipsak to monitor real transactions such as REGISTER and INVITE. Monit (`http://mmonit.com/monit/`) is another tool that you can use to monitor OpenSIPS from within. Using Monit, you can generate alerts about the status of the system and OpenSIPS daemon. A good tutorial on how to set up Monit with OpenSIPS can be found at `http://www.voip-info.org/wiki/view/OpenSER+And+Monit`.

Summary

In this chapter, you learned about some tools to test and monitor OpenSIPS. It is wise to stress test OpenSIPS before starting the production phase. Packet capture tools such as Wireshark and ngrep are very important and will be used on a daily basis, so be familiar with them, you will certainly need to use them. Finally, Monit can be used to monitor the processes and help you keep OpenSIPS up and running.

In the next chapter, we will cover accounting and CDR generation.

13
OpenSIPS Security

Security is one of the most important features for a SIP provider. OpenSIPS has an extensive list of features to help you prevent all types of attacks. The most relevant issues related to security are toll fraud, denial of service, and privacy violation through eavesdropping. Toll fraud is the unauthorized use of your telecommunication structure to make calls. Often, hackers make these calls to premium rate numbers paying a rebate. A toll fraud can easily go to hundreds of thousands of dollars in losses in a single month. The second most relevant issue is **Denial of Service (DOS)** or **Distributed Denial of Service (DDOS)**. A DOS/DDOS can bring your SIP server down to its knees, interrupting services to your customers. Sometimes, a customer sending a large amount of traffic in a short period can cause a DOS. In the last part of this chapter, we will cover security features to provide privacy and encryption, such as TLS and SRTP. These encryption technologies are very important for the corporate and government projects.

By the end of this chapter, you will be able to perform the following operations:

- Set up a firewall configuration for OpenSIPS
- See how to block multiple unsuccessful authentication attempts
- Use PIKE to detect and block SIP floods
- Prevent registration and DNS poisoning using blacklists
- Enable TLS for clients
- Apply the anti-fraud module

Configuring a firewall for OpenSIPS

Before we can even talk about security, it is important to configure a firewall between OpenSIPS and the Internet. I will also cover the rtpproxy daemon frequently used to provide a traversal of UDP over a relay NAT.

The default ports to open in a firewall for OpenSIPS are as follows:

Description	Source	Destination
SIP default UDP port	0.0.0.0/0	TCP 5060
SIP default TCP port	0.0.0.0/0	TCP 5060
SIP default TLS port	0.0.0.0/0	TCP 5061
RTP proxy ports defined in parameters — m and M	0.0.0.0/0	UDP Range m...M Default 35000-65000

Close all other ports for the world (0.0.0.0/0). Administration interfaces (port 80) and SSH (port 22) should be open for specific administration addresses only. Never allow indiscriminate access to web interfaces and SSH as they are frequently a vector for hacker attacks.

Blocking multiple unsuccessful authentication attempts

One of the most employed methods for toll fraud is the SIP brute force attack. If you start your server on the Internet, I can say that you will receive the first attack in less than 24 hours. These attacks are usually a series of registration attempts targeting a specific user and many different passwords. To prevent these attacks, many people employ the use of a utility called Fail2ban successfully. While Fail2ban is effective, it requires intensive processing of log files, possibly degrading the performance of the whole system. In 2012, at the ClueCon (developers' conference focused on open source VoIP), Vlad Paiu presented a simple script able to ban the attackers simply using OpenSIPS tools. I'm reprinting the script here:

```
www_authorize("","subscriber");
switch ($retcode) {
  case -3:  # stale nonce
  case -2:  # invalid passwd
  case -1:  # no such user
```

```
      xlog("Failed Auth\n");
      if ( cache_fetch("local","authF_$si",$avp(failed_no)) ) {
        if ( $(avp(failed_no){s.int}) >= 20 ) {
          xlog("SCRIPT: SECURITY ALERT: 20 failed auth from $si\n");
          send_reply("403","Forbidden");
          exit;
        }
        cache_add("local","authF_$si",1,60);
      } else {
        cache_store("local","authF_$si","1",60);
      }
    default:
      xlog("Challenging\n");
      www_challenge("", "0");
      exit;
      break;
  }
}
```

In the preceding script, we test for authentication failures by reading the $retcode variable after an authentication attempt. The return codes 1, 2, and 3 indicate a failure related to the username, password, or staled nonce, respectively, and we count the number of failed attempts. If it is higher than 20, we send a reply with code 403 and the reason Forbidden.

Preventing DOS using the PIKE module

One of the most annoying types of attacks is a Denial of Service. When it happens, it is frustrating and causes major headaches with customers. You can prevent and ban sources of SIP floods using the PIKE module described in this section. PIKE works in two modes: automatic and manual. In manual mode, you decide what to do when a certain IP passes a certain threshold in the number of requests per second.

PIKE in manual mode

To set up the module in manual mode, you have to set the following certain module parameters:

```
modparam("pike", "sampling_time_unit", 10)
modparam("pike", "reqs_density_per_unit", 500)
modparam("pike", "remove_latency", 120)
```

The `sampling_time_unit` parameter is the sample accuracy. Use a short period of time to detect fast spikes and a long one to detect consistent floods. Lower values lead to performance penalties. The `reqs_density_per_unit` parameter is the total amount of requests (also replies in automatic mode) in the sampling time. After passing the threshold for requests, PIKE will detect and mark this IP as flooding; the detection will last for the `remove_latency` time in seconds. In manual mode, PIKE does not block the requests by default. It is up to the scriptwriter to decide what to do when PIKE detects a flood.

To block requests, you can test the `pike_check_request()` function. This function returns the following values:

- `1` (true): No flooding detected
- `-1` (false): IP is the source of flooding, having being previously detected
- `-2` (false): IP is detected as a new source of flooding — first time detection

Following is an example of manual PIKE usage:

```
pike_check_request();
switch($retcode) {
  case -2:
    #simply drop the request
    exit;
  case -1:
    #drop the request and ban the IP, be careful not to drop
      gateways or valid #customers, this is an example, elaborate
      a little more for production.
    exec_msg("/sbin/iptables -A INPUT -s $si -p udp -j DROP");
    # The command above is valid only for Linux. It requires
    # root permission for execution.
    exit;
}
```

PIKE in automatic mode

In automatic mode, the module will catch all requests and replies even if they are malformed. In this mode, you need to assign `check_route` for the `PIKE` module to be executed for every request. In this script route, you can examine the sources to check whether flooding needs to be detected, usually excluding gateways and customers' IPs. When PIKE detects a flood, it drops the packet and generates an event and a log. To enable PIKE in automatic mode, simply set the module parameter, `check_route`:

```
modparam("pike", "check_route", "pike")

route[pike] {
```

```
#Avoid detection on customers (checking the source address) and
#gateways defined in the module drouting
if (!is_from_gw() && !check_source_address("0")) {
  #trusted, do not check it
  drop;
  #all other IPs are checked
  }
}
```

PIKE generates events using the event handler and logs the detections to syslog. You can check which IPs PIKE detected as flooding using the following command:

```
opensipsctl fifo pike_list
```

Preventing DNS and registration poisoning

DNS and registration poisoning are clever attacks, which use your SIP server infrastructure to send unauthorized calls. Actually, the attack is against the authorization process rather than authentication. Once a user has a valid account, it can send unauthorized calls to PSTN. Let's start explaining DNS poisoning, which is simpler. It exploits the possibility in a service provider to make calls to foreign domains. We will describe the following attack steps:

1. Get a valid account.

2. Make a legitimate call to PSTN and get the gateway's IP in the Contact header.

3. Change your DNS server to point a valid **fully qualified domain name (FQDN)** to the gateway's IP.

4. Initiate a call to the valid FQDN. In many places such as universities, the system allows you to make free calls to external domains, for example, calling to mit.edu from sip.edu.

Let's suppose that you want to make a call to an external international number such as +4423456789:

1. Once you have a valid account, make a call attempt to the number 4423456789 and register the gateway's IP address in the Contact header (for example, 1.1.1.1).

2. In a DNS server, Create a type A record pointing (for example, fakesip.freedns.org) to 1.1.1.1.

3. Make a call to +4423456789@fakesip.freedns.org.

The second type of attack called registration poisoning uses the same concept, but, instead of exploiting the authorization process to an external SIP address (in many providers, won't be authorized), it uses a fake registration to put a call. See the following steps:

1. Get two valid accounts.
2. Make a legitimate call to PSTN and get the gateway's IP in the Contact header.
3. Create a fake registration for a legitimate user passing the Contact as `external_number@gateways_ip`. A tool such as sipsak can be used for this.
4. Make an inbound call to the account with the fake registration.

Let's suppose that you want to make a call to an external international number such as +4423456789:

1. Once you have a valid account, make a call attempt to the number 4423456789 and write down the gateway's IP address in the Contact header (for example, `1.1.1.1`).
2. Create a fake SIP registration in the other account (for example, `sip:user2@opensips.org`) pointing to a Contact (for example, `+4423456789@1.1.1.1`).

   AOR: `user2@opensips.org`

   Contact: `sip:+4423456789@1.1.1.1`

3. Make a call to `user2@opensips.org`. The call will be completed at `+4423456789@1.1.1.1` (the address of our gateway) and will not be billed.

To prevent a DNS or registration poisoning, you have to use blacklists for your gateway's IP. Blacklists are part of the OpenSIPS core. One can define a blacklist using a core parameter called `dst_blacklist`. To filter out the gateways, you can define a list as follows:

```
# filter out requests going to ips of my gws
dst_blacklist = gw:{( tcp , 1.1.1.1 , 5060 , "" ),
   ( any , 1.1.1.1 , 0 , "" )}
# block message requests with known attack headers
dst_blacklist = msg_filter:{ ( any , 192.168.20.0/
   255.255.255.0 , 0 , "MESSAGE*friendly-scanner" )}
```

Each rule is defined by the following:

- Protocol: TCP, UDP, TLS, or any for anything
- Port: A number or 0 for any
- IP/Mask
- Test pattern is a filename such as matching (see man 3 fnmatch) applied to the outgoing request buffer (`first_line+hdrs+body`)

Once you create a blacklist, you have to apply it to the script. For DNS and registration poisoning, the following example would work:

This is for DNS poisoning:

```
dst_blacklist = gws:{( tcp , 1.1.1.1 , 5060 , "" ),
    ( any , 1.1.1.1 , 0 , "" )}

if (!is_uri_host_local()) {
  append_hf("P-hint: outbound\r\n");
  use_blacklist("gws");
  route(1);
}
```

This is for registration poisoning:

```
route[usrloc]{
dst_blacklist = gws:{( tcp , 1.1.1.1 , 5060 , "" ),
    ( any , 1.1.1.1 , 0 , "" )}

if (!lookup("location","m")) {
  switch ($retcode)
  ...
  use_blacklist("gws");
  route(relay);
}
```

When OpenSIPS blocks a destination in the blacklist, you will receive a reply, **473 Filtered Destination**.

If you use the `drouting` module to define tens of gateways, you can automatically insert them in blacklists using a module parameter. This saves a lot of time and keeps the blacklists from being hardcoded in the configuration file.

```
modparam("drouting", "define_blacklist", 'gws= 3,5')
modparam("drouting", "define_blacklist", 'media= 4,2')
```

 OpenSIPS uses gateway *types*, rather than gateway *numbers*, to create a blacklist.

Enabling Transport Layer Security

The **Transport Layer Security (TLS)** protocol is a security protocol able to protect the communication for web, e-mail, and many other systems. TLS is negotiated hop by hop, so it is possible to have TLS-UDP-TLS connections. This protocol provides you with privacy and data integrity between two applications. This occurs by authentication, encryption, and integrity protection protocols. The detailed explanation of TLS is beyond the scope of this book. You can search for detailed information in RFC 5246 (`https://tools.ietf.org/html/rfc5246`). Here, we will focus on how to apply TLS to your scripts and give you an example on how to implement it in popular softphones. Refer to your client device's manufacturer for details on how to use TLS in a particular IP phone or ATA.

To enable TLS, we will have to follow these steps:

1. Compile OpenSIPS with the `proto_tls` module.
2. Add the appropriate statements to the configuration script.
3. Create the certificate authority keys in your server.
4. Generate a server certificate.
5. Configure a client to connect using TLS.

Generating a script for TLS

For the first step, fortunately, you can use the script generator to create a valid configuration using TLS. You can copy and paste some sections of the examples to activate TLS. The first parts are the core parameters, module loading, and module parameters.

```
#You should have a listen statement for TCP and TLS
#TLS depends on TCP, so TCP is mandatory if you want to use TLS
listen=tcp:10.8.30.75:5060    # CUSTOMIZE ME
listen=tls:10.8.30.75:5061    # CUSTOMIZE ME


#In OpenSIPS 2.1 transport protocols are now modules
loadmodule "proto_tcp.so"
loadmodule "proto_tls.so"
```

In order for OpenSIPS to start in the new version, we need to configure some global certificates. We do this as a default match, something to match any domain.

```
modparam("proto_tls", "certificate",
   "/etc/opensips/tls/rootCA/cacert.pem")
modparam("proto_tls", "private_key",
   "/etc/opensips/tls/rootCA/private/cakey.pem")
modparam("proto_tls", "ca_list",
   "/etc/opensips/tls/rootCA/cacert.pem")
modparam("proto_tls", "ca_dir", "/etc/opensips/tls/rootCA/")
```

After the default matching, we will create a client domain:

```
modparam("proto_tls", "client_domain", "1=192.168.0.17")
modparam("proto_tls", "verify_cert", "1:0")
modparam("proto_tls", "require_cert", "1:0")
modparam("proto_tls", "ciphers_list", "1:NULL")
modparam("proto_tls", "tls_method", "1:TLSv1")
modparam("proto_tls", "ca_dir", "1:/etc/opensips/tls/rootCA/")
modparam("proto_tls", "certificate",
   "1:/etc/opensips/tls/user/user-cert.pem")
modparam("proto_tls", "private_key",
   "1:/etc/opensips/tls/user/user-privkey.pem")
modparam("proto_tls", "ca_list",
   "1:/etc/opensips/tls/user/user-calist.pem")
```

Creating the root certificate authority

You should decide to go with either self-signed certificates or commercial certificates. In most cases, it does not make sense to use a commercial certificate for OpenSIPS. You are the authority in the system, and if you are distributing and installing the root certificates in all the phones, it simply does not make sense to use a commercial certificate because you do not need a third party to verify you. The exception would be using a softphone that has certificate authorities from its own storage. The configuration from the phone can save you a lot of time in installing root certificates in notebooks and desktops. In our example, we will use a self-signed certificate. To do this, follow these steps:

1. Edit the `ca.conf` file

2. Generate the root certificate and private and public keys

The detailed procedure is explained in the following steps:

1. Edit the `/etc/opensips/tls/ca.conf` file and find the specific section to specify the information regarding your certificate:

   ```
   [ root_ca_distinguished_name ]
   commonName              = 192.168.0.17:5061 # Use here your
       domain or IP
   stateOrProvinceName = BU          # informational only
   countryName             = RO          # informational only
   emailAddress            = flavio@opensip.org  #informational
       only
   organizationName     = OpenSIPS      # informational only
   ```

2. Once you have edited the file, create the root authority using the following command:

   `opensipsctl tls rootCA`

3. This command will ask you for a password to protect the private key. After filling in the password, the system will generate the private key:

   `/usr/local/etc/opensips//tls/rootCA/private/cakey.pem`

4. The utility creates the certificate with the public key:

   `/usr/local/etc/opensips//tls/rootCA/cacert.pem`

Creating the server certificate

After this step, we have to create the server certificate. We will do this in two steps:

1. Edit the `user.conf` file

2. Generate the server certificate

Follow these steps:

1. Edit the `/usr/local/etc/opensips/tls/user.conf` file:

   ```
   [ server_distinguished_name ]
   commonName = 192.168.0.17:5061 #it has to match the server
     domain or IP
   stateOrProvinceName       = BU
   countryName               = RO
   emailAddress              = flavio@opensips.org # please
     update
   organizationName          = OpenSIPS
   organizationalUnitName = Training
   ```

2. Use the following command to generate the server certificate:

   `opensipsctl tls userCERT user`

3. Follow the instructions displayed by the command. The private key will be located at the following:

   `/usr/local/etc/opensips//tls/user/user-privkey.pem`

4. The server certificate will be located at the following:

   `/usr/local/etc/opensips//tls/user/user-cert.pem`

   The list of certificate authorities will be located at:

   `/usr/local/etc/opensips//tls/user/user-calist.pem`

5. Make sure that these locations match the module parameters specified in the script.

6. Restart your server to load the parameters.

Installing the root certificate authority in your softphone

Each softphone has its own way to handle certificates. While some use the root certificates from the operating system repository, others require you to load the certificates in its own user interface. We will give you an example of Blink (http://www.icanblink.com/). It is an open source softphone and supports TLS. Perform the following steps to enable TLS in the softphone; consult your phone manual on how to enable certification authorities and configure TLS for your specific phone. Phone interfaces change often, so check the manual for a divergence to the instructions provided here:

1. Copy the certificate from your certificate authority to your PC. This certificate is found at /usr/local/etc/opensips/tls/rootCA/cacert.pem. If you are using Windows, an easy way to copy is to use the WinSCP utility. For Mac users, use scp from the command line.

2. Create an account normally:

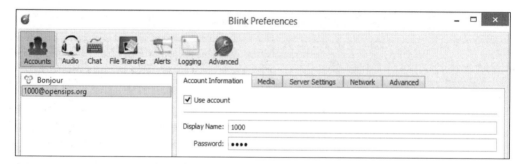

3. Select the **Outbound Proxy** server as the IP address of the server, **Port** as 5061, and **Transport** as TLS:

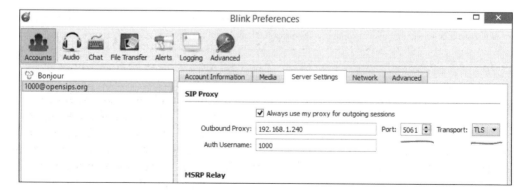

4. Add the **Certificate Authority** to your softphone and **Enable TLS** to port `5061`:

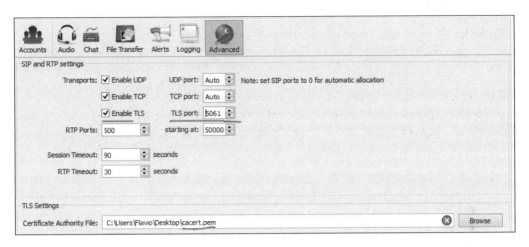

5. Restart the softphone and check whether the registration succeeded in the web server using `opensipsctl`:

```
root@bookosips:/etc/opensips# opensipsctl ul show
Domain:: location table=512 records=1
    AOR:: 1000@opensips.org
        Contact:: sip:04873219@192.168.1.101:5061;transport=tls Q=
            Expires:: 592
            Callid:: c56d9eeef494499f87945dc181bceb4f
            Cseq:: 2
            User-agent:: Blink 0.5.0 (Windows)
            Received:: sip:192.168.1.101:58331;transport=TLS
            State:: CS_NEW
            Flags:: 0
            Cflags:: NAT
            Socket:: tls:192.168.1.240:5061
            Methods:: 4294967295
            SIP_instance:: <urn:uuid:5916340c-e67b-415b-b67a-5ffc55d
```

Enabling Secure Real-time Protocol

While TLS is capable to encrypt the SIP signaling, it does nothing regarding the audio or video of calls. Someone can still eavesdrop on your calls and hear your conversations. There are many systems such as ucsniffer and wireshark that are able to sniff and record calls in local networks. To prevent this type of problem, you need to encrypt the RTP protocol. OpenSIPS has nothing to do with SRTP, and the phones are actually responsible for implementing SRTP. However, the key exchange often occurs over a TLS connection. There are different key exchange mechanisms for SRTP, and it is important to understand if phones are capable to interoperate encrypted calls. Here is a list of different key exchange mechanisms of SRTP.

SRTP-SDES

SDES is **Session Description Protocol Security Descriptions**. The key exchange occurs using fields in the SDP protocol. It is the most common way to implement SRTP and is found in the majority of IP phones and softphones in the market. Blink, Yealink, and many other manufacturers use SRTP-SDES. The system exchanges keys in the SDP protocol as follows:

```
v=0
o=root 201511111 201522222 IN IP4 192.168.1.1
s=call
c=IN IP4 192.168.1.1
t=0 0
m=audio 22711 RTP/SAVP 0 8
a=crypto:1 AES_CM_128_HMAC_SHA1_32 inline:WbTBosdVUZqEb6Htqhn+m3z7wUh
4RJVR8nE15GbN
a=rtpmap:0 pcmu/8000
a=rtpmap:8 pcma/8000
a=rtpmap:101 telephone-event/8000
a=fmtp:101 0-16
a=ptime:20
a=encryption:optional
a=sendrecv
```

DTLS-SRTP

The definition of DTLS-SRTP is **Datagram Transport Layer Security (DTLS)** extension to establish keys for SRTP. WebRTC uses DTLS-SRTP to encrypt VoIP traffic. It is slightly different from SRTP-SDES. The IETF standardized the DTLS-SRTP in RFC 5764. It is gaining ground in the shadow of the WebRTC phenomena.

ZRTP

This encryption standard is gaining ground in the market as the safest one. The encryption is end to end and uses the RTP protocol. Z comes from Philip Zimmermann, the inventor of the protocol, already famous by the invention of the consecrated PGP encryption protocol. Using SRTP-SDES poses a threat to privacy if the service provider captures the keys in the server traces. In other words, if a government agency requires a service provider, it can save the RTP traffic and decrypt it using the keys present in the SDP protocol. In the server, it is possible to see the SDP protocol unencrypted. Obviously, it can only be seen with the consent of the provider or if the server is compromised.

ZRTP is a new type of end-to-end encryption. It uses the RTP protocol to exchange keys. ZRTP also employs a mechanism called **Short Authentication String (SAS)** to detect man in the middle attacks. In Wikipedia, there is a mention of NSA creating a system to defeat the SAS mechanism. The status of this development is unknown.

Enabling SRTP

To enable SRTP is as simple as clicking a checkbox in the softphone; there is nothing to configure in the OpenSIPS server. The following is an example using Blink; you can set SRTP as disabled, optional, or mandatory:

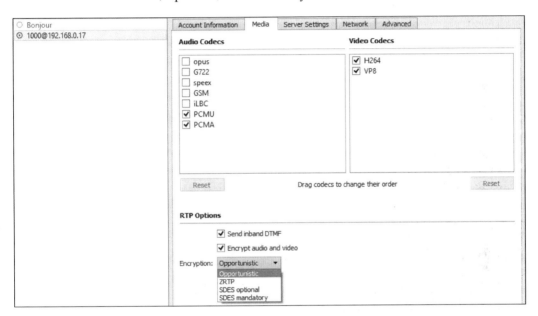

Enabling the anti-fraud module

Fraud has been one of the major problems for carriers. The CFCA (http://www.cfca.org/) has measured fraud in approximately eight billion dollars in 2013. There are many companies specialized in fraud systems for carriers. OpenSIPS now has a software module called fraud_detection (http://www.opensips.org/html/docs/modules/2.1.x/fraud_detection) that is able to substantially reduce the risks of fraud by defining alert levels on different metrics. This is a brand new module for OpenSIPS 2.1.

Using the `dialog` module, the fraud detection module monitors the following statistics:

- Calls per minute
- Call duration
- Total calls
- Concurrent calls
- Consecutive calls to the same destination

The module generates alarms at two levels, warning and critical, and you can create rules organized by the hour of the day and days of the week. The system stores the rules in a database as follows. You created this table when you installed extra tables in *Chapter 4, OpenSIPS Language and Routing Concepts*. The name of the table is `fraud_detection`:

rule id	profile id	prefix	start hour	end hour	days of the week	cpm warning	cpm critical	call duration warning	call duration critical
1	1	00	08:00	18:00	Mon-Fri	10	20	3600	7200
2	1	00	18:01	23:59	Mon-Fri	2	3	3600	7200
3	1	00	00:00	07:59	Mon-Fri	2	3	3600	7200
4	1	00	00:00	23:59	Sat,Sun	2	3	3600	7200

sequential calls warning	sequential calls critical	total calls warning	total calls critical	concurrent calls warning	concurrent calls critical
2	4	100	200	5	10
2	4	10	20	2	3
2	4	10	20	2	3
2	4	10	20	2	3

In the preceding table, we defined two groups: one is a policy for normal hours and another policy for after hours. The profile ID is **1**, so you can create a different set of rules using another profile ID. We know customers have different requirements, so create one profile ID per customer profile. You can be more restrictive for customers who rarely call overseas and another for customers making risky calls to high-priced destinations.

In this case, our policy for normal hours was to allow, for international destinations (**prefix 00**), a maximum of **10** calls per minute, duration of **one** hour, no more than **two** calls using the same caller ID to the same destination, maximum of **10** calls per current interval, and no more than **five** concurrent calls.

Once you have your policy created, you can integrate the module into your script. There two key concepts here: the `check_fraud()` command and the events. Let's have a look at the command first:

```
$var(fraudcode)=check_fraud(user, number, profile_id)
```

It is very simple. You should call this method when you want to check for calls to a given number. Pass a subset of the rules to the user using a pseudo-variable, usually $fU, the number dialed, usually $rU, and the profile ID.

The meaning of the return code is as follows:

- 2: No matching fraud rule found
- 1: Matching rule found, but there is no parameter above the rule's threshold (OK)
- -1: There is a parameter above the warning threshold (raised event)
- -2: There is a parameter above the critical threshold (raised event)
- -3: Something went wrong (internal mechanism failed)

Now that you have two mechanisms, you can take immediate action from the script by dropping the request, and using an external program, you can read events and take different actions such as sending a warning by e-mail, setting a rule in a firewall, or blocking a user.

Event generation

The system generates events and can send them to a queue such as RabbitMQ, where an external program can consume them and do something useful such as display on the screen, generate a warning by e-mail, or even activate a rule in a firewall. The fraud detection module generates the following events:

- E_FRD_WARNING

  The system raises an event whenever one of the five monitored parameters is above the warning threshold.

The event parameters are as follows:

- ∘ param: The name of the parameter
- ∘ value: The current value of the parameter
- ∘ threshold: The warning threshold value
- ∘ user: The user who initiated the call
- ∘ called_number: The number that was called
- ∘ rule_id: The ID of the fraud rule that matched when the call was initiated

- E_FRD_CRITICAL

  This event is raised whenever one of the five monitored parameters is above the warning threshold value.

  The parameters are as follows:

  - ∘ param: The name of the parameter
  - ∘ value: The current value of the parameter
  - ∘ threshold: The warning threshold value
  - ∘ user: The user initiating the call
  - ∘ called_number: The number that was called
  - ∘ rule_id: The ID of the fraud rule matching the call

 You can read more about these parameters here: http://www.opensips.org/html/docs/modules/2.1.x/fraud_detection

Script integration

It is not hard to integrate the fraud_detection module into our scripts. All we need to do is create the rules, load the modules, and insert the command, check_fraud(), just before sending the call to PSTN, usually just before the do_routing() command provided by the drouting module. The fraud detection module depends on the dialog and drouting modules.

To initialize the module, load the following mandatory parameters:

```
loadmodule "drouting.so"
loadmodule "dialog.so"
loadmodule "fraud_detection.so"
modparam("fraud_detection", "db_url",
  "mysql://root:123456@localhost/opensips")
```

Now, just before calling the do_routing() command, call the following function:

```
check_fraud("$fU","$rU","1");
switch $rc
{
  case 2:
    xlog("L_INFO","No matching rule found, call ok");
    break;
  case 1:
    xlog("L_INFO","Matching rule found, but call still ok");
    break;
  case -1:
    xlog("L_INFO","Possible fraud detected in warning level,
      please check events, but call will complete");
    break;
  case -2:
    xlog("L_INFO","Possible fraud detected in critical level,
      please check events, call will be dropped for security
      reasons");
    exit;
  case -3:
    xlog("L_INFO","Malfuntion in fraud detection module, please
      check, call not authorized");
    exit;
  default:
    xlog("L_INFO","Undefined return code");
    exit;
}
```

Summary

Security is a major concern for any VoIP provider or PBX administrator. A single flaw in the security police can easily bankrupt a small company. Frauds spanning hundreds of thousands of dollars are quite common and you can easily find many cases in the news. A solid security implementation is key for any VoIP service. In this chapter, you learned how to apply firewall policies for OpenSIPS, block multiple failed authentication attempts, use PIKE to prevent SIP flooding, prevent DNS and registration poisoning, enable TLS for security and privacy, and install and configure the fraud detection module. Pay thorough attention to this chapter before implementing any OpenSIPS system. It can save you a lot of trouble and money.

In the next chapter, we will cover advanced topics such as asynchronous processing.

Advanced Topics with OpenSIPS 2.1

OpenSIPS has evolved a lot since the first version. The OpenSIPS 2.1 is a major upgrade and has some very important new features. The major breakthroughs of this version are the asynchronous operations. Many features were also included that target better clustering, such as binary replication for registrations and NoSQL replication for dialogs and profiles. This chapter is dedicated to the following new and advanced features:

- Asynchronous operations
- Registration replication
- Dialog replication
- Support for TCP

Asynchronous operations

From the OpenSIPS script, you can perform a huge number of operations, including internal SIP message processing and routing as well as external entity queries such as external DB and **Representational State Transfer** (**REST**). Such queries will translate into I/O operations, where OpenSIPS will push a request/query to the external entity and then has to wait in order to receive a reply.

Until version 2.1, OpenSIPS implemented synchronous waiting for such I/O operations. This means that the process performing the query sits without doing anything until receiving the reply. Such an approach is inefficient. There is a fix and limited number of processes, which may be blocked doing nothing while waiting for an I/O operation to get completed.

Of course, an I/O-intensive script (with many DB operations, for example) will suffer from the lack of throughput as the processes will spend more time in simply waiting instead of handling the SIP traffic. It is very easy to detect this condition using the following command:

```
opensipsctl fifo get_statistics load:
```

If you see the number 100, all processes are waiting for an I/O or DNS operation and the server is not processing any requests or replies in this condition.

Starting with version 2.1, the internal architecture of OpenSIPS is now built around an asynchronous reactor. Such a reactor allows the implementation of asynchronous I/O operations, which means that a process can handle another task/job while waiting for an I/O to get completed. This leads to a 100% usage of the processing time, increasing the throughput and reducing the processing latency. The following figure shows the comparison of efficiency between the synchronous and asynchronous approaches:

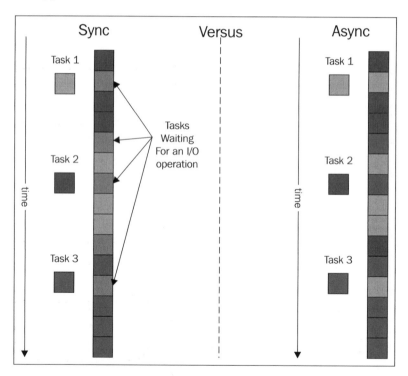

The asynchronous script operations are one of the key features of OpenSIPS 2.1. The main advantage of using them is the fact that they allow the performance of the OpenSIPS script to scale with a high number of requests per second even when blocking I/O operations, such as MySQL queries, exec commands, or HTTP requests.

Using asynchronous logic instead of simply forking a high number of children in order to scale (50 or more processes) also has the advantage of optimizing the usage of system resources. The system will require fewer processes to complete the same amount of work in the same amount of time. It is possible to minimize the context switching of processes and overall CPU usage is improved. Fewer processes will also eat up less system memory.

Even the asynchronous interface is provided by the OpenSIPS core and the whole mechanism to suspend the tasks waiting for I/O replies and resume the tasks when the reply is received is implemented in the TM module. You need to load this module if you plan to use asynchronous operations from your script:

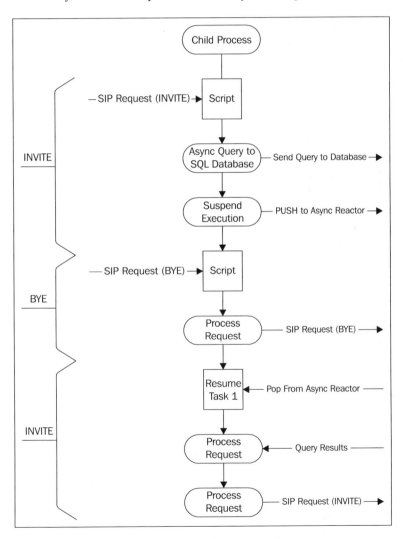

Asynchronous support in the OpenSIPS script

The usage is quite straightforward. Let's assume that you want to use a script function that internally performs some I/O operations (such as a DB query). First of all, you need to check whether this script function supports asynchronous mode. (See the respective module documentation for this.) Then, you can just throw it in the following function call:

```
async(script_function(...), resume_route);
```

Note that `resume_route` has to be a simple, named script, subroute. When a function is called in the asynchronous manner, the script is immediately halted, so any code that you write after the `async()` call will be ignored. OpenSIPS will launch the asynchronous operation; after this, it will continue to process any other pending tasks (queued SIP messages, timer jobs, or possibly other asynchronous operations). As soon as the asynchronous operation is complete and all the data is available, OpenSIPS will run the given resume route and continue processing with a minimum of idle time.

The return code of the function executed in asynchronous mode is available in the very beginning of the resume route in the `$rc` or `$retcode` variable. Additionally, all the output parameters (variables in the function parameters used to carry output values) will be available in the resume route:

```
route
{
  /* preparation code */
  ...
  async(avp_db_query("SELECT credit FROM users WHERE
    uid='$avp(uid)'", "$avp(credit)"), resume_credit);
  /* script execution is terminated right away! */
}

route [resume_credit]
{
  if ($rc < 0) {
    xlog("error $rc in avp_db_query()\n");
    exit;
  }

  xlog("Credit of user $avp(uid) is $avp(credit)\n");
}
```

After an `async()` call, your script will continue with the execution of the resume route, even in a situation where the actual I/O operation was never launched because of wrong parameters to the script function, parsing of internal errors, or any failure to meet the prerequisites to run the query. In such situations, the resume route will be executed on the spot, providing a negative return code to the script (via `$rc`).

Note that in some situations, the I/O query may end up being executed in a synchronous way; for example, if some asynchronous reactor issues were found (such as the number of maximum suspended tasks is reached). Nevertheless, from a scripting perspective, the behavior will be the same. The system calls the resume route when the synchronous I/O operation is terminated.

Even if the resume route intends to provide a transparent continuation of the script, there are certain types of data or certain mechanisms that do not survive an asynchronous jump (via a resume route):

- Data persisting after an `async()` call: The `$avp()` variables, message and branch flags, changes to your SIP message, and transaction state
- Data discarded after an `async()` call: The `$var()` variables, script flags, benchmarking sessions, blacklist bitmap, added SIP branches (by `append_branch()`), and per-message execution thresholds

Available asynchronous functions

Even if the asynchronous support is available for any function from any module, only a limited number of script functions were migrated to asynchronous implementation in OpenSIPS 2.1.

The criteria to select the functions to be migrated were as follows:

- How often are they used in OpenSIPS scripts?
- How many scripting scenarios can they cover?
- Do they cover as many OpenSIPS areas as possible (such as DB, exec, and so on)?

The current set of asynchronous functions is as follows:

- The `avp_db_query()` function from the `AVPops` module: This is a commonly used function as it provides a generic way of querying any SQL database
- The `rest_get()` and `rest_post()` functions from the `rest_client` module: It covers all the interactions with REST-based APIs
- The `exec()` function from the `exec` module: Any execution of an external script/binary can now be done in an asynchronous way

More functions will be migrated to asynchronous mode in the upcoming OpenSIPS version 2.2:

- The `radius_send_auth()` and `radius_send_acct()` functions from the `aaa_radius` module: They allow sending any RADIUS requests without any further blocking

- The `sleep()` and `usleep()` functions from the `cfgutils` module: Handling of a SIP message can be paused without any performance penalties

- The `ldap_search()` function from the `ldap` module: Querying LDAP databases in asynchronous mode

Binary replication

The **binary interface** (also called the **BIN interface**) provides you with an efficient way of internal communication between multiple OpenSIPS instances. It is a generic mechanism that allows different OpenSIPS modules to communicate data between different OpenSIPS instances transparently.

Engineers can use the BIN interface to replicate the data and state between OpenSIPS instances used for high-availability or clustering configurations.

To configure an OpenSIPS instance to be a receiver of BIN traffic, the following BIN parameters need to be configured:

```
bin_listen = 10.0.0.150:5062
bin_children = 2
```

The following figure shows how binary replication works in an OpenSIPS cluster:

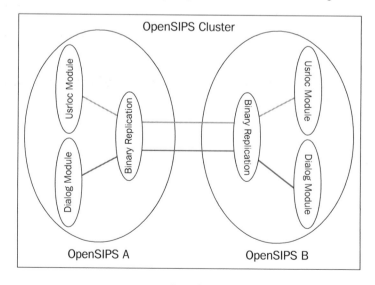

The BIN traffic is tagged with the name of the module generating it so that when received, OpenSIPS will automatically know which module to send the incoming traffic. For example, BIN packages tagged as generated by the `dialog` modules will be dispatched and consumed by the `dialog` module on the receiving OpenSIPS instance.

When it comes to replication, the BIN interface advantages are as follows:

- It provides real-time data/state replication
- It does not rely on external DBs
- It does not require any scripting logic (it is internal to the module)

Currently, `dialog` and `usrloc` are the first modules to make use of this interface, and they can now replicate all the runtime events (creation, update, deletion of dialogs/contacts, and so on) to one or more OpenSIPS instances.

Note that an OpenSIPS receiving BIN traffic will not perform any kind of checks on who is the sending party—no filtering or ACLs. Take care and address this issue at the network level via the necessary firewalling rules.

Dialog replication

Dialog replications means a full and real-time replication of the state of the SIP dialogs from one OpenSIPS instance (where the SIP traffic is received) to another (or many others).

To implement such dialog replication, you need to configure the **Master** or **Active** OpenSIPS to generate replication traffic based on the internal state of its dialogs:

```
modparam("dialog", "replicate_dialogs_to", "10.10.1.78:5062")
```

To replicate to multiple OpenSIPS instances, use one `replicate_dialogs_to` parameter per destination.

The OpenSIPS instances interested in receiving replicated dialog information must configure the following:

```
bin_listen = 10.0.0.78:5062
bin_children = 2
modparam("dialog", "accept_replicated_dialogs", 1)
```

The `dialog` module replicates the following changes in the dialog state:

- Dialog established (when a 200 OK was received)
- Dialog updated (after a re-INVITE or sequential request triggering changes in the dialog state)
- Dialog deleted (BYE received or internal timeout generated)
- Early dialogs or failed dialogs are not replicated at all

When the `dialog` module replicates the state, all the additional data is replicated as well such as dialog profiles, dialog flags, and dialog variables. So, be sure that you have the same dialog profiles configured on all the OpenSIPS servers involved in the dialog replication.

> Note that a replicated dialog may generate a timeout event if no dialog deleted event is received (from the OpenSIPS server performing the replication).

The usrloc replication

The usrloc replication via the BIN interface is a simpler and high-performance replacement for the old SIP replication by the `t_replicate()` function.

Similar to dialog replication, the usrloc replication works as one point to many points replication.

To implement the usrloc replication, you need to configure the **Master** or **Active** OpenSIPS to generate replication traffic based on the internal cache with contacts:

```
modparam("usrloc", "replicate_contacts_to", "10.10.1.78:5062")
```

> This contacts replication does not work in the DB_ONLY mode!

The OpenSIPS instances interested in receiving replicated usrloc information must configure the following:

```
bin_listen = 10.0.0.78:5062
bin_children = 2
modparam("usrloc", "accept_replicated_contacts", 1)
```

The following changes in the contact state are replicated by the `usrloc` module:

- Contact created (on initial registration)
- Contact updated (on reregistration)
- Contact deleted (on deregistration or timeout)

Along with the contact state, all the additional information attached to the contact is replicated, such as branch flags, network socket, User-Agent header, and others.

When using contact replication, be sure to configure all the servers with the same parameters for the `usrloc` and `registrar` modules regarding the definition of **Address of Record (AOR)** (see the `use_domain` parameter), which is the NAT `bflag` and contact matching mode.

On the receiving OpenSIPS nodes, depending on your database setup (if there is any replication or sharing at the DB level), you may want to avoid pushing the contacts received via replication to DB:

```
modparam("usrloc", "skip_replicated_db_ops", 1)
```

If the location table is shared between OpenSIPS instances generating and receiving the usrloc replication traffic, you should configure the receiving instance so as not to push any replicated contact information to DB in order to avoid conflicts at the DB level (duplicate keys).

TCP handling

TCP is gaining ground as a transport protocol for SIP. The limitations on the size of the UDP packet are creating challenges for applications, such as presence. Additionally, when a request traverses a large number of proxies with big SIP headers and SDP content, it is not uncommon to have overflows. To enable TCP on OpenSIPS is fairly straightforward; however, it is important to pay some attention to a few details.

Enabling TCP

TCP is now a module, so to enable TCP for use with OpenSIPS, use the following command:

```
loadmoduleproto_tcp.so
```

There are a few module parameters for TCP that deserve mention:

```
modparam("proto_tcp", "tcp_async", 0)
```

The preceding parameter sets OpenSIPS to handle the TCP connection asynchronously. The default setting is 1 (enabled). Handling the TCP connection asynchronously is key to have a good performance on SIP over TCP.

You can also define the number of child process for TCP using the following parameter:

```
tcp_children=4
```

TCP is a session-oriented protocol, so we will have a connection establishment before a client can end requests and/or replies. You can control the lifetime, in seconds, of the TCP sessions using the following parameter:

```
tcp_connection_lifetime=3600
```

OpenSIPS will close sessions that have been inactive for a time greater than the specified time. You can also set the TCP lifetime for the duration of the REGISTER expire value using the `tcp_persistent_flag` parameter of the `registrar` module.

Another important process for TCP is TCP keepalive. If a TCP connection is kept idle for a long time in a specific direction, some routers can close it. The TCP keepalive process is used to prevent this connection from closing. There are a few parameters controlling the process. OpenSIPS controls the keepalive using the following parameters:

- Enable/Disable `tcp_keepalive`: `tcp_keepalive = 1`
- Number of keepalives to send before closing: `tcp_keepcount = 3`
- Amount of time (in seconds) before sending keepalives, if the connection is idle: `tcp_keepidle = 30`
- Interval between keepalives (in seconds), if the previous one fails: `tcp_keepinterval = 8`

Summary

In this chapter, you learned two major improvements of the newer 2.x versions. OpenSIPS has become one of the major platforms used for flexible, high-performance, and high-volume SIP processing and routing. Cluster features such as binary replication are unique in the market and fundamental for this type of operation. On the other hand, asynchronous operations emerged to solve a very old problem of system blocking by slow I/O operations. This feature is key for the stability of the platform. OpenSIPS continues to evolve quickly and these are a few improvements that the platform has received since the version 1.x.

Index

B

backend
call end reason 222
selecting 216, 217
Back-to-Back User Agent (B2BUA server)
about 8
module 171
benchmark module
using 306
binary interface (BIN interface)
about 342
advantages 343
binary replication
about 342, 343
dialog replication 343, 344
usrloc replication 344, 345
blind call forwarding
access parameters, loading 265
AVPops module, loading 265
implementing 265, 266
Blink
URL 328
branch route 84, 85
built-in tools
about 298, 299
commands 298
BYEs 232

C

call forward
about 264
blind call forwarding, implementing 265
implementing 264
implementing, on busy 267
implementing, on unanswered 267
on busy 264
on no answer 264
testing 270, 271
unconditionally 264
call forward test
Asterisk Realtime, integrating with
OpenSIPS 271-275
integrated voicemail, implementing 271
user integration 271

Call Processing Language (CPL) 5
calls
counting, from MI interface 203
disconnecting 204
disconnecting, MI interface used 204
calls, receiving from PSTN
about 174
caller identification 176, 177
Gateway authentication 174
PSTN GWs, routing to 184
calls, sending to PSTN
about 178
Caller ID 183
PSTN calls, authorizing 179
PSTN calls, identifying 178, 179
call transfer
about 275
tips 294
unattended transfer 276, 283, 285
CANCEL requests
handling 147
capabilities, OpenSIPS
backend support 31
class 4 routing 29
class 5 routing 30
endpoint-oriented capabilities 29
feature-rich 28
flexibility 28
management and integration 31
media/RTP-related capabilities 30
performance 27
scripting capabilities 31
SIP-related capabilities 30
SIP security 30
SIP SIMPLE 30
transport-level capabilities 29
CDRs
about 232
CDRviewer, and extra accounting 225-227
generating 223, 224
generating, from accounting records 224
CFCA
URL 331
CNAME 41
codec 20
commands
sending, to management interface 165, 166

SIP Session Timer (SST) module
about 30, 210, 232
working 210-212
SIPTRACE
about 300
configuring 300, 301
SIP transactions 16, 17
software requisites, OpenSIPS 51, 52
startup options 72
start up route 89, 90
stateful mode 108-111
stateless mode 108-111
statements 103, 104
statistic variables, OpenSIPS
computed values 48
counter like 48
reference link 48
stress testing tools
about 307
SIPp (sipp.sourceforge.net) 308
sipsak tool 307
reference link 51
STUN
installing 243, 244
with symmetric NAT devices 245
subroutes 81
subscribers
managing 162
registration, verifying 163
system crash
troubleshooting 304

T

TCP
enabling 345, 346
handling 345
time-division multiplexing (TDM) 171
timer route 90
topology hiding (TH)
about 205
initial request after 206
initial request before 206
limitations 208
sequential request after 207
sequential request before 207

trace tools
about 300
script trace 301, 302
SIPTRACE 300
tracker, OpenSIPS
URL 32
Transaction Module (TM) 205
transformations 98-100
Transport Layer Security (TLS)
about 11
enabling 324
root certificate authority, creating 326
root certificate authority, installing in
softphone 328, 329
script, generating 325
server certificate, creating 327
troubleshooting, routing scripts
about 302, 303
benchmark module 306
packet capturing tools 311
stress testing tools 307
system crash 304
Trunking services 39

U

UAC (User Agent Client) 4
UAS (User Agent Server) 4
UA (User Agent) 4
unattended transfer 276, 284, 285
Uniform Resource Identifier (URI) 9
usage scenarios, for OpenSIPS
about 34
core side 38-40
egress side 40-42
ingress side 35-38
User Agent Server (UAS) 207
usrloc replication 344, 345

V

variables
about 94, 95
AVP variables 96, 97
reference variables 95, 96
script variables 97

VoIP provider
  about 24
  accounting and CDR generation 26
  media proxy or RTP proxy, for NAT
      traversal 25
  media server 25
  monitoring tools 26
  PSTN gateway 25
  SIP proxy 24
  user administration and provisioning
      portal 25

W

Wide Area Networks (WANs) 20
Wireshark 312-316

Y

Yate
  URL 25

Z

ZRTP 330

Thank you for buying
Building Telephony Systems with OpenSIPS
Second Edition

About Packt Publishing

Packt, pronounced 'packed', published its first book, *Mastering phpMyAdmin for Effective MySQL Management*, in April 2004, and subsequently continued to specialize in publishing highly focused books on specific technologies and solutions.

Our books and publications share the experiences of your fellow IT professionals in adapting and customizing today's systems, applications, and frameworks. Our solution-based books give you the knowledge and power to customize the software and technologies you're using to get the job done. Packt books are more specific and less general than the IT books you have seen in the past. Our unique business model allows us to bring you more focused information, giving you more of what you need to know, and less of what you don't.

Packt is a modern yet unique publishing company that focuses on producing quality, cutting-edge books for communities of developers, administrators, and newbies alike. For more information, please visit our website at www.packtpub.com.

About Packt Open Source

In 2010, Packt launched two new brands, Packt Open Source and Packt Enterprise, in order to continue its focus on specialization. This book is part of the Packt Open Source brand, home to books published on software built around open source licenses, and offering information to anybody from advanced developers to budding web designers. The Open Source brand also runs Packt's Open Source Royalty Scheme, by which Packt gives a royalty to each open source project about whose software a book is sold.

Writing for Packt

We welcome all inquiries from people who are interested in authoring. Book proposals should be sent to author@packtpub.com. If your book idea is still at an early stage and you would like to discuss it first before writing a formal book proposal, then please contact us; one of our commissioning editors will get in touch with you.

We're not just looking for published authors; if you have strong technical skills but no writing experience, our experienced editors can help you develop a writing career, or simply get some additional reward for your expertise.

Building Telephony Systems with OpenSIPS 1.6

ISBN: 978-1-84951-074-5   Paperback: 284 pages

Build scalable and robust telephony systems using SIP

1. Build a VoIP Provider based on the SIP Protocol.

2. Cater to scores of subscribers efficiently with a robust telephony system based in pure SIP.

3. Gain a competitive edge using the most scalable VoIP technology.

4. Learn how to avoid pitfalls using precise billing.

FreeSWITCH 1.6 Cookbook

ISBN: 978-1-78528-091-7   Paperback: 190 pages

Over 45 practical recipes to empower you with the latest FreeSWITCH 1.6 features

1. Learn how to create a fast and secure messaging and telephony system with FreeSWITCH.

2. Trap all the common functionalities of the telephony platform using popular communication protocols.

3. Move recipe by recipe to get the gist of the platform.

Please check **www.PacktPub.com** for information on our titles

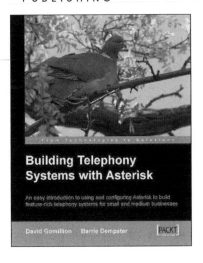

Building Telephony Systems
With Asterisk

ISBN: 978-1-90481-115-2   Paperback: 176 pages

An easy introduction to using and configuring
Asterisk to build feature-rich telephony systems
for small and medium businesses

1. Install, configure, deploy, secure, and maintain
   Asterisk.

2. Build a fully-featured telephony system
   and create a dial plan that suits your needs.

3. Learn from example configurations for
   different requirements.

Building Enterprise Ready
Telephony Systems with
sipXecs 4.0

ISBN: 978-1-84719-680-4   Paperback: 314 pages

Leveraging open source VOIP for a rock-solid
communications system

1. Learn how to plan, deploy and migrate an
   enterprise ready communications system
   with sipXecs.

2. Discover the different options for configuring
   phones, users and server features to get the
   best result for your organization.

3. Secure and maintain your sipXecs system.

Please check **www.PacktPub.com** for information on our titles

Printed in Great Britain
by Amazon